The Architecture of Madness

Architecture, Landscape, and American Culture

SERIES EDITOR
Katherine Solomonson
UNIVERSITY OF MINNESOTA

*A Manufactured Wilderness: Summer Camps and
the Shaping of American Youth, 1890–1960*

Abigail A. Van Slyck

*The Architecture of Madness:
Insane Asylums in the United States*

Carla Yanni

The Architecture of Madness

Insane Asylums in the United States

Carla Yanni

ARCHITECTURE, LANDSCAPE, AND AMERICAN CULTURE

University of Minnesota Press
MINNEAPOLIS • LONDON

Published in cooperation with the Center for American Places, Santa Fe, New Mexico, and Staunton, Virginia. www.americanplaces.org.

This book is supported by a grant from the Graham Foundation for Advanced Studies in the Fine Arts.

The author and the University of Minnesota Press gratefully acknowledge the support of the Faculty of Arts and Sciences and the University Research Council of Rutgers, The State University of New Jersey, in the publication of this book.

An earlier version of chapter 2 was previously published as "The Linear Plan for Insane Asylums in the United States to 1866," *Journal of the Society of Architectural Historians* 62, no. 1 (March 2003). Reprinted with permission of the Society of Architectural Historians.

The architectural plans in Appendix D were redrawn by Kevin Bell.

Published by the University of Minnesota Press
111 Third Avenue South, Suite 290
Minneapolis, MN 55401-2520
http://www.upress.umn.edu

Library of Congress Cataloging-in-Publication Data

Yanni, Carla.
    The architecture of madness : insane asylums in the United States / Carla Yanni.
        p. cm. — (Architecture, landscape, and American culture)
    Includes bibliographical references and index.
    ISBN 978-0-8166-4939-6 (hc : alk. paper) — ISBN 978-0-8166-4940-2 (pb : alk. paper) 1. Asylums—United States—Design and construction—History. 2. Psychiatric hospitals—United States—Design and construction—History. 3. Hospital architecture—United States—History. I. Title.
    RC445.Y36 2007
    725´.520973—dc22
                                                2007003766

Printed in the United States of America on acid-free paper

The University of Minnesota is an equal-opportunity educator and employer.

30 29 28 27 26 25 24 23 22   11 10 9 8 7 6 5

To my mother,

Joan K. Yanni,

the docent with the mocent

Contents

Acknowledgments

Architectural historian Joseph Siry suggested I write my undergraduate honors thesis at Wesleyan University on H. H. Richardson's Buffalo State Hospital for the Insane. An unusually dedicated thesis supervisor, he learned that I had been raised in Rochester, New York, near Buffalo, and that I was interested in social history and science. When I went to graduate school at the University of Pennsylvania from 1988 to 1994, I dropped the subject entirely, perhaps because I felt overwhelmed by its grimness. But I maintained an interest in science and architecture, and I pursued these interrelated endeavors in my first book on the architecture of natural history museums. The towers of Buffalo still loomed in my memory, and I was happy to return to the subject for this, my second book.

I have received generous intellectual guidance from titans in the history and sociology of medicine. Gerald Grob's enthusiasm for the project meant a great deal to me; readers will find frequent notes to a selected few of his twenty-odd books on the history of medicine. Andrew Scull read drafts of two chapters, and his advice helped me shore up the chapters that were most dependent on detailed knowledge of psychiatry in the nineteenth century. I thank Leslie Topp and Jonathan Andrews for inviting me to speak at "Space, Psyche, and Psychiatry," the best conference I have ever attended; it was a symposium designed with one session taking place at a time, so that all speakers were present at every talk,

and we were on the edges of our chairs. The other participants were wonderfully responsive, Sarah Rutherford, Jane Kromm, and Christine Stevenson, especially. Jeanne Kisacky's research on hospital architecture has helped me understand the key issues of ventilation and access to nature.

Annmarie Adams lavished attention on an early draft about the linear plan; my writing on this topic would be far less nuanced without her care. I thank the Society of Architectural Historians for permission to reproduce parts of an article published in the *Journal of the Society of Architectural Historians* in chapter 2. Caroline Elam read a draft of chapters 3 and 4, and Anne Cotterill cast her knowing eyes over the introduction. Therese O'Malley kindly offered her knowledge of landscape history. Cynthia Field encouraged me to rent a flat in her home, from which we shared many delightful conversations about buildings and cats. Robert Wozniak read early drafts and allowed me to peruse his extraordinary collection of one thousand postcards of insane asylums in the United States; it was a pleasure to view this wonderful repository in the company of his friendly golden retriever. Maureen Meister, Jeffrey Ochsner, and Frank Kowsky helped me understand the smaller points of H. H. Richardson's most massive building. I thank the anonymous reviewer for the Center for American Places and James E. Moran, who generously reviewed my book for the University of Minnesota Press.

Kate Solomonson was a thought-provoking series editor who guided my revisions in the final stages.

The Graham Foundation for Advanced Studies in the Fine Arts supported the book through a subvention grant, and Rutgers Research Council and the Faculty of Arts and Sciences matched the Graham Foundation's generosity. I owe a large debt of gratitude to the Center for Advanced Study in the Visual Arts at the National Gallery of Art, where I spent an academic year. Although my subject did not overlap with that of anyone else, I learned a great deal from my fellow scholars. I am certain that so many books on lunacy had never before darkened the doorstep of the CASVA interlibrary loan office; the librarians were puzzled but endlessly helpful. While in Washington, D.C., I had the honor of sharing my ideas with Richard Longstreth, whose breadth of knowledge of nineteenth-century buildings and cities aided the development of several chapters. I also had the pleasure of meeting E. Fuller Torrey, a research psychiatrist, and I wish him well in his passionate search for the biological causes of mental illness.

My friends and colleagues aided me along this journey. I thank Gregory Olsen, whose generous donations to the Rutgers Art History Department made much of this work possible and paid for the computer on which I am currently typing. Sarah Brett-Smith, Jeff Cohen, Emily Cooperman, Sandra Markham, and Susan Solomon all acted as sounding boards. Alison Isenberg has been a particularly great friend and colleague. Stephen Mirra, Peter Konin, and Angela Leone Konin, graduates of Rutgers's Art History Department, assisted me ably. Brian Clancy began as my Ph.D. student and has emerged as my most demanding and delightful editor. The students in two seminars on public architecture at Rutgers University also spurred me to new conclusions. It has been a pleasure to work with Geralyn Colvil and Cathy Pizzi in the art history office; they make the place hum. The Rutgers Center for Historical Analysis served as a useful ground for testing new ideas. I must thank Barry Qualls, associate dean of the humanities in the Faculty of Arts and Sciences, for creating an atmosphere at Rutgers in which research is respected, interdisciplinarity flourishes, and all things Victorian are justifiably venerated.

As always, my family has been supportive in every possible way, especially my brother Mark, who traveled with me to asylums in Tennessee, Alabama, and Illinois. We explored graveyards and barbecue joints, and he served as my all-time best research assistant. Back at home, he offered long-distance photographic assistance. My sister Barbara is always ready for an architectural adventure; my sister Palma introduced me to Dr. Theo Postolache, who invited me to St. Elizabeths, the first working psychiatric hospital I ever saw. Dennis Albert worked magic with Photoshop. My mother and father were curious, if dubious, about the unglamorous subject. After reading one chapter, my mother, the kind of person who does not like sad movies, chirped, "How nice, I thought it would be *more* depressing."

Bill Winfrey is an intrepid architectural tourist who nearly dragged me over the fence of Charenton before we realized it was easier to walk through the front gate. He also bounded with me along the streets of Gheel, as he bounds through life generally. I would like to thank his wonderful daughter, Moon, just for being herself.

In the course of my research I have used many libraries and rare book collections, too many to list here. All the librarians and archivists who made my acquaintance were helpful, especially Tony Mullin at the Library of Congress, Stephen Greenberg at the National Library of Medicine, and the tireless Diane Richardson at Oskar Diethelm. I also visited about twenty psychiatric facilities or related sites, including institutions in Kankakee, Illinois; Peoria, Illinois; Bolivar, Tennessee; Tuscaloosa, Alabama; Poughkeepsie, New York; Buffalo, New York; Binghamton, New York; Trenton, New Jersey; Greystone, New Jersey; Kalamazoo, Michigan; Middletown, Connecticut; Sheppard Pratt, Maryland; Green Door in Washington, D.C.; and Fountain House in New York City. I thank the staffs, doctors, patients, and members (in the case of the two clubhouses) for allowing me a glimpse into the spaces where they spend their days. The experience has been humbling. Carole Kraemer, who works at Green Door, introduced me to the clubhouse movement at a time when I was (without her realizing it) searching for an idea for the conclusion. I was looking for a hopeful note on which to end this book, and she—and the members of the club—gave it to me.

Insane asylums are not inviting or easy, although their weird appeal is increasing among local history buffs. Among art historians, the topic was not universally embraced—there's no great man in the title, no masterpieces spring to mind, these buildings don't appear in textbooks. I have encountered raised eyebrows and furrowed brows along the way, and thus I feel that I owe a tremendous debt to those people, both scholars and friends, who never wavered in their support.

Introduction

In 1853, Dr. Horace Buttolph, the superintendent of a respected lunatic asylum, proudly described the institution he managed as "reposing in the midst of the most beautiful scenery in the valley of the Delaware, combining all the influences which human art and skill can command to bless, soothe, and restore the wandering intellects that are gathered in its bosom. The state may proudly point to this asylum, as a noble illustration of that charity, which, borne from above, diffuses itself in blessings of the poor and unfortunate."[1] It hardly sounds like New Jersey. But the doctor did not embellish. The New Jersey State Lunatic Asylum, its official name, was located in a once-beautiful valley. From the architect, to the builders, to the medical experts, it was a work of human "art and skill." The state was proud. And the charitable *impulse* to construct the hospital was "borne from above," even if the outcome was less than providential.

The Architecture of Madness explores the participation of architecture in this grand project to "bless, soothe, and restore . . . wandering intellects." It considers the New Jersey State Lunatic Asylum in Trenton among others in an exploration of architecture for the care and treatment of the insane, over a period slightly longer than one hundred years. The stately towers of insane asylums were once a common sight at the edge of American towns, and about three hundred were built in the United States before 1900. Given the current reputation of insane asylums, variously called loony bins, funny farms, nuthouses, and booby hatches, these are not institutions that make later generations swell with pride. Indeed, today they are grim reminders of an often inhumane system. But it was once believed that an improved environment could cure insanity, and during those times these institutions and the buildings that housed them exemplified civic munificence. These much-maligned institutions occupied buildings ranging in style from Greek temples to medieval castles to Arts and Crafts cottages, and, in their day, they attempted to communicate a message of generosity. Their founders felt a sense of Christian kindness toward those less fortunate. Even so, the buildings represented the conflicting values of nineteenth-century America.

For most of the nineteenth century, doctors believed that between 70 and 90 percent of insanity cases were curable, but only if patients were treated in specially designed buildings. *The Architecture of Madness* demonstrates that nineteenth-century psychiatrists considered the architecture of their hospitals, especially the planning, to be one of the most powerful tools for the treatment of the insane. Architects were challenged by this novel building type, which manifested a series of tensions between home and institution, benevolence and surveillance, medical progress and social control, nature and culture.

Insanity as an Interaction of Social and Biological Forces

The dual nature of mental illness—that it is both medical and social, both biological and constructed by societal norms—is one of the starting points for my study. In *Mind-Forg'd Manacles,* historian Roy Porter presented the problem of insanity as a complex interaction between medical and socially constructed realities: "Insanity is both a personal disorder (with a kaleidoscope of causes, ranging from the organic to the psychosocial), and is also articulated within a system of sociolinguistic signs and meanings. This complexity is made quite clear by the historical record. For pre- and early industrial English society had little difficulty in accepting that—generically speaking—lunacy existed, yet actually demarcating the insane often remained controversial in the particular case."[2] Diagnoses were inconsistent, people fell in and out of sane states, doctors introduced new terms and flooded their journals with hypotheses. Varying publics interpreted insanity in many different ways, and responses ranged from cautious tolerance to swift incarceration. So we are left wondering: what was insanity? Even Porter, the most confident of scholars, refused to define insanity in *Madness: A Brief History;* as he stated, he made no attempt to "define true madness" or "fathom the nature of mental illness." Instead, he "rested content with an . . . account of its history."[3] To the extent that my book makes an original contribution to the discourse on lunacy, it does so by accounting for the history of the buildings that housed the insane, and stops short (as many others have) of offering a definition of insanity that carries through the nineteenth century.

In Victorian America, one might easily find experts who agreed that insanity existed, but it would have been difficult to get them to agree on a single definition. There were some behaviors, however, that were frequently ascribed to insane people. Annual reports of lunatic asylums described the arrival of new patients, articles in the *American Journal of Insanity* gave longer case histories, doctors reported on the signs that were interpreted as evidence of a disordered mind, and legal documents revealed indications of insanity. People tried to kill themselves, threatened their children, destroyed their property, talked to themselves, and claimed imaginary

friends. Some individuals thought they were Jesus or Abraham Lincoln or the Queen of the Nile. Others evinced no need for sleep. There were individuals who scoured their hands, and cases of nonstop hair pulling, praying, and hoarding. Emotional reversals, rhythmic shaking of the limbs, extreme sex drive, gambling binges, inexplicable paralysis, rapid talking, flatness of affect—all of these appeared. There were cheerful women who plummeted into darkness after the birth of a child. To call these behaviors "symptoms" would be historically presumptuous, because it would impose our values and present medical language on the nineteenth century. Such indications of insanity existed in a social context and carried different meanings in different contexts.

Nineteenth-century doctors did not agree on the causes of insanity any more than they agreed on what insanity was. They would have concurred that the causes were multiple. Doctors, friends, family members, clerics, and legal officials called some people's behavior insane because of religious bias. (For example, annual reports listed Mormonism as a cause of insanity, and spiritualism was cited as a symptom.) Such reports also hypothesized about the many nonphysical causes of lunacy, such as idleness or bad luck, luxury or poverty, sunstroke, religious excitement or atheism, or the death of a loved one.[4]

Doctors also assumed there were physical causes, as yet unseen or unidentified by medical science. If a patient received a blow to the head, this would constitute an exceptionally identifiable physical cause. Most alienists assumed odd behaviors to be manifestations of an underlying disease affecting the brain.[5] One important doctor, John P. Gray, took this view seriously: his theory was that insanity was entirely dependent on physical disease and that moral causes (like religious excitement) affected the mind only when the body was already weak.[6] Hereditary factors were a common concern. One Victorian doctor opined that "a hereditary constitutional defect" was the predisposing cause of the "disease of the brain, on which insanity is always based."[7] The state of the brain after severe childhood disease could also make a person more likely to become insane. Neglect of the physical training of young people and the excessive gratification of their capricious feelings impaired the nervous system. Intemperance was frequently cited. And if a patient had a tendency toward insanity, environmental conditions (pressure at home, maltreatment in the county jail, or neglect in the almshouse) would exacerbate the problem. In the nineteenth century, insanity came to be seen as an interaction between biological and environmental factors.

Even if doctors could not agree on what exactly insanity was, or what caused it, they could agree that their treatments improved upon the past. By the middle of the nineteenth century, as far as doctors were concerned, the shivering madman of the eighteenth century was an apparition from long ago. He had been released from his shackles, and he no longer huddled on a cold, dirty floor chained to a wall (Figure I.1). He now had the opportunity to live on a clean, orderly ward, dress in decent clothes, and go out-of-doors. Importantly, for the time period discussed in chapters 2, 3, and 4, insanity was not seen as an unkind visitation from God, a religious taint that no human intervention could overcome. In the minds of Anglo-American reformers, lunatics were transformed from beastly persons into

sick ones. In Daniel Hack Tuke and Charles Bucknill's *Manual of Psychological Medicine* of 1858, we see a sympathetic depiction of the mentally alienated, categorized roughly by type of disease (Figure I.2). These are the patients as doctors envisioned them. How they saw themselves is a different question.

One specific cause of insanity was thought to be civilization itself. Thus the insane hospital, which on the one hand symbolized the progressiveness of a civilized nation, also announced the corruption caused by industrialization, urbanization, and the quest for profit. The very fact that modern society required asylums pointed to the high cost of progress, a sad side effect of the growth of industry and commerce. Nineteenth-century thinkers believed that civilization caused insanity through a subtle process of mental disease preying on society's weakest individuals. Generally, it was agreed, civilization strengthened the nervous system through its demanding disciplinary and educational processes. But there were some people, fragile from the outset because

Figure I.1. *Madness,* as illustrated in Charles Bell, *Anatomy and Philosophy of Expression as Connected with the Fine Arts* (London: George Bell and Sons, 1806), 160. Courtesy of Wellcome Library, London.

Figure I.2. Daniel Hack Tuke and Charles Bucknill,
Manual of Psychological Medicine (London: J. & A.
Churchill, 1858), frontispiece. The patients depicted
here have greater dignity than the figure in *Madness*;
the woman in the center was said to have
"monomania of pride."

of "some defect in organization, inherited or acquired,"[8] who fell to the wayside. Psychiatrist Henry P. Stearns, writing for *Scribner's* in 1879, reported that "Christianity has taught us to pick them up and try to nurse them to strength for further battle. She has built hospitals and asylums, and these weaker ones drift into these refuges from the storm."[9] Many writers contended that modern society was overstimulating and adversely affected the mental state of the populace.[10]

The insane hospital, like so many other social institutions, was a microcosm of the values of society at large. Daniel Tuke noted that both the higher mental feelings, such as religious yearning and moral sentiment, and the lower proclivities, like lustfulness, were subjected to "an amount of excitement unknown to savage tribes."[11] Freed slaves lost their reason, supposedly, as the pressure of owning land and earning wages bore down upon them.[12] Thus, freedom for some was a cause of insanity. Once incarcerated, the races were treated differently, too. Like race, class figured greatly in the supposed causes of insanity and in the practice of asylum medicine. Dr. Stearns identified class stratification caused by urbanization as a root of insanity:

> Another condition incident to civilization which tends largely to develop and increase insanity . . . is *the unequal distribution of the means of living*, especially in the large cities and manufacturing communities. . . . Impure air, from overcrowding, the effect of which upon the delicate tissue of the nervous system is deleterious in the highest degree; the lack of all facilities for bathing; the insufficient, irregular, and often unwholesome food-supply, and its improper preparation for use; . . . immoral practices which grow out of such surroundings and practices, all tend strongly in one direction.[13]

That direction, of course, was toward madness. In practice, wealthy patients paid fees to stay in state hospitals, but unlike indigent patients in the same institutions, upper-class inmates could bring their own furniture, books, and even servants. The poorest patients were not allowed to mix freely with the wealthy; those who were accustomed to good food and fine furnishings were accommodated on the best-maintained wards. As medical historian Charles E. Rosenberg wrote of the modern hospital, it is an "institution that reproduces values and social relationships of the wider world and

yet manages at the same time to remain isolated in its particular way from the society that created and supports it."[14] Much the same can be said of the nineteenth-century asylum.

The Rise of the Asylum

Scholars in the history of psychiatry concur that asylums increased in number over the course of the nineteenth century. Historian and sociologist Andrew Scull has searched for grand economic and societal causes for the rise of the asylum, and maintains that an overall uptick in affluence, the shift to a service economy, and nascent consumerism (which he places in the eighteenth century for England), partly explain the asylum's heyday. Social forces acting upon the family made commitments more likely than in earlier times. Historian Gerald Grob explains, "In its origins, the mental hospital—irrespective of its medical role—was primarily an institution designed . . . to assume functions that previously had been the responsibility of families."[15] The geographical separation of the workplace from the home tended to create smaller and more specialized families and "undermined their capacity to care for needy and especially elderly members."[16] It was time-consuming and expensive for anyone to care for a relative; assuming healthy, concerned persons needed to work for a living, they would have to pay for private nurses to tend their ill relatives while they were out working, or they would have to seek treatment for them in an asylum. As the numbers of displaced and family-less people increased with industrialization, so did the need for state care. Insane asylums housed a disproportionately high number of single people compared to the general population. These were precisely the people who had no one to turn to when they fell ill. (A less generous interpretation voiced at the time was that such people were, by dint of their lunacy, not at the front of the line for spouses.)[17] Porter makes a more general point in *Mind-Forg'd Manacles:* families gradually started to pay for many services that had never been part of the market economy, and hiring experts to care for an insane relative was one of those services.[18] All of these are reasons why the number of asylums increased over the course of the nineteenth century.

Scull concludes that "the asylum provided a convenient and culturally legitimate alternative to coping with 'intolerable' individuals."[19] Asylums were "culturally legitimate" because doctors claimed that insanity could not be treated outside the home and that cures could only be achieved in institutions. This was a powerful incentive for families to commit a relative. Scull notes that the asylum "created the demand for its own services."[20] Of course, the doctors would have denied any such self-serving motive, claiming that they were only trying to help society's most miserable dependents. They promulgated a medical theory, albeit somewhat tautological, that lunacy needed to be treated shortly after the onset of the disease; a lunatic could be cured only in the asylum; therefore, time spent at home led toward an incurable state. By separating the lunatic from the home, the morbid associations of his or her previous life would be broken down, and, in the orderly halls of the asylum, mental disturbances would be replaced by feelings of a more healthful nature.[21] Also, the domestic scene could have been an environmental cause for the patient's mental instability. Alienists frequently maligned the well-intentioned friends and relatives who kept an ill person in the family domicile. A British alienist summed it up: "All persons who have managed lunatics advise removal from the home."[22]

To put it succinctly, mentally ill people were "both disturbed and disturbing," as Scull points out:

> [T]hey were often themselves in great distress and simultaneously the source of great stress on the lives of those forced to interact and cope with them. Unquestionably, they constituted a threat, both symbolic and practical, to the community at large. They were the source and harbingers of commotion and disarray in the family; social embarrassment and exclusion; fear of violence to people and property; the threat of suicide; the looming financial disasters that flow from the inability to work or the unwise expenditures of material resources.[23]

The threat to society was both symbolic and practical, and so was the threat to the individual family.

The Victorian era reveled in the sanctity of the home and the nuclear family as the primary social unit; therefore, when an insane relative threatened the day-to-day life of the family, he or she might be shifted out of the home and into the hands of strangers. If the very existence of the family unit was perceived to be under siege, family members would be compelled to commit a relative.[24] Nineteenth-century doctors were conscious of the fact that families struggled with committing a relative, and they sought to ease the family's concern through reassuring domestic language in their annual reports. However, doctors faced a paradox. The institutions they managed were large, and seemingly unwelcoming, but doctors needed their patients' families to have confidence in them. The paradox is evident in the architecture of linear plan asylums: the exteriors of large asylums projected a civic presence, while the interiors were broken up into smaller rooms, even though the long corridors do not resemble a farmhouse, cottage, or rowhouse.[25] Thus, a simple dichotomy (home vs. institution) is not sufficient to frame the complicated relationships among homes, asylums, doctors, patients, and families.

Historian James E. Moran acknowledges the "impressive growth in institutionalized care for the insane," but he also states that "it is evident that many Americans considered to be insane in the antebellum United States were never sent to the asylum."[26] In 1855, a report on the insane in Massachusetts stated that there were 1,348 lunatics in institutions and 1,284 at home.[27] The census of 1880 calculated that of 91,959 insane persons in the United States, 50,879 were incarcerated and the rest (about 45 percent) were "at home or in private care."[28] Historian David Wright has quite reasonably attempted to divorce the history of confinement from the history of psychiatry. He and Moran both remind us not to take the doctors' rhetoric about removal from the home as fact. Their research has aided me in thinking about the asylum as one possible site for a lunatic to survive, recover, or expire, but it was one site among many, and not the social necessity historians have often assumed.

The Professionalization of Psychiatry in the Asylum

The practice of medicine took on great significance in public life during the nineteenth century. The first psychiatrists in the United States emerged as superintendents in insane asylums, beginning in the 1770s, with a sharp upturn in their professional ranks in the 1830s. For a period of time, psychiatrists boasted greater social stature than physicians. In 1800, physicians had little more social status than snake oil salesmen, whereas by 1900 the activities of medical men, doctors, surgeons, and pharmacists were recognized as socially beneficial. In the United States, from about 1830 on, psychiatry was actually known as "Asylum Medicine," and psychiatrists created a professional organization (the precursor to the American Psychiatric Association) called the Association of Medical Superintendents of American Institutions for the Insane (AMSAII), whose name suggests that they defined themselves as caretakers of large organizations. The robustness and status of those organizations gave doctors legitimacy within the medical profession and society. While local family doctors served the needs of insane people in their homes, the professionalization of psychiatry *as a specialty* took place in asylums. (A patient did not need the asylum to be a lunatic, but a doctor needed the asylum to be a psychiatrist.) Psychiatric specialists practiced primarily in insane hospitals—they did not make house calls, hang a shingle in town, or hold the equivalent of today's office visits.

Superintendents were autocratic leaders within their asylums, and they often used their power to shape architecture. In my view, it is correct to assume that the establishment of psychiatry as a legitimate branch of medicine was advanced by the construction of elaborate state-funded hospitals, although I do not go so far as to conclude that the rise of elaborate asylums was an outright conspiracy of empire-building doctors. (One of the challenges in writing this book was to avoid belittling, aggrandizing, and apologizing for physicians, but, instead, to present their ideas as part of mainstream medical and social systems of belief.) Officially sanctioned medical journals were replete with articles on architecture, a constant preoccupation for asylum superintendents. Doctors did not shape these environments by themselves, but rather in collaboration with architects. The history of asylum architecture does not make sense without explicating the doctors' motivations and intentions, but, at times, the gap between rhetoric and achievement yawns. Wright has concluded that the medical superintendents were less important medical figures than historians have surmised: "Alienists were glorified

administrators, inspecting the most interesting cases, attending medico-psychological conferences."[29] Wright is convincing about the relatively minor role played by superintendents in recruiting new patients, but, for the art history I am writing here, these aptly named "glorified administrators" were crucial as architectural patrons.

The Architecture of Madness, will, I hope, make a contribution both to the history of psychiatry and to the history of architecture. A recent group of historians of medicine has tackled such issues as legal cases, boarding-out policies, the resistance of individuals, and community reaction to mentally ill individuals.[30] I optimistically include myself among these recent historians of lunacy and hope that my research on architecture adds depth to their studies on social policy, law, kinship relations, and historical epidemiology. My research on architecture does not undercut or radically alter recent conclusions in the history of psychiatry, but rather enriches the discourse through sustained and detailed study of changes to this building type over time.

In architectural history, my work builds on that of Jeremy Taylor, Christine Stevenson, and Leslie Topp, who analyze the ways in which psychiatric hospitals were potent forces in the treatment of mental illness. Stevenson has advised that "asylum appearances mattered in the same way their plans did; actively, instrumentally, in themselves therapies."[31] The historical record makes it clear that architecture was considered essential to the cure. Indeed, historians of psychiatry share the opinion that architecture was of signal importance to the asylum project.[32] Historical documents corroborate this position. For example, in the middle of the eighteenth century, the head physician at newly opened St. Luke's Hospital in London, William Battie, published his "Treatise on Madness," which contained an early unambiguous statement that the asylum itself could be therapeutic. Battie claimed that insanity was as curable as "many other distempers," and he wrote confidently in 1758: "[R]epeated experience has convinced me that confinement alone is often times sufficient, but always so necessary, that without it every method hitherto devised for the cure of Madness would be ineffectual."[33] So it seems clear that architecture participated in cures and treatments, but how and why the environment determined behavior are much larger questions.

The Idea of Environmental Determinism

The idea that the environment, including architecture, shapes behavior has been called "environmental determinism," and it remains a concept, however elusive, in architectural discourse today. In the case of asylums, nineteenth-century thinkers clearly believed the environment could not only influence behavior but also cure a disease. David Rothman noted the prevalence of environmental determinism in the context of Jacksonian America:

> American environment had become so particularly treacherous that insanity struck its citizens with terrifying regularity. One had only to take this dismal analysis one step further to find an antidote. Create a different kind of environment, which methodically corrected the deficiencies of the community, and a cure for the insane was at hand.[34]

Degraded environments, such as cities, produced degenerate populations.

To American historians, the preference for agrarian life over the bustle of the industrialized city will have a familiar ring. Andrew Jackson Downing and before him Thomas Jefferson idealized life lived close to the land. Jefferson located his beloved University of Virginia in Charlottesville, then a small town, to protect the young wards from the bad influence of city life. Jefferson placed the university's pavilions—"pavilion" being a term taken from hospital design—facing one another across a grassy lawn in an attempt to control behavior in his academic village.[35] He apparently was brokenhearted when the students got into fistfights and other mayhem in the year 1825. Jefferson hoped the environment would lead them away from crime, not toward it. Crime was among the greatest social ills that Enlightenment thinkers hoped to eradicate through the force of improving environments.

Environmental determinism is the thread that connects three other buildings types to the asylum. This book will explore attempts to educate healthy minds through university buildings, and to reeducate unhealthy minds through asylum design. Both colleges and asylums faced questions of whether to house all the activities in one building, or to spread them out in a cluster of smaller buildings with different purposes. This comparison is especially important because it illustrates that colleges used architecture to construct a cultural norm (healthy students) and insane asylums used architecture to instruct the inmates on achieving normality. Mental hospitals will also be compared to prisons, which faced related challenges of surveillance and organization of inmates. A third theme is the comparison of mental hospitals to medical hospitals—the most obvious comparison but in some ways the most unexpected. Since injured and contagious people in medical hospitals were confined to bed for much of their stay, there are surprising differences between the spaces for the ambulatory lunatic and those for the bedridden patient. Also, the trajectory of mental health institutions was in some respects the opposite of the path of medical hospitals. Medical hospitals increased in prestige toward the end of the nineteenth century, but insane asylums declined as the twentieth century began. The early success of the asylum represented a departure from traditional attitudes toward regular hospitals, which were regarded as places of last resort for the poor. The context of these other building types is important because they were all newly invented institutions that watched over, controlled, housed, and categorized their inhabitants. In the prison, university, medical hospital, and asylum, builders expected the human-made environment to determine behavior.

Environmental determinism as a concept may be found in discourse about all these building types, as well as gardens. Landscape historian Therese O'Malley has written that "the botanic garden developed in part as a response to the new empirical sciences and to the new understanding they fostered of the influence of environmental conditions. . . . the notion that environment exerted an influence on human character had a long tradition in social theory."[36] Hector St. Jean de Crèvecoeur, an eighteenth-century farmer in Pennsylvania, wrote:

> Men are like plants; the goodness and flavour of the fruit proceeds from the peculiar soil and exposition in which they grow. We are nothing but what we derive from the air we breathe, the climate we inhabit, the government we obey, the system of religion we profess, and the nature of our employment.[37]

O'Malley goes on to say: "This quotation is a particularly cogent expression of environmental determinism, pervasive in America, where a new nation that proclaimed itself to be in compliance with 'natural law' was in its formative stages. The botanic garden was perhaps the clearest attempt to construct an improving environment."[38] It is my hope that the research for this book continues O'Malley's work. Just as the botanic garden was a good example of an improving environment, so too were insane asylums. In nineteenth-century America, university builders, social reformers, park enthusiasts, and asylum doctors shared many values: that nature was curative, exercise therapeutic, and the city a source of vice.

Frederick Law Olmsted believed that the most powerful effect of nature took place by an unconscious process. Olmsted's father loved natural scenery and often took his son on horseback trips to enjoy the picturesque views. The Olmsteds' family minister, Horace Bushnell, used the phrase "unconscious influence" to describe the effect of one person on another, and the effect of the environment on an individual. Words were not necessary—the silent emanation of a man's good character would have a subtle influence on those around him. Olmsted adapted these ideas to theorize about the sway of beautiful scenery on the mind, concluding that the land was a force for good, smoothing the rough edges of humankind. As landscape historian Charles E. Beveridge described it, Olmsted decided that scenery "worked by an unconscious process to produce relaxing and 'unbending' of faculties made tense by the strain, noise, and artificial surroundings of urban life. The necessary condition for such an experience was the absence of distractions and demands on the conscious mind. The effect came not as a result of examination, analysis, or comparison, nor of appreciation of particular parts of the scene; rather, it came in such a way that the viewer was unaware of its workings."[39] Olmsted participated in the design of five asylum landscapes. He believed, as did many, that the workings of the sane mind and the insane mind were not so different. The fact that the environmental influence was unconscious suggested that it could operate even on those who had apparently lost their reason. The subtle, positive influence of nature on healthy people could be applied to sick people, and what was an enhancement for the healthy might be an out-and-out cure for the sick.

Good food, exercise, walks in the brisk air, plenty of sleep, and the absence of too much intensity—these were all considered appropriate for healthy people and were also used as treatments for the insane. Dr. John Galt wrote in 1855: "[T]here is not any great difference between the rules for the government of the sane mind and those applicable to a mind diseased. And, indeed, it has been a doctrine advanced by standard authority, that the best policy in the general management of the lunatic consists in deviating as little as possible from the ordinary daily life and habits of the sane."[40] Although this book focuses on habitations for the mentally ill, the research described here illuminates more than the plight of the afflicted. In fact, we can learn a great deal about nineteenth-century attitudes toward the supposedly normal human mind by studying attitudes toward the deranged.

Terminology

The use of historically grounded language is the convention among historians of medicine. I grant that words such as "asylum" and "lunatic" are hurtful to modern sensibilities, as I suppose that our words for awkward subjects will seem callous to future generations. In this book, terms appear more or less in chronological order, so, for example, "madman" appears in the chapter that considers the eighteenth century, but the word is phased out in favor of "patient" and "insane person" in later chapters. In this way, the terms help re-create the cultural context for the reader. To vary diction, some generic modern terms, such as "the mentally ill" and "psychiatric hospital" are incorporated throughout. A lengthier note on terminology may be found in Appendix A.

The Historiography of Madness

The historiography of madness is fraught with dissent, and even though the debates are well known to medical historians, other readers may benefit from a summary of the key historiographical issues. In the first half of the twentieth century, Whiggish historians pronounced asylum doctors to be compassionate men in search of reform. The discoveries of doctors and the improvements in treatment were evidence of the forward march of progress.[41] Progress-minded historians presented the pre-Enlightenment period as a dark age for the mentally ill, and they further suggested that asylum practices were positive steps on the path toward modern psychiatry.

In 1961, with the publication of *Madness and Civilization,* Michel Foucault drew attention to the dialectical nature of reason and madness, stating that each was defined in terms of the other. The age of reason, in Foucault's edgy formulation, was not at all reasonable, but was rather a fierce regime of oppression that subjected those who had lost their reason to a massive confinement based on trumped-up moral grounds. For historians of psychiatry, Foucault's limits as a historian are familiar. Scholars who study the Middle Ages concur that the well-known metaphor of the Ship of Fools was just that—a metaphor—but Foucault claimed there were actual ships set afloat with lunatic cargo.[42] Another of Foucault's memorable and oddly pleasing images is the happy pre-Enlightenment wandering lunatic or village idiot, whose lack of reason threatened no one and who was supposedly left to his own devices or even cared for by the community. Unfortunately, this picture was a figment of Foucault's imagination. As Scull has explained, "Where the mad proved troublesome, they could expect to be beaten or locked up; otherwise they might roam or rot. Either way, the facile contrast between psychiatric oppression and an earlier almost anarchic toleration is surely illusory."[43] My position is aligned with those historians who view the plight of the insane as serious, and who concede that asylums, while deeply flawed, were an improvement over dark, wet cellars, holes in the ground, or cages. And although it continues to be a subject of intense debate among historians, I tend to agree with those scholars who think that, most, but not all, of the people in psychiatric hospitals in the nineteenth century had severe mental illnesses.[44]

Madness and Civilization relies on the idea of a "great confinement" of deviants affected by centralized capitalist states. During Foucault's so-called Classical Age (1650–1800), absolutism, under the guise of rationalist social organization, caused beggars, criminals, lunatics, and wanderers to be lumped together through the agency of the state. Porter has explained that such "lumping together" might have happened in France, but not in Britain or the rest of Europe. Readers of Foucault are left with the impression that "the state" confined lunatics, in the sense that proto-policemen locked up vagrants who eventually were placed in asylums. In fact, recent scholarship shows that "the majority" of inmates were "admitted by family members."[45]

In spite of the complaints, most scholars agree that Foucault's challenging ideas pressed historians to ask new questions and seek better answers. Melling has referred to Foucault's "extravagant historical errors,"[46] but he also acknowledges that Foucault's taunting approach inspired many historically minded authors to study insanity in detail, with an eye toward its shifting and socially constructed meanings. Scull further explains: "On a purely mundane level, it was surely the reception accorded to Foucault's work, and the stature he came to occupy in both the academy and café society, that played a major role in rescuing madness from the clutches of drearily dull administrative historians and/or psychiatrists in their dotage, thus giving the whole topic the status of a serious intellectual subject and thus attracting us to it in the first place."[47] In sympathy with Foucault, most historians, including this one, agree that insanity exists in a dialectical relationship between reason and unreason, and that it is more than a medical disease marked by physiological signs that lead to clear diagnoses.[48] So the knife of Foucault cuts two ways, both spurring further historical research and causing great confusion.

Rothman's important book, *The Discovery of the Asylum,* first published in 1971, concisely summarized *Madness and Civilization* as dealing with "ideas alone, never connecting them to events."[49] Rothman's book has become a standard introduction to the theme of social control in the new republic, and its challenging ideas have stimulated historical debate. Rothman claimed that the development of the asylum was exceptionally American, that the changes wrought by the Jacksonian era and fears of the increasingly diverse, urban, and modern America led social reformers to confine deviants. Many authors, including Porter and Scull, rejected this exceptionalist view, because they found too many similarities in Great Britain and Canada during the same period to pin the "discovery of the asylum" on the anxieties of Jacksonian America.

Most assuredly, however, Rothman's contributions are many. First, he denounced prisons, almshouses, and insane hospitals, noting that although prisoners' chains were removed, the systems of control under which they lived were "highly regimented and repressive."[50] In my attempt to attain a level of architectural specificity, I differentiate between prisons and asylums, but Rothman emphasizes their similarities, which is valuable, too. Both institutions offer evidence of a society grasping for ways of managing difficult populations, even though, as Rothman points out, doctors wished to avoid associating asylums with jails. At a basic level, both prisons and asylums rejected the pre-Enlightenment method of chaining deviants to walls in favor of elaborate architecture. Indeed, Rothman focused on architecture when he wrote, "The institution itself held the secret to the cure of insanity. Incarceration in a specially designed setting, not the medicines that might be administered or the surgery that might be performed there, would restore health,"[51] and he noted the doctors' calls for a linear asylum to be materially different from "ordinary habitations."[52] Rothman analyzed the metaphor of the family as used by doctors, but his book might leave the reader unaware of segregate (cottage) and congregate asylums, even though he explains the different types of prisons. He called attention to moral treatment's layers of control: the classification of patients, organization of their daily routines, the punctuality demanded by the ringing of bells. He convincingly portrayed the asylum as an institution that allowed medical superintendents to create a microcosm of their vision of a proper society.

By studying legal cases, Moran has developed a more nuanced picture of how societies defined and managed the insane; his research cleverly illustrates the blurred boundary between sane and insane and, and while his work does not lend itself to architectural history, it is important for the reader to know what happened to lunatics who were not behind asylum walls. Moran shows that a span of possibilities existed. For instance, when a farmer was deemed unable to care for his land, a group of neighbors might ask for the formation of a commission in lunacy, similar to a jury, but made up of twenty-four landowning men. This commission would decide whether the allegedly crazy farmer was truly insane: but if he were found insane, he was not

necessarily sent to the state asylum. He might be allowed to work his own farm as a wage laborer, while neighbors acted as guardians.[53] Moran also identified a situation in which a madman's appointed guardians had deserted their duties by allowing him to roam half-naked around town, which in turn caused the townspeople to ask a local judge to petition the neglectful guardians.[54] Even in this case, the townspeople did not request that the man be institutionalized, only that his guardians live up to their legal duties. In another case, a farmer was considered to be slightly deluded but was allowed to keep his farm because he was well enough to perform his social duties and conduct business. These cases also exemplify a version of community care of the insane, in that relatives and friends maintained insane people without sequestering them.[55]

Keeping in mind the many lunatics who lived outside the asylum, one might still argue that a reorganization of society into sane and insane was represented by the very existence of these large-scale structures. Architecture performed a kind of cultural work through these buildings by making such categories obvious. The construction of a colossal stone asylum in Utica in 1841, for example, would have communicated at the time a division between those inside the walls (insane) and those outside (probably, but not necessarily, sane). However, in the nineteenth century, the categories were not stable. Edgar Allan Poe's story "The System of Dr. Tarr and Professor Fether" (1845), in which the protagonist, upon visiting an asylum, only gradually realizes that the lunatics have taken over the madhouse, is one of countless examples that not only recognized but celebrated the blurry line between sanity and insanity.

Asylums were expensive public buildings, and as such, legitimized psychiatric knowledge. Indeed, in comparison to other charity cases, lunatics consumed the most state funds in the United States in the nineteenth century. Aside from prisons and state capitols, asylums were among the only state-funded buildings in Victorian America. They were technological marvels that demonstrated advanced fireproof construction, state-of-the-art heating and ventilation, and fresh water delivery systems; some had their own railroads. They were surrounded by well-designed, picturesque gardens that predate many public parks. According to Dr. Henry M. Hurd, who compiled a four-volume history of mental institutions in 1916–17, there were 297 institutions for the insane in the United States, and 32 in Canada, including both public and private.[56] Asylums deserve careful scholarly attention for these basic historical reasons alone.

It was not my goal to produce a catalogue raisonné of American asylums.[57] Rather, I selected specific cases to demonstrate significant changes in the development of the building type (for example, Trenton) or a change in theories about architecture for the insane (Kankakee) or an utter disaster (Peoria). This is primarily a book of architectural history, and the facilities themselves are the starting point of my study. In a few examples, I selected buildings that are still standing rather than similar ones that have been demolished, since it seemed reasonable to concentrate on structures I could visit and that might stand a chance of adaptive reuse. (The now vanished California State Hospital at Napa from 1875, for example, duplicates issues raised by Greystone in New Jersey.) Accomplished architects, including John Notman, Samuel Sloan, Thomas U. Walter, Frederick Clarke Withers, Calvert Vaux, and H. H. Richardson, designed asylum buildings. Downing and Olmsted designed grounds. But, again, my goal was to write a social and cultural history of a building type. It was almost an ancillary benefit that the rich subject allowed me to explore "big name" architects working within the constraints of this prescriptive building type. In some ways, I faced the same challenges that Abigail Van Slyck stared down in *Free to All: Carnegie Libraries and American Culture, 1890–1920*. As she explains in the introduction to that book, the Carnegie libraries fell into a methodological gap between histories of architectural innovation and vernacular architecture studies. Asylums fall into the same gap. They are too large, expensive, formal, and professional to attract historians of vernacular architecture. And they have not been of much interest to traditional architectural historians, for at least three reasons. The architects were not famous. Or, when famous architects did design asylums, they appeared to be following a preset plan. Finally, architectural historians see themselves as conveyors of refinement and culture, an image that does not accord well with skulking around psychiatric hospitals during research sabbaticals. It is necessary to find a place for buildings that lie between vernacular and traditional architectural histories; as Van Slyck suggests, we would do well to "look at buildings as evidence of social processes in which a variety of attitudes are negotiated in specific social and cultural settings."[58]

Such studies as this one need boundaries. I chose not to write about small private sanatoria, like the one managed by George Cook in Canandaigua, New York, because while they are fascinating as examples of alternative extra-asylum treatment, a very small percentage of patients were treated in them, and mainstream doctors disparaged the oversized houses for being poorly planned and not purpose-built. One doctor wrote, "Speaking generally . . . they are badly arranged, and only in very few particulars well fitted to serve as residences and hospitals for the insane."[59] For example, houses tended not to have central heat or advanced ventilation, two mainstays of asylum construction; doctors made a sport of finding fault with private madhouses that had clumsy fittings and appliances worse than those in state-run asylums for mere paupers.[60] But, other scholars might well take on the reuse of mansions for madhouses. A brief review of private hospitals appears in chapter 4, but, in the United States, state-funded care of the insane dominated the psychiatric world, and thus I considered those more fully.[61] I hesitated to repeat the error commonly made by architectural historians of recognizing only those structures that were innovative, but I did decide for this building type, which has never been studied before, to focus on moments of change.

Other types of charitable institutions, not discussed here, are certainly worthy of further study. For example, inebriate asylums conveyed values about drinking, drunkenness, and immigrant groups once strongly associated with alcohol, primarily the Irish. Some social reformers claimed that inebriates were clogging up the county jails and disrupting the already messy life of the insane asylum, and several doctors proposed dedicated institutions for the care of inebriates. The pattern of first medicalizing a condition, then constructing separate confining buildings for its treatment, follows a general tendency in the nineteenth century.

Asylums for the feebleminded, also called idiot asylums, were a different matter. Sadly, the so-called feebleminded, today defined loosely as the developmentally disabled or the mentally handicapped, were beneath the notice of most institutional psychiatrists, who discerned that those born with limited mental faculties were not going to recover. For example, the chromosomal condition later named Down's syndrome was evident at birth and never changed during a person's life. Similarly, autism manifested in young children, and its symptoms did not appear to improve. Most of the doctors discussed in this book were fixated on a finding a cure; therefore, they did their best to keep non-insane incurable people out of their supposedly therapeutic hospitals. The advocates for the developmentally disabled emerged around 1870, later on the scene than the supporters of the mentally ill. These reformers found, to their dismay, that the state's funds were allocated unfairly in favor of the insane. The goal of the idiot asylums was not to cure but rather to provide education and comfort. In this

way, their goals were similar to asylums for the incurable, or euphemistically, "chronic," insane.

Outline

Chapter 1 examines the architecture of Bethlem and leads into the late eighteenth century, the same time when Battie worked at St. Luke's. The purpose-built asylums at Williamsburg, Virginia, and Columbia, South Carolina, represent early attempts to house America's madmen. Chapter 1 introduces moral management or moral treatment, the method by which psychiatrists inculcated their subjects with self-control and positive thoughts. Diverting activities such as walking in the grounds, boat trips, acting in skits, and sleigh rides

Figure I.3. Attendants and patients out for a sleigh ride, Hudson River State Hospital, Poughkeepsie, New York. Lantern slide, no date. Courtesy of Oskar Diethelm Library, Institute for the History of Psychiatry, Weill Medical College, Cornell University.

were part of the cure and part of the internal culture of the asylum (Figure I.3). Establishing a cure was Dr. Thomas S. Kirkbride's career-long preoccupation. Kirkbride, a Philadelphia Quaker, believed good architecture was essential for the comfort, security, and recovery of lunatics. His work completes chapter 1 and forms a bridge to chapter 2. Chapter 2 focuses on the development of the linear plan, also known by Kirkbride's name. The plan is peculiar to the United States. The linear plan was really not all that linear: asylum plans did not dictate a long straight building, but rather one in which the wards were set back *en echelon*. As the century moved along, the plans became even less linear, with wards that turned at ninety-degree angles. (In spite of the term's faults, I thought it best to use the nineteenth-century phrase "linear plan," which I use interchangeably with "Kirkbride plan.")

This book spans a longer period, from 1770 to 1894, but the Kirkbride plan dominated in the United States from 1840 to about 1880. The first freestanding hospital for the insane was built in 1770; the year 1894 was the fiftieth anniversary of the Association of Medical Superintendents of American Institutions for the Insane, and a speech given by S. Wier Mitchell marked a downturn in the prestige of institutional psychiatry. But even while the Kirkbride plan held sway, doctors carried on conversations about other modes of housing the insane. Some doctors claimed that large monolithic asylums had not lived up to expectations, and as an alternative, they suggested that new cottages be arranged as in a village. An even more radical suggestion was to house lunatics in the community, a notion inspired by the Belgian town of Gheel, whose residents had looked after mentally ill people for centuries. Dr. Merrick Bemis caused a rift among the self-named "brethren" of asylum superintendents when he recommended a farm colony for the Worcester State Hospital in Massachusetts. The alternatives to linear plan hospitals are described in chapter 3. Surprisingly, the program for large mental hospitals did not change much between 1840 and the century's end, nor did it change much at cottage and linear plan hospitals. A combination of medical treatments and moral management dominated care; when some patients were shuttled off to asylums for the incurable, their caretakers claimed the same diversions to be beneficial.

As we learn in chapter 4, in the second half of the century, asylums exploded in number and size: Kirkbride and his colleagues had originally limited the institution to 250 patients, but the AMSAII increased the allowable number of inhabitants to 600 in 1866. Architects responded with plans for state hospitals in a range of then-fashionable styles. Calvert Vaux designed a private hospital that resembled side-by-side villas, Frederick Clarke Withers built a sprawling High Victorian Gothic building on an original plan, and H. H. Richardson refined the tenets of the Kirkbride plan with a massive Romanesque pile. These grand structures are the subjects of chapter 4. The organization of this book may seem to imply an evolution from one institution to the next, but there was no such teleological progression. Indeed, the time period for chapters 3 and 4 overlaps.

As an architectural historian greatly interested in reception, I would have jumped at the chance to understand the buildings through the inmates' eyes.[62] But other than a few accounts written by falsely committed people who hated their doctors and despised their asylums, I have found little fodder for reception study. Even so, chapter 2 includes the stories of Ebenezer Haskell and Elizabeth Packard, who believed themselves to be unfairly imprisoned by cruel relatives. A third complainant, Francis Delilez, wrote a book about his imprisonment in a Wisconsin state asylum. These fascinating tales from the inside offer some glimpse into the role of space and power from the patient's point of view. The undercover reporter Nellie Bly's *Ten Days in a Mad-house* offered evocative details about patients, nurses, and doctors, but Bly commented little on the spaces she occupied during her research, when she posed as a lunatic in order to write her exposé.

It is a truism of architectural history that powerful people build big buildings, and asylums were big. Thus, my historical lens has remained regrettably somewhat focused on the socially powerful: patrons, state officials, public advocates, doctors, and architects. There is not that much evidence about whether the spaces of these buildings were used in the ways the doctors proposed, but the few reception studies show that there was often a messy slippage between the shape of a place and how it was really used.

In addition to the patients' testimonials, plans and vintage photographs offer much evidence of the spatial sequences of the asylum, and some indication of the patient's place in those interiors. Doctors left behind by far the greatest number of historical documents; annual reports of hospitals, doctors' papers, periodical publications such as the *American Journal of Insanity* were all valuable sources.[63] One unexpected source was Robert Wozniak's collection of more than one thousand postcards of insane hospitals. Perusing that number of images allowed me to look at the exteriors of buildings from coast to coast and to select representative case studies. I also chose three patrons, Drs. Kirkbride, Gray, and Buttolph, who were involved in commissioning two asylums each; their patronage shows development of the building type over time.

The Kirkbride plan was the cutting edge of medical architecture in the 1840s and 1850s, and the treatment enacted there, moral management, was similarly forward-looking. Doctors thought their buildings would operate instrumentally, but they did not always. The AMSAII held fast to the Kirkbride plan even while cottages were being constructed in the 1870s and tentative experiments with community care were under way in the 1880s. At the time of the debates between Kirkbride plan proponents and cottage promoters, both groups adhered to a general principle, namely, that an improved environment could enhance people's lives, and moral management was attempted in both architectural types. Alienists did not completely abandon their belief in the therapeutic environment when the linear hospitals became overcrowded and impersonal. Rather, they asked for different environments and made claims about comforting, not curing, their unfortunate tenants.

Doctors thought that architecture was a part of the *cure* for patients who were likely to improve, and part of the *treatment* for the chronically ill. Major aspects of moral management continued in all manner of buildings, and medical interventions (opiates and laxatives) persisted throughout the nineteenth century, but the architectural component of the cure changed. In the 1890s, when neurologists mocked asylum doctors for their lack of scientific research, institutional psychiatrists continued to construct giant state hospitals. Medical culture and material culture did not always proceed apace.

In many ways, these buildings gave physical form, however imperfect, to the ideals of their makers. But psychiatry moved on, and by the middle of the twentieth century, Victorian buildings had no medical credibility. Most were run-down, if still in use; others were dilapidated, empty ghosts of what they had once been. This desperate obsolescence is one of the central issues in architecture and science. Science depends upon currency for legitimacy, and medicine is the same. Nineteenth-century alienists relied upon the newness of their buildings to establish the legitimacy of their nascent profession. Even the cottages of segregate asylums, which evoked familiar surroundings, were medically new. (Nobody wants to be treated at Ye Olde Psychiatric Research Center.) Nostalgia may have a role to play in the design of houses, churches, shopping malls, and entire neotraditional suburbs, but a longing for the past has a limited place in medical buildings. There is a re-created asylum at Colonial Williamsburg, but no smiling actor in period costume giving out laudanum. Psychiatry is uncomfortable with, even embarrassed by, its own history.

Both as an institution and as a type of architecture, the asylum mediates between a person and his or her society. The asylum and its architecture regulated life, limited interaction, controlled activity. It was a place of struggle. Its history does not offer up any grand narratives or totalizing schemes, and I chose to accept that this story would be rife with contradictions. I have always been skeptical of histories that are more about the author than the subject; it seemed to me that this subject, especially, required respectful distance. If I have not pushed the historical evidence as far as others would, if I have not performed feats of scholarly acrobatics, that is intentional, and, I believe, appropriate, for this is a book about places that witnessed a great deal of suffering.

Dr. William Dean Fairless stated in 1861 that "we all have some idea of what an asylum would be, and we hold that as the treatment of the insane is conducted not only *in*, but *by*, the asylum, so no architect is competent to plan the building unless he possesses some knowledge of the treatment of the inmates."[64] The architect who wished to design asylums had to possess knowledge of the treatment of the insane, and so must the architectural historian who wishes to understand them.

1

Transforming the Treatment
ARCHITECTURE AND MORAL MANAGEMENT

It is a proposition, the truth of which cannot perhaps be questioned, that, in proportion as a nation advances in intellectual cultivation; its practical benevolence assumes a loftier standard.

:: Pliny Earle, *A Visit to Thirteen Asylums for the Insane in Europe, with Copious Statistics* (1833) ::

Americans began building lunatic asylums in the eighteenth century, in the wake of reform movements and compelled by a sense of civic and religious duty. They built asylums with increasing speed as the nineteenth century progressed, and soon, in the 1840s, the United States developed its own plan for hospitals for the insane. Nineteenth-century doctors typically placed their benevolent approach to the treatment of the insane against the picture of the brutality of earlier epochs. In constructing new hospitals, they attempted to reject the horrors of Bethlem and include new ideas from England and France that were intended to ameliorate the poor treatment that the insane had suffered until the Enlightenment. To understand the reforms and architecture of the nineteenth century, we must grasp the complex earlier history of these easily criticized institutions.

Notorious Bethlem

By far the most famous and infamous of asylums was London's Bethlem. As the best-known institution for the insane in the English-speaking world, it deserves to be considered here, but not as an architectural model. In fact, American doctors used Bethlem as a counter-example. Bethlem introduces some themes that carry through to the end of the nineteenth century, and hence through this book: Were purpose-built structures

necessary? How should an asylum relate to its city? And should a lunatic asylum be magnificent or modest?

At the close of the nineteenth century, Bethlem was the oldest psychiatric institution in Europe, dating back 650 years. The Priory of St. Mary of Bethlem was founded in 1247 in the City of London as a means to raise funds for the Order of Bethlehem, crusaders in the Holy Lands. The priory was located on Bishopsgate Street, on the north-south road leading to London Bridge. In times of plague, the priory took in sick, indigent victims. It also collected and distributed alms. Records indicate that in 1403 there were six madmen and the following instruments of control: six iron chains with locks, two pairs of stocks, four sets of manacles, and some additional chains. Nineteenth-century charity reformers concluded from the ironmongery alone that the treatment was "wretched indeed."[1] The conditions were cold and damp, inmates slept on the floor, and the place was seldom cleaned. In 1598, it was filthy, with the water supply coming only from a cistern in the backyard.[2] Recent scholars surmise that Bethlem first became known for the treatment of the insane in the sixteenth century, even though the numbers were small: in 1598, there were just twenty madmen housed at the former monastery. In 1650, there were fifty patients, males and females were separated, and servants were forbidden to beat the inmates. This injunction may not sound like much of a humanitarian intervention, but considering the way people were treated in profit-making jails, it was.[3]

New Bedlam in Moor-fields.

Figure 1.1. Robert Hooke, Bethlem, Moorfields, London, 1674–76 (demolished). Courtesy of Wellcome Library, London.

The polymath and architect Robert Hooke designed an improved Bethlem hospital in Moorfields, near Bishopsgate, in 1674. Although it was destroyed in the early nineteenth century, Hooke's fascinating structure and its setting were well known (Figure 1.1). The building's site made it an ornament at the head of Moorfields, one of the largest open spaces then in London. Inmates were not allowed to use the front lawn, which stretched out toward the street, was contained by low walls and a row of evenly spaced trees, and was bisected by a wide path. Airing courts were located at the sides of the structure. Hooke designed a bilaterally symmetrical building composed of a central structure, flanked by two long ward blocks punctuated by central pediments, and bookended neatly by forward projections. At the time, the composition was admired for breaking up what might otherwise have been a tediously long facade.[4] A long range of shallow structures with a French-style pitched roof, it slightly resembled the Tuileries Palace, as some contemporary commentators noticed. Art historian Christine Stevenson regards Londoners as likely to take an odd pride in the fact that their charitable institutions looked like palaces, while their palaces looked like pauper hospitals.[5] A corridor ran the length of the building, with cells on one side, allowing for a gentle breeze through the halls. Critics admired the breezy hallway as early as 1676, offering clear evidence that keepers believed fresh air was healing. When wings were later added perpendicular to the main buildings, these had double-loaded corridors, which were more economical but not as good for ventilation. Hooke improved the sanitation at Bethlem by including cisterns on every floor (except the top) and by locating outdoor latrines at either end of the yard. Servants were required to clean the inmates and the facility. The structure included warming rooms, or stove rooms, which, from the 1760s on, had evolved into parlors.[6] Working in the midst of these architectural improvements, attendants nonetheless restrained the patients with leg locks and handcuffs.[7] The construction was completed quickly, and it was one of the great sights of London, lauded in many a guidebook.

This is the Bethlem that came to be known as "Bedlam," with all that word's connotations of terror and chaos. Later reformers drew themselves up with pride when they discussed its horrors. Writing in 1871, one American alienist decried "the *bedlams* which had been a disgrace to Christendom."[8] "The asylums of today are not the bedlams and mad-houses of former times," wrote another superintendent in 1885.[9] Dark rooms, whippings, food shortages, and general mistreatment characterized the place, and later generations were determined to advance beyond the image of Bedlam.

Bethlem's population rose, and the Moorfields building was quickly overcrowded. The institution moved to Southwark in 1815, where the architect James Lewis demonstrated his up-to-date knowledge of architectural style (Figure 1.2). Lewis was accused of sacrificing the needs of the insane for the doctors' requirements of public show. The Ionic portico and dome were grand, but the lowest level, where the sickest patients lived, was perpetually dark and gloomy. One opinionated architect criticized Lewis's grand portico for casting shadows on some interiors.[10] Lewis's Bethlem was an urbane and long building with one single-loaded corridor, thus borrowing the plan of Hooke's 1676 Bethlem. The northern, public side of Bethlem was pressed up against the street, presenting a rank of windows to the city outside. Given that there were many hospitals and asylums in which patients shared beds, Bethlem's individual cells were duly acclaimed.[11] Lewis's building, then, is the one nineteenth-century American alienists visited and, almost universally, condemned.

Asylums presented an architectural paradox. On the one hand, it was possible to assert that asylums should be unassuming and utilitarian, expressing the economic

NEW BETHLEM HOSPITAL
St George's Fields

Figure 1.2. James Lewis, New Bethlem, London, 1815. Courtesy of Wellcome Library, London.

constraints of the state. On the other hand, they might better offer magnificence, thereby enhancing the hospital's status in society and enticing the public to respect them as civic enterprises. After all, a certain degree of dignity and grandeur would encourage the families of patients to assume that their relatives were wards of a beneficent state-appointed family. Stevenson has convincingly analyzed the powerful theme of the manor house as it relates to British lunatic asylums.[12] She points out that the long corridor opposite the cells, used for interior strolling, was known as a gallery—the same term used for the longitudinal picture galleries of posh country houses. The doctor recalled the lord of the manor; the attendants were like the domestic staff of butlers, maidservants, cooks, and so forth; and the patients were like serfs, owing everything to the lord. Asylums even regularly entertained visitors, a social role that was equally expected of manor houses. Social hierarchy was replicated inside the asylum walls.

If one knows anything about Bethlem, it is probably that the place operated as a kind of freak show and human zoo, with paying customers gaping at the inmates. Although visiting was a popular pastime, recent scholarship has revised and tempered the famous myth. The lavish architecture was a large part of the spectacle. Visitors did not actually pay admission, although they were asked to give alms, and hollow figural sculptures served as poor boxes just inside the door of Hooke's Bethlem. Bethlem was not alone in asking for alms: all kinds of charities used spectatorship to encourage philanthropy—other hospitals, almshouses, and orphan asylums did the same. Many of the visitors to Bethlem were family members bringing clothing, blankets, books, pens, paper, and extra food. The governors of Bethlem encouraged upper-class visitors, who would set a good example, cheer the lunatics, and leave tips for the poorly paid staff. According to Jonathan Andrews, the lunatics, in turn, offered an object lesson in providential authority and became exemplars of the pain wrought by ignoring God's wishes.[13]

In 1770, the overseers forbade any visitor who was not approved by the governor and issued tickets only to carefully selected spectators. The stated reason was to shield the lunatics from prying eyes, but Andrews has intimated that the patients were better off in the days of freer access, because the public's arbitrary visits may have served to protect the patients from the attendants. While the public was allowed in, Bethlem was a relatively porous institution; but once officials clamped down on visiting, the patients "were subject to a considerable degree of isolation from friends."[14] Andrews also suggests that "it is at least arguable . . . that the termination of general visiting did no good to the patients: behind locked doors, they had more to fear from the depredations of the staff than previously from the public."[15] Spectators chosen by the superintendent were welcomed, because visits from dignitaries worked to bolster the image of the institution among the philanthropic class, and to assure the public that all was well behind its doors. In later American asylums, public rooms and selected wards were better decorated than the rest of the institution, and these were the areas on a visitor's tour.

British Asylums at the End of the Eighteenth Century

The tension between grandeur and practicality, evident at Bethlem, remained unresolved in St. Luke's hospital for the insane in London designed by George Dance the Younger. Opened in 1787, the structure dated back to a competition held in 1777 (Figure 1.3). All the entries in the competition incorporated barrel-vaulted cells with high lunette windows, nine feet above the floor, for the patients' bedrooms.[16] The barrel vaults dampened sound, and the high windows eliminated noisy distractions from the close-in city. St. Luke's tall foundations served to keep the lunatics at a height above passersby. The round-arched windows, bricked from their lower edge up to the level of the springing of the arch, were its most distinctive external design element. Lunettes above the bricked-in lower portion of the windows were grilled but had no glass; this peculiar fenestration allowed fresh air and some light into the cells, but did not allow outsiders to stare. Sir John Soane noted the intense emotions evoked by the structure, when he recounted a physician's remark at a dinner party: "[A]lthough he had occasion very often to visit [St. Luke's], he never discovered any beauty in it. It always excited in him no other idea but that of an hospital for the reception of mad persons. Every

Drawn by Tho H. Shepherd.
Pl. 135

Engraved by J. Gough.

LUNATIC HOSPITAL, ST. LUKE'S.

Figure 1.3. George Dance the Younger, St. Luke's Lunatic Hospital, London, 1787, as illustrated in an engraving by J. Gough after Thomas H. Sheppard. This building was the second home for St. Luke's Hospital. Courtesy of Wellcome Library, London.

member of the company observed that a greater compliment could not be paid to the powers of architecture."[17] Indeed, the round-arched bricked-in windows gave St. Luke's character—it *looked* like a madhouse—and it was admired for its communicative power.[18] The idea of character, prominent in French theory of the same time, placed a high value on architecture that seemed to speak.

Augustus C. Pugin and Thomas Rowlandson illustrated St. Luke's interior in their *Microcosm of London,* an elaborate guidebook of 1808 (Figure 1.4). Here we see a juncture of a wide main corridor with one of the short transverse wings. Corridors were used as day rooms, so although it appears as if the inmates had escaped from their cells, this is not the case. The patients were supposed to be in the corridors during the day,

and their cells were used for sleeping only. A manic patient on the left throws her arms in the air and wails. A woman seated on the floor pulls her hair with her right hand and tugs at her foot with her left hand. (It is rather apparent that the patients have not been cured yet.) But the architecture comes off well in this famous picture, with light streaming through the cells into the hall, sturdy masonry walls, and a generous quantity of open space for the number of people, especially if one considers the cramped quarters that paupers usually inhabited.

The Scottish Enlightenment led to the founding of many unusually forward-looking institutions, and in the first two decades of the nineteenth century, the rival cities of Glasgow and Edinburgh competed to construct the most advanced lunatic asylums in the world.

Figure 1.4. Dance, St. Luke's Lunatic Hospital, women's ward, interior, as illustrated in Augustus Pugin and Thomas Rowlandson, *Microcosm of London* (London: Ackerman, 1808–11; reprint 1947). Courtesy of Wellcome Library, London.

Figure 1.5. Robert Reid, Edinburgh Lunatic Asylum, 1807. This elevation shows one side of the quadrangle. The center three-story building was connected by covered passages to flanking two-story corner pavilions. Courtesy of Wellcome Library, London.

These two buildings were not copied very frequently in the United States, but they illustrate a sophisticated Enlightenment discourse about asylum architecture, as well as attention to categorization and social class. The Edinburgh Lunatic Asylum's foundation stone was laid in 1809, and it opened to patients in 1813 (Figures 1.5 and 1.6). The architect Robert Reid adapted the round-arched, mostly blind fenestration from St. Luke's, repeated in unvarying rows, and the asylum's quadrangular plan presented four flat edges to the city.

Stevenson has noted that most of the inhabitants were wealthy (the poor were not admitted until 1842).[19] Reid carefully considered the subdivision of space and the categorization of patients in the Edinburgh asylum, settling on a quadrangle, each side of which was composed of a three-story center building, with hyphens to

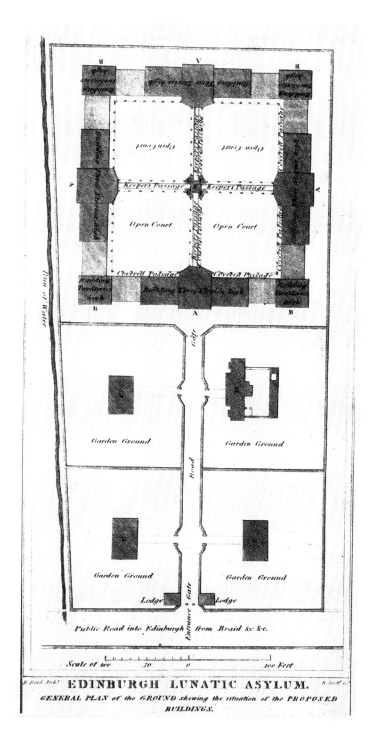

Figure 1.6. Reid, Edinburgh Lunatic Asylum, plan. Courtesy of Wellcome Library, London.

either side, leading to two-story blocks at the corners. This plan allowed Reid to divide inmates by severity of disease and by social class. The corner houses were for persons of high rank, as he explained:

> This plan consists of various buildings, detached one from each other. In it are four distinct houses, for accommodation of 40 patients in each, with a keeper's house, and lodging for the servants, and also separate cooking-spaces, and other conveniences. These buildings, together with four corner buildings, of smaller dimensions, form the four sides of a square, within which are four separate open courts, or airing-grounds. The four corner buildings are proposed for the accommodation of patients of a higher rank in life than either of the classes lodging in any of the large buildings, and who might be permitted to walk and amuse themselves in the garden ground.[20]

One of the many challenges facing asylum designers was to create spaces that mirrored the class stratification of society. Asylum builders simply assumed that paupers would not desire or benefit from the luxuries that were essential for the cure of the wealthy. As Stevenson notes, the "old ideal of the extended rural household offered the closest model for this society, which was both integrated and stratified."[21]

The exterior and silhouette of Reid's Edinburgh Lunatic Asylum were relatively modest, compared to the domed edifice for lunatics that was about to take shape in neighboring Glasgow. The Glasgow Lunatic Asylum, by William Stark, opened in 1814 with a Greek cross plan and a circular staircase at its center (Figures 1.7 and 1.8). Airing courts filled the wedge-shaped spaces between the arms of the cross. The central stair made it impossible to see through the middle of the cross,[22] so although it is tempting to think that the design fostered surveillance, there were no sight lines across the center. This central area was illuminated by natural light coming from a remarkable, tall dome, made largely of glass, a crystalline recollection of the shallower dome over the new Bethlem hospital in London. These two Scottish hospitals classified patients by severity of disease. Stark even presented the categories and locations of patients in a table showing each category's distance from the center point of the building. The plan published in 1807 demarcated half the space for men, half for women. Stark divided those parts into "higher rank"

and "lower rank" (by which he meant social wealth), and those divisions were again subdivided into "convalescent" (meaning likely to improve) and "ordinary state." Deeply ingrained class distinctions stood out in high relief in asylum organization.

Moral Treatment

As historians have often noted, at the time of the Enlightenment, social reformers sought to remake all of society's institutions: schools, colleges, medical hospitals, prisons, and insane asylums took on new forms to express their novelty, rationality, and heightened presence in American life. The insane asylum was one of these many relatively new institutions that shaped daily life in the nineteenth century. Historians have traditionally given credit to two late-eighteenth-century men, William Tuke and Philippe Pinel, for releasing madmen from their chains. They worked separately, apparently unaware of the other's reforms. These doctors are linked to the moral treatment, a translation of Pinel's *traitement moral*. Somewhat confusingly for English readers, the *moral* in moral treatment (also moral management) did not connote that it was morally superior therapy. The term meant rather that the new therapies applied to the mind, not the body, of the patient. *Traitement moral* referred to a benevolent approach to caretaking, in which reformers called for patients to develop self-control under the guidance of paternalistic doctors.

Pinel, who hailed from a village in southwestern France, came to Paris during the Revolution. He worked first at a private madhouse before he took up the job of supervising the Bicêtre pauper hospital in 1793 and Salpêtrière two years later. In these asylums, indigent insane and the mentally handicapped were jumbled together with petty criminals. But Pinel believed that insanity could be treated, and he began his new regimen by giving lunatics freedom to walk around the hospital grounds. He is known for making the dramatic gesture of releasing mad people from their chains. Other restraints such as straitjackets and leather muffs were used in lieu of chains, so the event was perhaps not as earth-shattering as later accounts would have it, but Pinel's well-publicized work in Paris suggested to

Figure 1.7. William Stark, Glasgow Lunatic Asylum, 1807–1814, view of grounds and hospital, showing two arms of the Greek cross plan and the tall glass dome. Courtesy of General Research Division, New York Public Library, Astor, Lenox, and Tilden Foundations.

Figure 1.8. Stark, Glasgow Lunatic Asylum, plan, as illustrated in William Stark, *Remarks on the Construction of Public Hospitals for the Cure of Mental Derangement.* Courtesy of General Research Division, New York Public Library, Astor, Lenox, and Tilden Foundations.

future generations that an asylum ought to be a curative, not punitive, place. Pinel's follower, Jean-Étienne Esquirol, pressed the reforms further, transforming the asylum into a therapeutic community where doctors and patients lived together, and at his private clinic, certain patients even dined at the family table. The doctor's family served as a model family in contrast to the patient's real one: Esquirol believed patients needed to be separated from the outside world in order to establish a calming distance from the distractions that caused their disease. The idea was to imitate normal life so that the disturbed associations would be replaced with healthy ones.

These two French hospitals are cases in which medical practice outpaced the architecture, at least in the opinion of the American alienist D. Tilden Brown. He admired Esquirol and Pinel as reformers, but found France's two pauper lunatic asylums, Salpêtrière and Bicêtre, to be unacceptably backward buildings. Salpêtrière and Bicêtre served as counterexamples for American hospital designers, in somewhat the same way Bethlem did, but perhaps with less antipathy. The

hospital at Salpêtrière began in 1656 as a replanned saltpeter factory (Figure 1.9). In its mid-seventeenth-century incarnation, it housed people with venereal diseases, the elderly poor, the mentally ill, able-bodied but lazy boys, and girls in danger of debauchery.[23] As such, it was not purpose-built for lunatics, a fact that would have offended later American visitors, who believed asylums needed to be purpose-built. The placement of a chapel at the center of an asylum continued all the way through to the twentieth century. Loges, back-to-back rooms with doors that opened directly to the outside, were added in 1789 (Figure 1.10). The walls of the rooms did not rise to the level of the ceiling, but rather stopped short, allowing the passage of air across the tops of the rooms to a central ventilation tower. These short walls allowed noise and contagious clouds of disease to waft overhead at all times. Patients slept two to a bed.

At Bicêtre, a large main building was surrounded by newer constructions, including a three-sided quadrangle, became a new standard beginning in the 1820s. Colonnades stretched the length of the parallel arms,

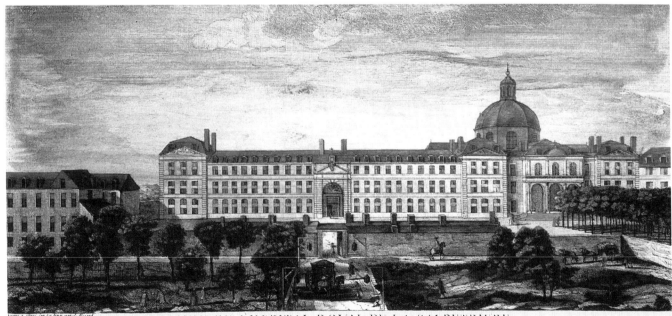

VUE DE L'HOPITAL ROYAL DE LA SALPETRIERE
du Hopital general hors de Paris a une petite promenade de la porte Saint Bernard.

Figure 1.9. Louis Le Vau, hospital at Salpêtrière, Paris, begun 1656, replanned factory, main building. Liberal Bruant, chapel at the hospital at Salpêtrière, 1670–77. The dome marks the chapel, which is in the shape of a Greek cross. Courtesy of Wellcome Library, London.

Figure 1.10. Charles François Viel, loge added to site of the hospital at Salpêtrière, 1789, as illustrated in Georges Guillain and P. Mathieu, *La Salpêtrière* (Paris, 1925). Small-scale buildings were added to the site of Salpêtrière, but none found favor with American doctors. In these loges, rooms were back to back with doors opening directly to the outside. Courtesy of Oskar Diethelm Library.

and although the room doors still opened directly onto a courtyard, at least they were covered by the roof of the colonnade. There was no heating or ventilation system here. Brown dismissed these two, the most famous institutions for the insane in France, as "caravanseries [*sic*] for the poor" when he visited in 1863.[24] The comparison to *caravansaries* was reasonable insofar as the typical plan of a *caravansary* was a sequence of rooms around a courtyard. But Brown used the term derogatively to insinuate that the French asylums were inappropriately foreign and derived from the wrong purposes: in his mind, *caravansaries* sheltered mysterious eastern travelers, not lunatics on the mend.

The York Retreat

Unlike the asylums so far discussed, the York Retreat of 1796, designed by John Bevans, was an important architectural model for American asylums beginning

with the Friends Asylum in 1817. The Quaker William Tuke was regarded as kindly and humane, and like Pinel, he was famous for rejecting mechanical restraints such as chains and straitjackets. Tuke's Retreat resembled a domicile (Figure 1.11).[25] The term "retreat" suggests a haven, a refuge from the ills of society. Medical practices such as feeding the patient well, maintaining bodily hygiene, encouraging sleep, and insisting on a daily regimen were required. Tuke intended to use kindness to evoke affection in the patients, who would later be returned to society. In contrast to the many small, family-run private asylums of its time, which were fitted into old houses, the York Retreat was purpose-built.[26] A brick structure at the crest of a hill, the Retreat offered excellent views. Its land was unencumbered by high walls or a fence, and cows grazed within its hedge-trimmed borders. The plan included a central structure for both administration and for the superintendent's home, to either side of which were double-loaded corridors lined with single bedrooms, the same on both

PERSPECTIVE VIEW of the NORTH FRONT of the RETREAT near YORK.

Figure 1.11. John Bevans, York Retreat, 1792, perspective view of the north front, as illustrated in Samuel Tuke, *Description of the Retreat, An Institution near York, for Insane Persons of the Society of Friends* (York: W. Alexander, 1813).

stories. Like Pinel, Tuke sought to treat the whole person, and he offered homey meals in addition to his family's company. He had noticed that in healthy people a hearty meal including cheese and meat, not to mention port, made folks drowsy, so he instituted the same routine for the insane.[27] Compared to the sizable St. Luke's and the eerie Bethlem, Tuke's Retreat was a country farmstead rather than a grandiose urban edifice. And this quality was part of its therapeutic power.

Samuel Tuke, William's grandson, wrote a description of the Retreat that was published in 1813. He regretted that his grandfather had not used single-loaded corridors, because he found the ground floor corridors to be "rather gloomy," and he felt the downstairs halls could have benefited from a bank of windows along one side.[28] Set back slightly from the prominent

two-story wings, almost invisible in the perspective drawing, were more tightly secured wards for the most violent patients. To the rear of the building, where the ground sloped down, airing courts were laid out as two quarter circles on either side of a central path. These airing courts were furnished with animals such as rabbits, seagulls, and chickens, because it was believed that interacting with these creatures awakened benevolent feelings in the patients.[29] Beyond the quarter circles, the remaining irregular spaces were assigned to the outer wards. In the garden, low walls separated men from women (Figure 1.12). The York Retreat's doctors eschewed harsh medical treatments such as bloodletting, emphasized comfort, encouraged outdoor activity, and insisted upon kindness toward their self-styled family members.

Although conventional histories of British psychiatry elevate Tuke as the father of psychiatry, Roy Porter's analysis of earlier eighteenth-century care of the insane indicates that many of Tuke's ideals—separation from society, orderly daily regimen, and avoidance of mechanical restraints—were already common before the Retreat. These therapies grew up in small private clinics, to which the patients voluntarily committed themselves. As in so many other areas of human enterprise, change was gradual, and society had to be ready for the reforms to take hold. That said, almost every nineteenth-century reformer drew a sharp line between the improved moral and medical treatments of their century and the corporeal terror and intellectual neglect of previous centuries.

The First American Institutions for the Insane

In 1770, the same year that Bethlem forbade open spectatorship at its venerable hospital, city folk in Philadelphia could still peer into the windows of the Pennsylvania Hospital, where lunatics had been unwittingly entertaining crowds for two decades (Figure 1.13). Benjamin Franklin and physician Benjamin Rush had organized the Pennsylvania Hospital to manage both medical and mental cases; the hospital accepted curable medical cases and some citizens who "unhappily became disorder'd in their Senses," as Franklin put it.[30] The earliest part of the building predates the York Retreat; passersby would even taunt

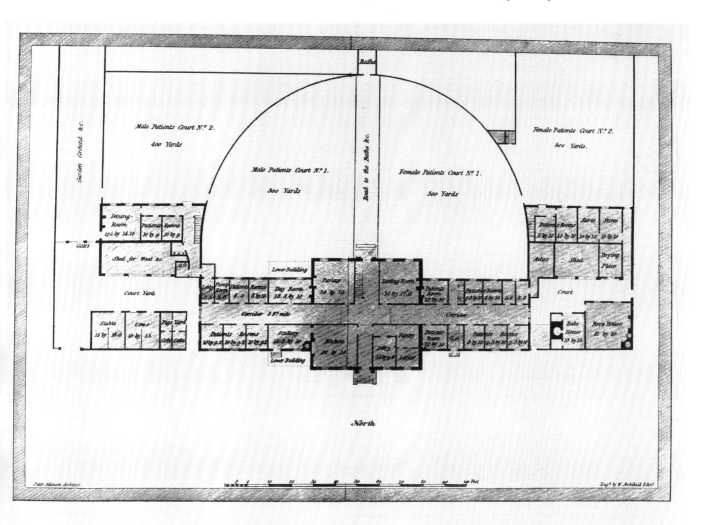

GROUND PLAN of the RETREAT near YORK.

Figure 1.12. Bevans, York Retreat, plan, as illustrated in Tuke, *Description of the Retreat.*

the chained inmates, which was not allowed at the York Retreat.[31]

Like many large institutions, the Pennsylvania Hospital had been built in stages. First the hospital officers constructed the T-shaped east wing (1756) and later a similarly shaped west wing (1796). The central building (1797–1805) connected these two wings and contained a fine foyer, grand staircases, a library, steward's office, apothecary's shop, parlor, and residences for the staff.[32] The lying-in department (a maternity ward for poor but honorable married women) was located on the second floor of the central structure. The third floor contained the three-hundred-seat operating theater,

surmounted by a dome with a glass oculus and thus offering generous overhead light for the surgeons. The surgical and medical wards of the Pennsylvania Hospital consisted of largely uninterrupted interior spaces, open wards along either side of the main building.[33] These rooms, with beds lined up along the walls, could be used for people who were recovering from a noninfectious disease or recuperating after surgery.

By 1832, the center city facility housed 249 patients, 126 of whom were considered insane.[34] The insane cases were housed separately: "On the basement story, are a long hall in which a majority of the insane patients take their meals; eleven sleeping rooms for this class of

SOUTH EAST VIEW OF THE   PENNSYLVANIA HOSPITAL

Figure 1.13. Samuel Rhoads and Joseph Fox, Pennsylvania Hospital, Philadelphia, ca. 1755–60 (engraving, 1820). Insane patients were housed in the basement of the hospital until 1841, when they were moved to a new hospital in west Philadelphia. Courtesy of National Library of Medicine.

patients, and their attendants, and some store rooms."[35] The west wing was occupied from basement to attic by "insane persons and their attendants." The men and women came in close proximity to one another; of the four dayrooms on the first floor, those on the north were used by men and those on the south by women.[36] Harsh medical treatments, however, were common; attendants attempted to deplete the madman's bodily systems, and thus caused patients to bleed, blister, and vomit. The hospital's chronicler and librarian, William Gunn Malin, described a "long garret" for twelve to fifteen males to sleep in and another garret for fourteen females in 1832.

The Pennsylvania Hospital was located in the Center City area of Philadelphia. By the 1830s, it was a crowded urban neighborhood, and thus the air that surrounded it was not considered salubrious for a medical or mental hospital. Also, it was too hemmed in by neighboring buildings to allow for picturesque views, and with the exception of 150 feet of iron fence on Pine Street, it was surrounded by a brick wall. Significantly, Malin saw the wall as an advancement that protected against "elopement," as escaping was called. He also celebrated a gap in the wall for being "furnished with an iron railing, which affords a view of the south front of the building."[37] Malin was proud of the view *inward* that allowed Philadelphians to see the fine hospital building, whereas later doctors insisted that patients have a view *outward*. Its quarters were hardly exemplary, but by comparison to the other options, it was a reasonably safe place for the early American lunatic. Most colonial madmen were confined in jails or almshouses, which were considerably worse than the Pennsylvania Hospital. Other lunatics lived in bleak conditions among their families, or they were cast out to roam the country roads. In spite of the hospital's importance in medical history, the Center City facility of the Pennsylvania Hospital did not serve as an architectural model for other institutions, even though it must have loomed in the mind of reforming doctor Thomas Kirkbride, who worked there from 1833 to 1841.[38]

In Virginia, the colonial government offered a better option for the "maintenance and support of ideots [*sic*], lunatics, and other persons of unsound mind," but the legacy of the Public Hospital was as limited as the commingled medical and mental facilities at the

Pennsylvania Hospital. Furthermore, as a purpose-built structure, it marks a turning point in the American context. It was not a curative institution, though, and it did not hint at the highly specialized plan that would emerge in the 1840s. In 1766, Francis Fauquier, governor of the colony of Virginia, decreed that it was the proper role of a "civilized Country" to care for those of unsound mind, to take them to a place where they could be "confined, maintained, and attended by able Physicians, to endeavor to restore to them their Lost Reason."[39]

Designed by builder-architect Robert Smith, the structure was sturdily constructed (Figures 1.14 and 1.15). Thomas Jefferson, who generally disparaged the redbrick colonial architecture of Williamsburg, listed the lunatic hospital along with the capitol, the governor's mansion, and the College of William and Mary as one of the four monumental works of interest in the town.[40] Upon entering the building, visitors encountered a center hall containing a stair and the keeper's one-room apartment. Double-loaded corridors with single cells flanked the hall. The second and third stories resembled the first, although above the keeper's apartment was a meeting room for the hospital's directors. To either side of the thin building were airing courts with high walls. The boxy brick building could easily be mistaken for a college, a town hall, or an orphan asylum. Indeed, the Williamsburg asylum resembles two of Smith's other structures: Nassau Hall at Princeton University and the Walnut Street Jail in Philadelphia.[41] This lack of specificity in the exterior is typical of the time and does not suggest any meaningful associations among the three buildings' inhabitants.

The plain brick walls could have enveloped a medical hospital, but the interiors were different from a typical medical arrangement. Eighteenth-century medical hospitals usually contained wards (long rooms with several beds) rather than the single rooms of this early asylum. Builders of medical hospitals focused their attention on providing ventilation to the wards. One way to maximize the fresh air pouring through the wards was to place hospitals on salubrious sites, usually on the outskirts of town, removed from swamps, marshes, cemeteries, or sewage-filled city streets.[42] Smith's hospital was relatively small, and its numerous doors and windows provided natural ventilation to sweep away

Figure 1.14. Robert Smith, Public Hospital, Williamsburg, Virginia, 1771–73. Reconstructed in 1986, Travis McDonald, restoration architect. Photograph by the author.

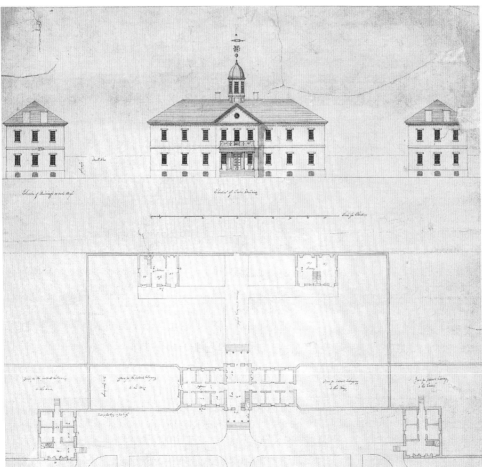

Figure 1.15. Smith, Public Hospital, Williamsburg. Plan and elevation, probably drawn by A. Dickie Galt, superintendent of the Eastern State Hospital for the Insane, successor to the Public Hospital. Courtesy of the Library of Virginia.

effluvia and foul emanations. But since the primary purpose of this asylum was to confine, the builders used single rooms. Single cells also appear in private asylums as a luxury that afforded more privacy, but here they were akin to prison cells. Single rooms had different meanings in different local contexts.

Scholars usually give credit to the transatlantic community of Quakers for bringing moral treatment to the United States.[43] Founded in 1817, the Friends Asylum requires a look back to the York Retreat, William Tuke, and William's grandson, Samuel. Samuel corresponded with some American Friends about starting an asylum based on his grandfather's successful experiment in York, and the result was the Friends Asylum in Frankford, outside Philadelphia.[44] This institution brought to the United States the supposed promise of the new system based on internalized self-respect and limited use of harsh bodily treatments. The Friends Asylum was a linear structure with a central houselike building and two ranges of rooms to either side along single-loaded corridors. The single-loaded corridors were an improvement upon the York Retreat and show the direct influence of the younger Tuke. It accommodated about sixty

patients (Figure 1.16). Men lived on one side of the central building, women on the other. The central building housed male and female parlors as well as a reception room and office. This most basic plan, consisting of a central building with wings, was already in place in 1817 and it survived through the end of the nineteenth century.

The keepers at the Friends Asylum were particularly proud of the light, airy space, since proper ventilation was considered absolutely critical for both psychological and bodily care:

> [T]he free admission of light and air [and] their influence on organic and inorganic bodies, requires no elucidation. The free circulation of air, the great supporter of life, is of primary importance; —without proper ventilation, the resources of medicine may be developed in vain; the miserable sufferers are suffocated in the effluvia of their own bodies, and a long train of physical evils are added to their mental miseries.[45]

This near obsession with ventilation may be found in almost all written works about asylum and hospital construction, reflecting the widely held miasma theory

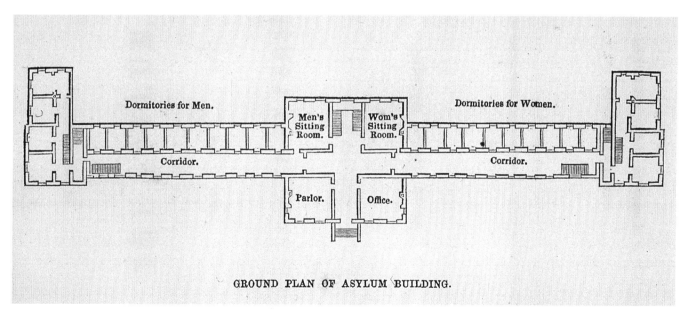

GROUND PLAN OF ASYLUM BUILDING.

Figure 1.16. Friends Asylum, Frankford, outside Philadelphia, 1813–17, as illustrated in Robert Waln, *An Account of the Asylum for the Insane established by the Society of Friends near Frankford in the Vicinity of Philadelphia* (Philadelphia: Benjamin and Thomas Kite, 1825). This private asylum for Quakers was the first U.S. institution to emphasize the moral treatment of the insane. Courtesy of National Library of Medicine.

Figure 1.17. Friends Asylum, plan, as illustrated in Waln, *An Account of the Asylum for the Insane established by the Society of Friends* . . . Courtesy of National Library of Medicine.

of contagion, the medical assumption that noxious exhalations from humans polluted the air and caused disease. The single-loaded corridors represented a generous use of space, given that for each individual bed the amount of shared space (that is, the corridor) was relatively high. Assuming the patients' doors were open, the single-loaded corridors allowed for lateral air flow from the exterior wall on the front of the building, across the corridor, through the patients' rooms, and beyond. For nineteenth-century doctors, ventilation was not just a matter of comfort; it was a matter of life and death.

Entertainment was a part of moral management, and one of its manifestations is visible in contemporary prints of the Friends Asylum (Figure 1.17). This illustration shows a circular rail immediately in front of the

building; next to the rail is a small hut and a wagon. The contraption was intended for play. It is the equivalent of a modern amusement park ride, and its purpose was to divert the patients from negative thoughts. In addition to these rides, hospitals for the insane included billiard tables in the dayrooms and croquet courts on the lawns; some even offered nine-hole golf courses. All these amusements were considered part of successful moral management, and doctors lobbied for their inclusion in state hospitals throughout the nineteenth century. However, state lawmakers were not always sympathetic. For example, at the public asylum in Columbia, South Carolina, the legislators forced the asylum's builders to eliminate amusements and occupational opportunities, regarding such things as frills.[46] The doctors, in turn, argued that these amenities might have attracted paying patients who could have helped offset the cost of treating impoverished people.

Unlike the Public Hospital in Virginia, but in sympathy with the Friends Asylum, the asylum in Columbia, South Carolina, was intended to be therapeutic and was based on the principles of moral management. At its start, the asylum offered its services to both indigent and paying patients, but eventually, as more paupers were admitted, the wealthy ceased to commit themselves or their relations, and its inhabitants came more and more from the lower classes. This pattern was typical of nineteenth-century asylums. A group of reformers hoped that the patients would regain their reason and return to society.[47] The architect Robert Mills incorporated all-stone vaulted construction for fireproofing, and he employed the basic plan of a central structure with flanking wings (Figures 1.18, 1.19, and 1.20).

The cornerstone was laid in 1822, but the first patient did not arrive until 1828. The state legislators were frustrated by the slow construction and stopped allocating funds in 1826.

Mills presented the public with a learned classical edifice. He received the commission because he was employed as acting commissioner of the Board of Public Works,[48] and in its time the asylum was intended to be the largest building in the state. Although inspired by the York Retreat, the South Carolina building was far more grandiose than its parent. Compared to the flatness of the York Retreat's facade, which lacks a portico or even a modest porch, Mills's asylum projected Palladian importance. Mills designed a handsome redbrick and white stone–trimmed building, with a six-columned Doric temple front surmounted by an attic and a cupola; a rusticated arcade supported the north-facing temple front. Flanking the arcade, curved side

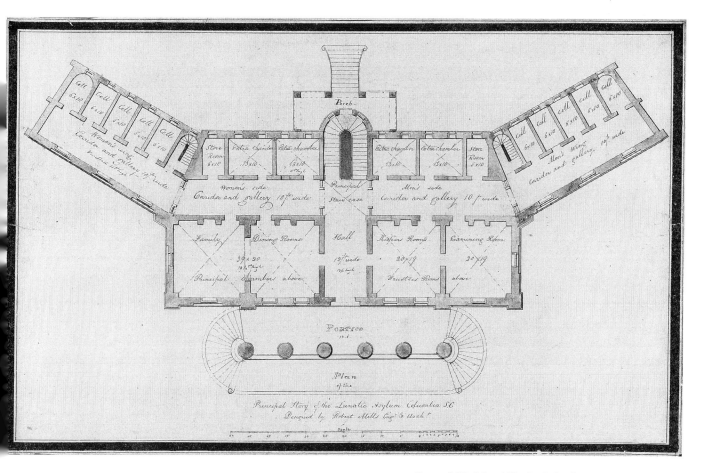

Figure 1.18. Robert Mills, South Carolina Insane Asylum, Columbia, South Carolina, 1821, plan (drawing, 1828). From South Carolina Department of Archives, Map Collection box 17, folder 10.

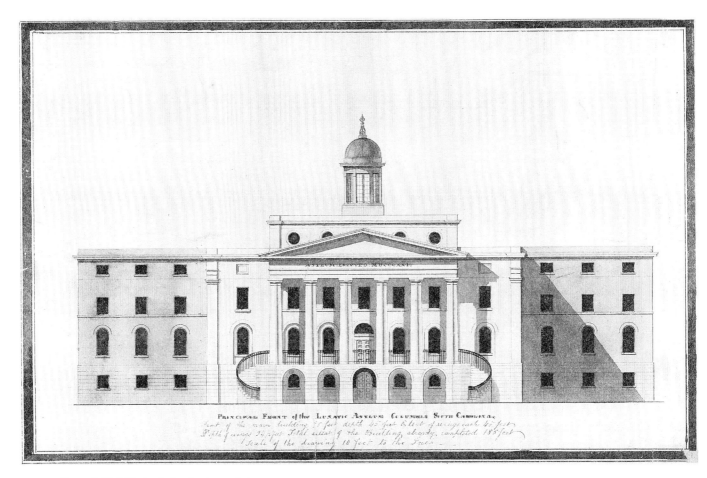

Figure 1.19. Mills, South Carolina Insane Asylum, front elevation (drawing, 1828). The roof terrace covered just the central portion. From South Carolina Department of Archives, Map Collection box 17, folder 10.

staircases allowed access to the *piano nobile*, distinguished by round-headed windows. The placement of the stairs resembles the setting of the rectilinear steps on either side of the entrance to Palladio's Villa Foscari of 1570. The circular cupola had sash windows to allow ventilation.[49] Mills himself described it as combining "elegance with permanence, economy, and security from fire. The rooms are vaulted with brick and the roof covered with copper."[50]

In plan, the two-and-a-half story structure included a central edifice and wings on either side that broke away at an obtuse angle from the facade. These wings were not originally for dividing men from women, unlike the plans of later asylums; rather sixty males and sixty females were housed on different floors. Each wing contained a single-loaded corridor lined by five ten-by six-foot cells. Again, as at the Friends Asylum, by placing rooms on one side of the hall, designers could achieve better ventilation than by choosing the more economical option of having rooms on both sides. The wide corridor also served as an indoor exercise area, in which patients could stroll on rainy days. The central portion of the structure included public rooms at the front and smaller service rooms at the rear; its central hall led directly to a curving stone interior staircase for access to additional patients' rooms. There were ten cells in the basement forming a ward for those who were most violent and difficult to control.

The landscape plan was dominated by wedge-shaped airing courts defined by low walls (Figure 1.21). Neither plantings in geometric patterns nor picturesque rolling hills were offered to these inmates. Rather indecorously, the lavatory (the last stop for the contents of the chamber pots used throughout the building) was

Figure 1.20. Mills, South Carolina Insane Asylum, exterior. Photograph by Ann M. Keen.

Figure 1.21. Mills, South Carolina Insane Asylum, plan of exercise yards, also called airing courts (drawing, 1828). The building as constructed is at the lower edge of the drawing. From South Carolina Department of Archives, Map Collection box 17, folder 10.

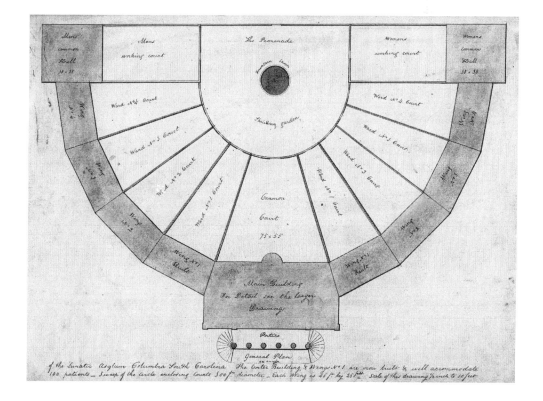

in the courtyard.[51] The garden plan shows that Mills imagined a series of wings that could be added in sequence, forming a semicircle. Decorum demanded that men not be able to ogle the women, so the view from one yard to the next needed to be blocked; he achieved this using both walls and a shrubbery garden. He described the yard, saying, "[T]he whole is surrounded by a lofty enclosure."[52] Such "lofty enclosures," or high walls, were anathema to doctors later in the century. The balance between decorum and surveillance was difficult to find.

Among the building's most notable innovations was its roof garden, or as one historian has described it, "the earliest roof in America designed for recreation."[53] The walkway over the main building, enclosed by a parapet wall, offered views over the building itself and its grounds. It was to be used exclusively by visitors, not patients. (A stickler for safety might think of several reasons why madmen should not be allowed to play on the roof.) The South Carolina Insane Asylum was far more advanced than many hospitals for the insane in terms of technology, spaciousness, and comfort. In particular, the single cells lining single-loaded corridors were spacious. And each wing contained five patients only, so the amount of communal space per bed was extremely generous. The design of the asylum in Columbia was seldom imitated; in spite of its fireproofing, central heating, and elegant facade, it did not engender many copies, almost certainly because of the rising influence of America's foremost asylum doctor, Thomas S. Kirkbride.

Thomas Story Kirkbride's First Hospital for the Insane

Dr. Thomas Story Kirkbride, a physician and member of the Society of Friends, believed fervently that establishing a new building type was essential for affecting a cure. He supervised a high-profile hospital, advised many doctors and architects, influenced the architectural guidelines published in 1851 by the AMSAII, and wrote a book on the architecture of insane hospitals in 1854. For most of the nineteenth century, from about 1840 to about 1880, he was the single most important nineteenth-century psychiatrist when it came to matters

of architecture. (This is not to suggest that his authority was absolute, but his ideas were the standard against which alternatives had to be tested.) Kirkbride was devoted to moral treatment, which required a change of daily habits—regular schedules were intended to make patients internalize self-control. Not surprisingly, the spaces within hospitals and the circulation patterns reinforced this control. Patients would live a regimented life, eat healthy food, get exercise, avoid the vicious city, and visit daily with the superintendent or his wife, the official matron of the institution. Additional principles included that patients should be unchained, granted respect, encouraged to perform occupational tasks (such as farming, carpentry, or laundry), and allowed to stroll the grounds with an attendant. Early-nineteenth-century American doctors believed patients were inherently good, despite their outward behavior; and they offered the mentally ill the promise of return to society after a stay in the purpose-built asylum. In spite of the powerful shift toward moral treatment in nineteenth-century America, almost all the doctors included in this study used medical treatments as well. They typically administered opiates, warm baths, cold baths, and an arsenal of laxatives.

Kirkbride presided over the private Pennsylvania Hospital for the Insane, a long, thin building west of the Schuylkill River, then a mixed rural and industrial area (Figure 1.22). He moved his workplace and all of his patients out of the Pennsylvania Hospital in Center City (see Figure 1.13) in 1841; they went west together, to a purpose-built facility for the mentally ill on Forty-ninth and Haverford streets. A pastoral site afforded picturesque views. Land was cheaper there, too.

While some historians have illustrated the Pennsylvania Hospital for the Insane as an exemplar of Kirkbride's theories, this exemplification is not exactly correct. Historian Nancy Tomes has explained that the first hospital for the insane on the west Philadelphia site was put up before Kirkbride was given complete supervisory duties.[54] The English architect Isaac Holden began construction, but the building was finished by Samuel Sloan. Young and opportunistic, Sloan worked as journeyman carpenter on the Eastern State Penitentiary and the Blockley Almshouse in the 1830s, and he was working for Holden in 1838 when illness compelled the Englishman to return to his mother country.[55]

Figure 1.22. Isaac Holden and Samuel Sloan, Pennsylvania Hospital for the Insane (first hospital on the west Philadelphia site, now demolished) 1841. Thomas Kirkbride's first hospital was built on a narrow site. When a second, similar hospital was built facing this one, women were housed here and men were housed in the new building. Courtesy of Oskar Diethelm Library.

When Holden left, the new asylum was only half completed. Sloan finished the structure in 1841, topping the central administrative building with a lantern, flanking it with three-story pavilions, and marking each pavilion with its own smaller lantern.[56] Both the eastern and western fronts had Doric porticoes in stone, but the rest of the edifice was stucco-covered brick.[57]

Originally, the hospital included fully detached, one-story, U-shaped buildings made of stone to serve as refractory wards, the areas reserved for the most violent and noisy patients, in this case about twenty of them.[58] Tomes's research has shown that families often requested that their sick relatives be spared the noisiness of other inmates: "[S]hould it be practicable and not infringing on your rules," the family would prefer "if you will let her rooms be out of hearing of any shrieking you may have."[59] Since it would have been difficult for attendants to manage them as they wandered the grounds, refractory patients gained access to the out-of-doors in an interior courtyard. Outdoor activity was an important part of moral management, requiring in this case a specific architectural solution—an easily defensible courtyard for the most disturbed patients (Figure 1.23).

The interiors were well furnished and spacious. The transverse corridors were twelve feet in width, and the longitudinal corridors were even wider, at fourteen feet. Carpeting covered the floors of the wide corridors, offering sound insulation: "[M]ost of the corridors have a handsome carpet, six feet wide, in their whole extent . . . contributing materially to the quiet of the house, by diminishing the sound made by their being used as a promenade during the day."[60] Six-foot-wide interior stairs were constructed entirely of iron. On the second floor of the central structure, "two parlours, similar in size to the large rooms on the first floor, [were] handsomely furnished and intended for the better class of convalescent patients." The purpose of the parlors was to allow patients' families to visit. (At most asylums, the central building, which housed administration offices and parlors, among other functions, was nicknamed the "center main.") Certain patients were allowed into the center main, where physical proximity to the superintendent and his family was cherished. The family members served as role models of normal behavior who might impart their reason by their good example.

Borrowing directly from the York Retreat, which was known for its normal-looking but powerfully built windows, the sashes here were cast iron and the window panes just six by fifteen inches. "[B]y its peculiar arrangement, the hospital presents neither bars nor the extra sash which is almost universally met with."[61] Doctors agreed that patients needed light-filled halls and rooms, so they desired an abundance of windows. Small panes of glass and the avoidance of grates or bars on the windows were representational strategies: such gestures indicate that the imagery of the asylum was important for all its users. The doctors appeared caring, the morale of the patients could be bolstered, and the public would not see metallic evidence of confinement.

The dome on the Pennsylvania Hospital for the Insane held iron tanks, from which "water is conveyed to every part of the building," and at the same time it served as an observation deck. From its summit, Kirkbride explained, "the panoramic view is one of great beauty." It seems reasonable to assume that no one other than a high-ranking visitor was allowed to gaze out on the Schuylkill and Delaware rivers, at the as yet unfilled grid of Penn's great town.

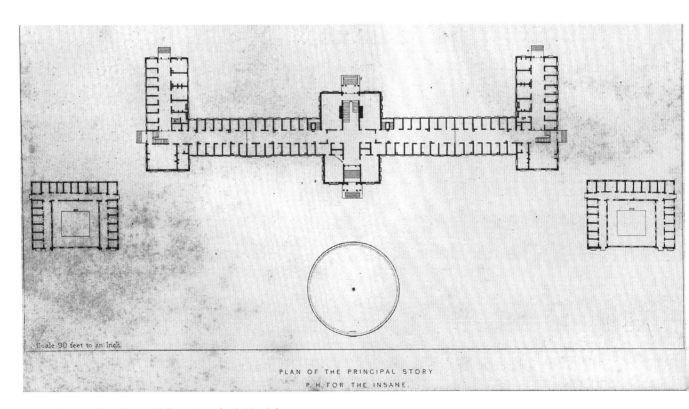

Scale 90 feet to an inch

PLAN OF THE PRINCIPAL STORY
P. H. FOR THE INSANE.

Figure 1.23. Holden and Sloan, Pennsylvania Hospital for the Insane, first building, later Department for Females. The symmetrically placed, detached U-shaped buildings were intended for the most deranged patients. Courtesy of Oskar Diethelm Library.

Balancing Surveillance and Circulation: Pavilions, Quadrangles, and U-Shaped Plans

For the best ventilation, designers of universities, hospitals, and asylums preferred a series of detached pavilions—completely separate structures—grouped in some orderly way. Again the miasmic theory of disease helps explain designers' decisions: clouds of concentrated foul air needed to be dispersed in order to prevent illness. The invention of the pavilion was one of the major architectural developments in the history of hospitals. The challenge posed by pavilions, however,

was that they were good for ventilation but bad for surveillance.

The Royal Naval Hospital at Stonehouse, Plymouth, completed in 1762, was widely recognized for its detached pavilions connected by an open arcade (Figures 1.24 and 1.25). Fully detached structures grouped in a square were also used by many of the entrants in the competition for the new Hôtel Dieu in the 1780s. Ideally, pavilions would be entirely freestanding and of only one story. Often designers incorporated some sort of covered walkways into pavilion plans, to shelter employees who needed to go from ward to ward in bad weather.

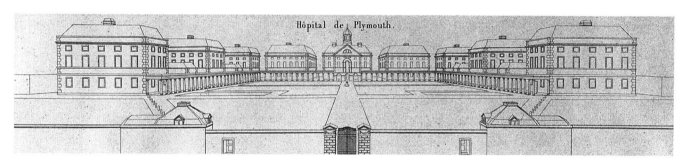

Figure 1.24. Attributed to William Robinson, Royal Naval Hospital at Plymouth, Stonehouse, 1756–65, view, as illustrated in John Howard, *The State of Prisons in England and Wales* (1784), detail. Courtesy of Wellcome Library, London.

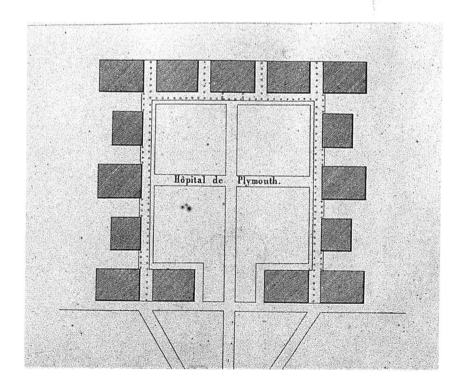

Figure 1.25. Attributed to Robinson, Royal Naval Hospital at Plymouth, plan, as illustrated in Howard, *The State of Prisons in England and Wales*. The two front pavilions are shown in the plan but not the perspective view; in the perspective view, they appear as outlines on the ground only. Courtesy of Wellcome Library, London.

Both the Hôtel Dieu competition and the hospital at Plymouth have been cited as sources for Jefferson's University of Virginia, where, of course, the miniature temples that served as classrooms and apartments are known as pavilions. "Hospitals and universities both accommodate large resident populations; both institutions also raise issues of discipline, sanitation, flammability, and circulation," Mary Woods has explained.[62] Jefferson consulted Benjamin Henry Latrobe about the architecture for the university, and Latrobe's response included a sketch showing small structures around three sides of a lawn, anchored by a domed edifice. As Woods has reported, Latrobe also proposed pavilions arranged in a U for other national institutional complexes, including a naval hospital (1811–51) and a national university (1816), although these projects were not widely known. Latrobe worked on a hospice for infirm retired navy veterans, from 1811 to 1815, and for the naval hospital he looked to Wren's Royal Hospital and St. Luke's Asylum for precedents.[63]

The quadrangle was a related formal arrangement that suited institutions. A quadrangle needed wings short enough for brisk ventilation; the form also conveniently creates a protected interior courtyard. Two of the earliest state-funded lunatic hospitals were in Massachusetts and New York State, and they were both versions of a quadrangle. (Thus they contrasted with Kirkbride's linear hospital in Philadelphia.) Indigent patients were moved to these state asylums from almshouses and prisons, with counties paying a part of the cost. Upper-class patients would have paid a fee for their medical care directly. In Massachusetts, the asylum in Worcester was U-shaped. Economy was the primary concern at the pauper hospital at Worcester: it had to be built cheaply. Horace Mann appealed to the state legislature to give funds for the hospital out of a sense of Christian benevolence, but he also indicated that since the institution would cure the poor lunatics, they would return to society as contributing citizens, and thus ultimately alleviate the burden on the state.[64] Worcester was built quickly; critics abhorred its shoddy construction. It did not spawn many followers.

The New York State Lunatic Asylum in Utica was also a modified quadrangle, with three sides containing wards, and one side made up of service buildings.

William Clarke designed the hospital in 1841; he was not an architect by trade but rather a local entrepreneur who achieved the rank of captain in the army and afterward embarked on a career running a legal lottery in Utica.[65] Clarke was one of the commissioners for the new state asylum, and he put forth a design for a square building with chamfered corners forming an octagonal court. It was 550 feet long on each side, covering about thirteen acres of land, with connecting verandas. It included three sides of a quadrangle for the wards, and on one side, at the rear of the courtyard, services such as the laundry, bakery, and workshops (for sewing, blacksmithing, carpentry, etc.) were housed in small brick buildings. The foundations were constructed in 1837, but the dimensions were overlarge, and the state chose not to complete all four sides of the quadrangle. Kirkbride visited in 1845 and remarked that the "original plan, which was to occupy 13 acres and to contain 1000 patients, has been abandoned."[66] A more modest arrangement prevailed, and in 1844, brick side wings were constructed that were half as long as Clarke had intended.[67] Even so, the structure was colossal for its time and its place, a small town in upstate New York.

The principal structure, parallel to the road, accepted 276 patients during its first year of operation, 1843. The imposing facade captured architectural historian Henry-Russell Hitchcock's patriotic eye: "No European edifice has a grander Greek Doric portico than that which dominates the tremendous four-story front block of the Lunatic Asylum in Utica" (Figures 1.26 and 1.27).[68] The facade presents unrelenting ranks of windows. The portico was placed in front of the director's offices and parlors for families. At the rear of the main building there were porches that looked into the courtyard, the center of the plan. Patient rooms lined the double-loaded front halls and one side of the corridors perpendicular to the street, with dining rooms halfway down the corridors to break up the rows of rooms. Attendants would have had to walk through the dining rooms to get to the patients on the far side. Chapels were common in asylums, and were usually located on an upper level of the main building—the fourth floor in this case. Some patients had single rooms, while others shared bedrooms. At Utica, there were 380 single rooms and 20 so-called associated dormitories, as

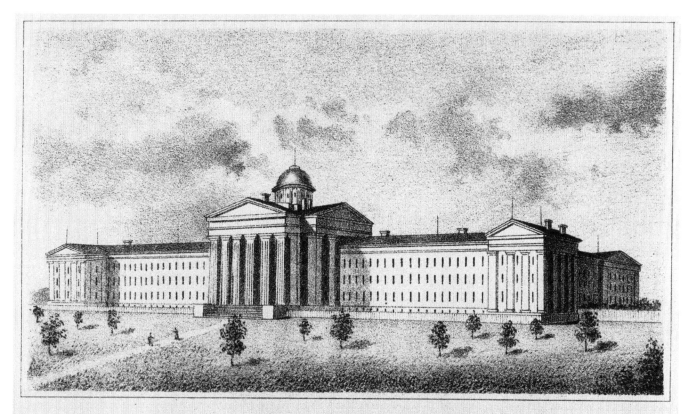

STATE LUNATIC ASYLUM
Utica N.Y.

Figure 1.26. William Clarke, New York State Lunatic Asylum, Utica, 1844. Courtesy of Pennsylvania Hospital Architectural Drawings Collection, on long-term loan to the Athenaeum of Philadelphia with the support of the Pew Charitable Trusts.

the large, shared bedrooms for six to eight were called; the majority had the option of single bedrooms while the remainder, less than a third, shared bedrooms.[69] The ratio of single rooms to associated dormitories was not stable during the course of the nineteenth century. The combination of room types was not so much for therapeutic reasons as for patient management; it was a reflection of early attempts among superintendents of state asylums to attract a range of social classes by offering a range of accommodations.

In 1842, the landscape theorist Andrew Jackson Downing was asked by the Utica asylum's managers to improve their property, making it "as beautiful as the most cultivated and refined taste could desire."[70] Downing produced two designs, one curvilinear, and the other (the choice of the managers) axial with grand elms lining the driveway (Figure 1.28). He added peripheral

plantings to soften the effect of the tree-lined drive,[71] but the earliest prints of the grounds at Utica show an almost empty field with an unflinching drive that aims straight for the temple-fronted entrance. The site posed other problems. It was flat and therefore not picturesque. It had no stream, spring, or canal. (To provide water, the asylum officials constructed a well, sixteen feet in diameter, with a horse-powered pump that forced water into a reservoir in the building's attic, but its yield was not great enough to meet the institution's needs.)[72] The lawn met the street abruptly and soon required a highly visible fence along the road. Kirkbride, who soon came to dominate ideas regarding asylum construction, did not favor this U-shaped plan. From his later publications we know he preferred shorter wards, a greater separation of the sexes, and an unfettered view of the landscape from all rooms.

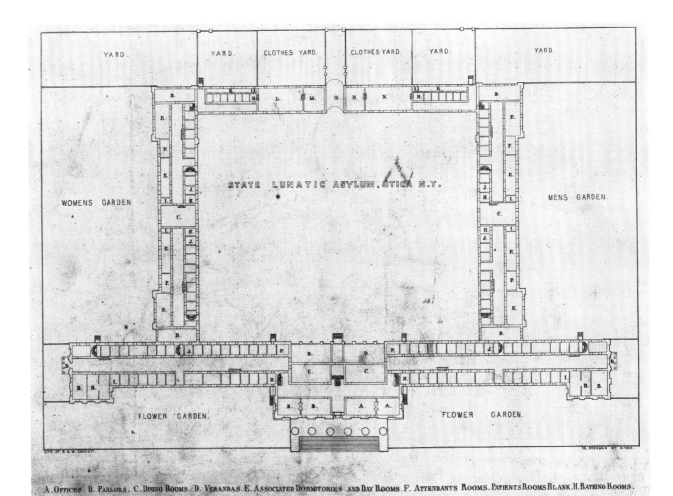

YARD.   YARD.   CLOTHES YARD.   CLOTHES YARD.   YARD.   YARD.

STATE LUNATIC ASYLUM, UTICA, N.Y.

WOMENS GARDEN   MENS GARDEN.

FLOWER GARDEN.   FLOWER GARDEN.

A. OFFICES. B. PARLORS. C. DINING ROOMS. D. VERANDAS. E. ASSOCIATED DORMITORIES AND DAY ROOMS. F. ATTENDANTS ROOMS. PATIENTS ROOMS BLANK. H. BATHING ROOMS.
I. WATER CLOSETS. J. CLOTHING ROOMS. K. STRONG ROOMS. L. LAUNDRY. M. BAKERY. N. SHOPS. O. CARRIAGE WAY.

Figure 1.27. Clarke, New York State Lunatic Asylum, plan. Courtesy of American Institute of Architects Collection, Athenaeum of Philadelphia.

State Hospital, Utica, N. Y.

Figure 1.28. Clarke, New York State Lunatic Asylum, postcard ca. 1920, showing rows of elm trees as designed by A. J. Downing. From collection of the author.

The influential British asylum doctor John Charles Bucknill visited Utica, among other hospitals, in 1875. Although he did not set out to criticize hospitals for the insane, it was, as he explained, a natural consequence of his devotion to his field of medicine, that when he arrived in the United States he contacted like-minded men of his profession. Bucknill possessed a keen sense of his surroundings and a sharp eye for detail. He commented on the architecture of nearly every building he visited, evidence of the importance of the built environment in the treatment of the insane. Although the main building at Utica was actually made of gray limestone, Bucknill admired it for its "Doric portico of granite [which] is a lasting testimony to the liberal ideas of its constructors."[73] Utica is an interesting example of a building that was not an architectural model, even though it was a site of up-to-date medical treatment and even psychiatric research. When its chief physician, John Gray, got the chance to build a lunatic asylum from scratch, he constructed a colossus entirely unlike the one in Utica; he was the major patron for H. H. Richardson's Buffalo State Hospital for the Insane, discussed in chapter 4. In the intervening years, Gray absorbed the tenets of the linear plan.

Asylums and Prisons: Architecture and Social Control

Asylums and prisons have often been compared by contemporary observers, since both building types exemplify architecture in the service of social control: individuals are managed and categorized through the use of surveillance. A comparison of the two types, however, will illustrate why nineteenth-century doctors saw them as distinct. Any building can be manipulated to control and survey its inhabitants, but perhaps the most famous example of architecture designed for control is Jeremy Bentham's Panopticon, which was tailored to the subjugation of criminals. As is well known, the Panopticon plan of 1791 was a six-story doughnut-shaped building with a tower, or inspector's lodge, at the center; the guard in the lantern looked out through slit windows toward the backlit cells that surrounded him (Figure 1.29). From there he could see each prisoner. This

powerful form of control was not achieved through manacles and leg irons, but through sight—through the power of the gaze. When the guard slipped out, he replaced his physical body with "an opaque object"; thus the inmates did not actually know whether they were being watched. Michel Foucault proposed that the Panopticon amounted to social control given physical form. As Foucault pointed out, this was not simple surveillance but the fear of potential surveillance—the notion that the prisoners would internalize the mechanism of control and therefore become self-policing was crucial for the Panopticon.

Bentham changed the plan in subtle ways over a decade or so as he struggled to get a true panopticon prison built, but he never succeeded. Fascinating though it is, the Panopticon has been much more influential in critical theory than in actual prison building. The panoptical idea illustrated an extreme example of how surveillance and the possibility of surveillance could be used as a control mechanism. Historians have noted a few prisons and one mill building that were constructed in eighteenth- and nineteenth-century Britain using the Bentham system. Latrobe's Virginia State Penitentiary, begun in 1787, employed a Benthamite semicircle and a guard's house at the center, but lacked the unending surveillance because its cell doors were opaque.[74] Prison historians concur that the most influential part of Bentham's work was his insistence on solitary confinement.[75] Although solitary confinement was used to calm, and probably punish, the most violent of lunatics, it was certainly not an official aspect of the doctors' curative rhetoric.

Nineteenth-century psychiatrists in the United States did not consider the Panopticon as a diagram for the construction of asylums—it did not allow for the separation of men and women, nor was it possible to keep noisy patients removed from the quiet ones. Ease of vision was a boon for wardens but a nuisance for alienists. Although Bentham described a convoluted system of partition walls that would prevent sight lines from one cell to another, it seems likely that whatever partitions jailers devised, the round form would have still allowed views across the building. These sight lines would have distressed the doctors, who wrote often (and with little humor) about the tendency of lunatics to remove their clothing.

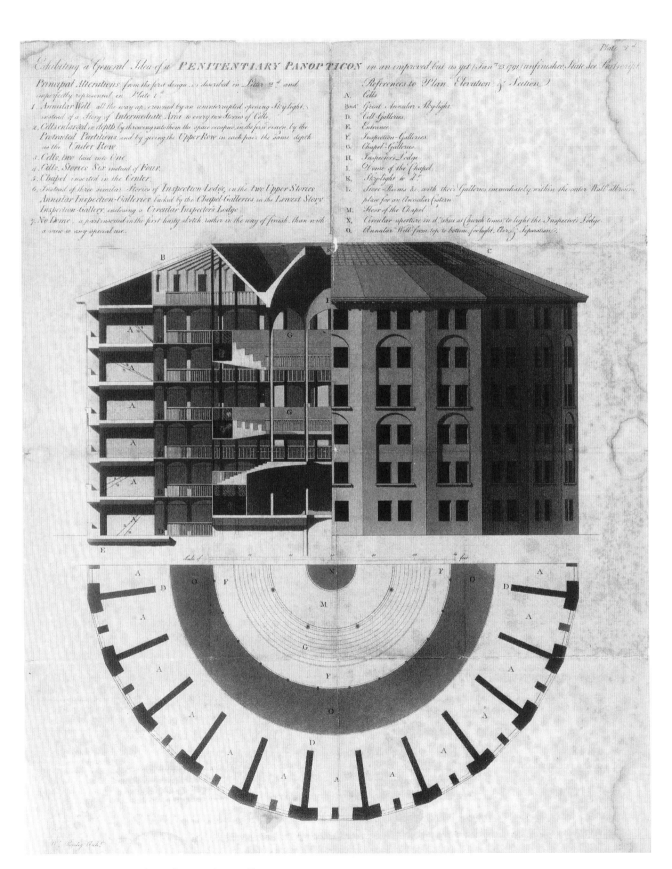

Figure 1.29. Jeremy Bentham, *The Panopticon; or, The Inspection House* (London: T. Payne, 1791). Bentham Papers, University College London, UCL Library, Special Collections, London.

Figure 1.30. William Brittin, Auburn Prison, State Prison for New York, begun in 1816, interior cells, as illustrated in U.S. Bureau of Prisons, *Handbook for Correctional Institution Design and Construction* (Washington, D.C., 1949), 9.

The prisons constructed in the United States in the decade after Bentham published his ideas were less idealistic and more practical. American prison design relied more heavily on the theories of John Howard than on those of Bentham. Existing congregate jails held eight to twelve prisoners, and often many more, in one room. The state prison in Charlestown, Massachusetts, by Charles Bulfinch, was a typical example from around 1800: small windows dotted the facade, behind which single-loaded corridors allowed the inspector to walk past the cells without ever turning his back on a prisoner.[76] In 1816, New York State began construction of a more influential prison at Auburn, which was based on the principle that prisoners could

encounter one another but not speak to one another. This came to be known as the silent (as opposed to the separate) system. The designer, a local carpenter named William Brittin, built the first cell block and served as the first warden.[77] Auburn was built in several stages, with inmates laboring on the north wing (1825), which contained 550 tiny cells, each one seven feet six inches by three feet eight inches.[78] In contrast, the size of a single room in an asylum was usually nine feet by twelve feet. Single cells or single bedrooms held different meanings in prisons and asylums. It was much more expensive to house each prisoner or patient in his or her own room. But single cells in a prison prevented conspiring and forced contemplation or possibly even repentance; single rooms in an asylum offered a more homelike setting and much-desired privacy.

At Auburn prison, each range of cells had a three-foot balcony, or gallery, so that guards could walk past the cells; there were five stories in similar arrangement (Figure 1.30). The basic design concept consisted of "multileveled cells stacked back-to-back, opening onto a space from ground to roof that separated the cells from the exterior cellblock walls."[79] Cells were deep inside the structure; thus they had no windows, the outer cell block wall had meager openings for light, and there were no toilets or heating ducts in individual cells. It was too dark to read the Bible, or anything else for that matter. Casual modern observers might think prisons and asylums were the same, but when seen in its historical contexts, Auburn's prison plan was not a model for a therapeutic hospital.

The radial plan, a wheel with spokes, had more potential as a layout for lunatic asylums, and the most famous radial prison was in the City of Brotherly Love,

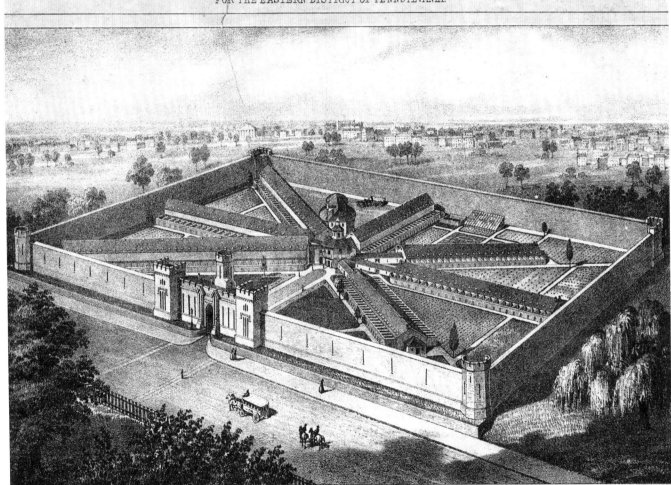

THE STATE PENITENTIARY,
FOR THE EASTERN DISTRICT OF PENNSYLVANIA.

drawn by a convict N° 2954.   Entered according to Act of Congress in the year 1855 by Richard Vaux, in the Clerk's Office of the District Court of the Eastern District of Pennsylvania.   P.S. Duval & Co's steam lith.pres.

Figure 1.31. John Haviland, Eastern State Penitentiary, Philadelphia, 1823–29, as illustrated in P. S. Duval and Company lithograph, 1855. This view distorts the lengths of some of the cell blocks, but still gives an overall sense of the size and shape of the institution and its relationship to the surrounding countryside. Courtesy of The Library Company of Philadelphia.

Kirkbride's hometown (Figure 1.31). In Dickens's 1842 tour, the attractions he most desired to visit were the Eastern State Penitentiary in Philadelphia and Niagara Falls. The stone structure sat on land that was outside the crowded city, although today it is surrounded by residential neighborhoods. The British-born John Haviland won the commission by architectural competition in 1821, and he worked on the design and construction of the prison until 1836. Haviland was familiar with contemporary reformist prisons in England. Its imposing walls communicated to passersby that life within was much worse than life outside. The prison represented idealistic notions of how to reform human behavior, similar in some ways to the panopticon but differing in many more significant ways. At its core was the principle that solitary confinement would lead the prisoner to repent. Rooms were warmed by a central heating system, and the original cells had skylights offering enough light to read the Bible and a flush toilet with pipes that led to a central sewer beneath each corridor.[80] Each inmate had his or her own exercise yard, available for one hour a day. A central tower made it possible for a guard to observe some of the exercise yards, but not all, and the guard could not actually see the prisoners in their cells: Bentham's notion of surveillance and Foucault's concept of internalized control were not quite activated here. Rather, it was the isolation of the person, the total distance from others, that would serve to control. The radial plan was copied more by European than by other American prison builders, and Eastern State became known as a tourist attraction; in 1839, four thousand visitors, including schoolchildren, toured the prison.[81]

The prison commissioners admonished: "The exterior of a solitary prison should exhibit as much as possible great strength and convey to the mind a cheerless blank indicative of the misery which awaits the unhappy being who enters within its walls." Indeed, Haviland effectively used the walls, square towers, iron gates, and crenellations to communicate the penitentiary's moral strength, but others saw those additions as expensive decoration. When Alexis de Tocqueville and Gustave de Beaumont visited the United States in 1831, they calculated that the cost of Eastern State was around $1,800 per cell, while a more modest prison in Connecticut cost only $151 per cell.[82] Tocqueville and Beaumont were quick to point out the irony that American political rhetoric emphasized personal freedom, and yet the young country's prison system was unusually harsh.

Asylum builders rejected the doughnut-shaped Panopticon, but some gravitated toward the radial plan, such as William Stark in his lunatic hospital in Glasgow. Radials had many advantages over panopticons.[83] First, they had hallways whose purpose could be reassigned to dayrooms. Second, wards could be made short enough to allow for a ventilating breeze. But in a pinwheel arrangement one could not separate the most deranged patients from the quieter ones except by a wedge-shaped airing court. The separation was therefore less effective than in a long thin asylum, in which the noisiest patients were placed at the farthest distance from the administrative offices and—it should be noted—the doctor's family apartment. Every room in a radial plan building had a limited view, which was not a problem for designers of prisons. (Offering a picturesque vista to hardened criminals was not high on the wardens' list of priorities.) But asylum doctors, steeped in the nineteenth-century belief that nature was curative, wanted their patients to have views toward nature when they were not actually enveloped by the parklike grounds during their daily walks. A spoke-and-wheel plan caused a constriction of space toward the center, so that the rooms could never be equally served by fresh air and light, and most rooms could not have a vista. A British observer noted that a radial asylum plan in Genoa, Italy, was particularly loathsome—"a mass of lunatics sweltering in a building constructed in the shape of a wheel with many spokes."[84] One can speculate that in Kirkbride's Philadelphia, with Eastern State looming over the city, the radial plan itself symbolized imprisonment and represented solitary confinement, the opposite associations from moral treatment.

While moral management could, with difficulty, be employed in an old mansion or adapted almshouse, this situation was considered a sad compromise. Old buildings had neither proper ventilation nor the orderly arrangement of rooms that were expected of new asylums. A few doctors employed moral treatment in preexisting buildings, but as they refined their needs, the professional society of superintendents began to argue for purpose-built structures that would serve the patients and staff. Once Americans had new asylums to work in, they rejected European asylums for their eccentricity. American doctor Pliny Earle visited many European asylums in 1839, and condemned all the old buildings he visited. He particularly disliked former almshouses and old hospitals, such as Salpêtrière in France, and he objected to the *palazzi* and monasteries of Italy. Of the asylum at Malta he wrote, "[T]he building is old, and as an almost necessary consequence, very incommodious for the present method of treatment."[85] Another American doctor, D. Tilden Brown, observed that a Scottish private hospital in an ancient baronial residence was "picturesque" but "not peculiarly convenient for its present uses."[86] Brown particularly disliked the French asylums he visited, noting that they neglected that most basic of architectural desiderata: shelter. The French designers, he said, approached their task as if everyone were going to live outside: "The prevailing mode of construction seems founded on the supposition that the insane, like the sane population, are to live out of doors most of the year, and that therefore it is useless to waste much thought on their dwellings."[87] If old buildings could not be adaptively reused, then new ones had to be built. Old buildings would not do—newness counted.

As moral treatment grew in public recognition, the building type developed, broadcasting the values of reform. The Williamsburg Public Hospital of 1773 and the New York State Lunatic Asylum of 1841 illustrate a remarkable transformation of asylum architecture over a seventy-year period. Doctors and architects together refined the generic plan and facade of colonial institutions into the highly specialized hospitals of the 1840s. During this period, asylum builders could shape their hospitals in a variety of ways because there was no centralized organization to mandate planning, site selection, or materials. Doctors banded together to discuss the management of these diseases, and their publications reveal a strong interest in architecture. In the following chapter, we will see a much more rigidly codified system, sponsored by Kirkbride and endorsed by the leading medical superintendents.

2

Establishing the Type

THE DEVELOPMENT OF KIRKBRIDE PLAN HOSPITALS AND
HOPE FOR AN ARCHITECTURAL CURE

It is now generally considered that external impressions such as arise from cheerful landscapes and
handsome architecture have a happy effect upon this class of unfortunate persons.

:: *Independent Monitor* (Tuscaloosa, June 25, 1857) ::

The idea that "cheerful landscapes and handsome architecture" profoundly affected patients was at its height during the 1840s and 1850s. Before those decades, American doctors had no set plan, no rules to follow, when they embarked on the raising of a new asylum. But in the middle of the nineteenth century, new construction became codified per the instructions of Dr. Thomas Kirkbride. This chapter will consider the rise of the Kirkbride plan, using certain key buildings to illustrate the paradoxes of asylum life. It will explore the importance of landscape in treating the insane; visit a few individual patients and their perceptions of the asylums in which they lived; and consider the role of work and recreation as components of moral treatment.

Generally, large asylums in which all the patients lived under one roof were called congregate hospitals. The Kirkbride plan, also known as the linear plan, was a type of congregate plan, made up of short but connected pavilions, arrayed in a shallow V. The Kirkbride plan was distinctive: no other nineteenth-century American institution used a plan like it. Contemporary medical hospitals in Britain and Europe relied on pavilions but did not adopt the echelon arrangement. Short wards were common in European and British medical hospitals, asylums, and prisons, but in such cases the pavilions were incorporated into two parallel rows, a U shape, an E shape, a grid, or a cross, but not a V.

In the United States, as a result of the power of the Association of Medical Superintendents of American Institutions for the Insane, who published architectural guidelines in 1851, and bolstered by Kirkbride's widely consulted 1854 publication, the plan became standard. The AMSAII held annual meetings, published a journal (the *American Journal of Insanity, AJI*), and guided states in the establishment of hospitals. It had been founded three years before the American Medical Association, and the alienists declined membership in the latter organization because they argued that ordinary physicians were less professional than AMSAII members. Medical doctors, especially neurologists, would later deride the founders of the AMSAII for their lack of scientific rigor—and for their obsession with their buildings. But in the 1840s, the organization represented a prestigious and tight-knit cadre who shared many interests, including architecture. As Nancy Tomes explains, the asylum was a doctor's "most impressive asset."[1] The AMSAII is important for this study because the members acted as a collective client—they shared information on new buildings through the journal and celebrated each other's successes. Although the editors of the *AJI* allowed for debates about various types of plans, by and large, the AMSAII supported Kirkbride in the development of the linear plan. The organization exemplifies the way in which a powerful and systematic group of patrons could set exacting architectural standards, although this was not necessarily to its advantage in the end.

The New Jersey State Lunatic Asylum

Each new state asylum was a feather in the cap of Dorothea Dix, a charity reformer who considered the asylum in Trenton to be her earliest success. She later called it her "first child." Although legislators had discussed the possibility of a state mental hospital for seven years, from about 1838 to 1845, it was Dix's petition that catalyzed the process. Formerly a schoolteacher, Dix traveled across the United States reporting on the desperate situation of almshouses and prisons. A Unitarian, she believed that within each person dwelled the possibility of continued spiritual development. She effectively coerced legislators in several states to fund asylums for the mentally ill. Generally, Dix's appeals to state legislatures were filled with emotional descriptions of the conditions of dehumanized, pauper lunatics shivering in the cold of foul-smelling, dangerous almshouses. She did not speak herself, because women were not allowed to address state legislatures, but she prepared statements that were read aloud by sympathetic politicians. Her entreaties on behalf of "those who . . . are incapable of pleading their own cause" convinced many lawmakers.

According to Dix, the situation for poor, mentally ill people was dire. Without institutions specifically for the insane, impoverished lunatics ended up in almshouses. County officials placed insane people in poorhouses when they were disruptive to the community, were dangerous to themselves, or carried some additional illness bringing them to the brink of death. Dix promoted the economic benefits to society of building therapeutic hospitals. If the insane could be cured, and it was widely believed they would be, it would cost the state less to support them for a short time in a hospital than to pay for them to reside for a lifetime in an almshouse. Besides, counties and states looked uncaring when poorhouses burned to the ground, as happened in New Jersey just a week before Dix's petition was presented to the state legislature.[2] No one died in the fire, but it served to illustrate that old buildings were unsafe and could not be adapted to this new purpose; since moral treatment required a changed setting, a new building was the only way to house the nascent reform institution.

The New Jersey State Lunatic Asylum was recognized by most American doctors for its innovative planning. Its superintendent, Horace Buttolph, almost certainly worked with Kirkbride when he penned an article called "Modern Asylums" in 1847 outlining many key architectural issues.[3] Buttolph's asylum in Trenton was the first shallow-V-plan asylum in the United States (Figures 2.1 and 2.2). It had a pristine plan, simple and compact, each part directed specifically to the perceived needs of the insane patient. The Trenton asylum was intended to house 250 patients, a number considered small enough that the superintendent could visit all the male patients and his wife all the female patients daily.[4] The July 1849 issue of the *American Journal of Insanity* explained that the New Jersey state commissioners had "adopted the draft of design by Dr. T. S. Kirkbride, of the 'Pennsylvania Hospital for the Insane,' from which a working plan was subsequently made by the architect, J. Notman."[5] Kirkbride later explained: "The general features of the first linear plan which has been described, were originally prepared by the writer [Kirkbride, referring to himself] at the request of the commissioners for putting up a State Hospital for the Insane in New Jersey."[6] The *American Journal of Insanity* published a plan of Trenton in 1847 and again in 1849. The design for the New Jersey State Lunatic Asylum was under way before the AMSAII published its propositions in 1851.[7] These groundbreaking propositions outlined the principles by which a lunatic asylum should be constructed, and they described an institution much like the one in Trenton.

The sheer size of the building, the use of stone, and the formality of the entrance suggested the stability of a state institution. State officials were impressed by the well-educated Scotsman John Notman's redesign and enlargement of the New Jersey State House, which encouraged them to select his design for the state hospital in 1847.[8] Notman's neoclassical middle block originally housed the superintendent and his family in addition to having public parlors and a chapel (Figure 2.3). The central administrative block stood in advance of two setback three-story wings. Notman described the monumental building's style as Tuscan:

The exterior will be in the simplest style of architecture. A Tuscan portico of six columns marks the centre and entrance.

Figure 2.1. John Notman, New Jersey State Lunatic Asylum, Trenton, 1848, perspective view with gardens. Courtesy of Oskar Diethelm Library.

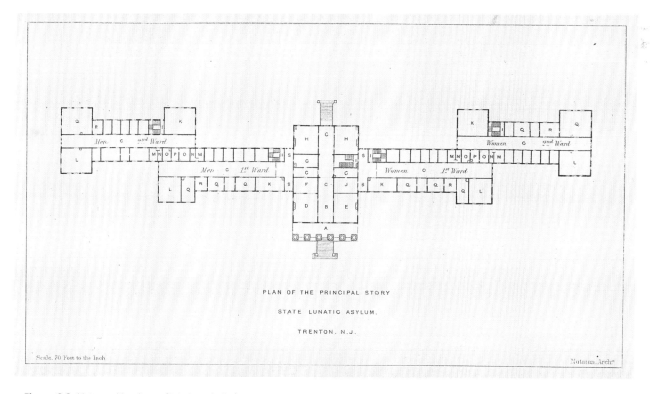

Figure 2.2. Notman, New Jersey State Lunatic Asylum, plan. Courtesy of Oskar Diethelm Library.

A boldly projecting cornice of the same style will be continued around the whole. . . . its architectur[al] effect will be good, from its great size, the well-arranged advancing and receding disposition of the wings, the variety in height, and the fine proportions of the several masses of the building.[9]

The exterior of Notman's Tuscan temple, with its ebb and flow of massive stone walls, was decidedly undomestic.

Many of the patients would have come from cramped, dark urban row houses, others from old farmhouses; even the upper-class patients hailed from Victorian houses with many small rooms. These cramped home environments would have contrasted with the long corridors and broad dayrooms of the asylum. One contemporary doctor wrote that "in many instances patients received into an asylum are taken from close confinement at home, or from dark disagreeable rooms in a jail. Being admitted from such situations, if the asylum is comfortable and pleasant, the mere change itself is soothing and restorative."[10] Even for paupers moving to a hospital from an almshouse or jail, the brightly lit spaces and orderly plan would have been unlike any prior setting. The exterior of a linear state hospital could never be mistaken for a poorhouse, prison, or domicile, and neither could the interior, although the

Figure 2.3. Notman, New Jersey State Lunatic Asylum, exterior. The central building has been demolished, but the wings are still standing. Courtesy of Oskar Diethelm Library.

interior made an attempt at domesticity with its parlors, dayrooms, and single bedrooms. Not all antebellum lunatics ended up among hundreds of other patients in an asylum set within a picturesque landscape garden, but for the ones who did, it was an environment unlike home.[11]

No Place Like Home

According to Kirkbride, institutionalization, separating the patient from his or her home and family, was an unfortunate demand of the cure, and he maintained that insanity could be treated most effectively in an institution:

> Most other diseases may be managed at home. Even with the most indigent, when laboring under ordinary sickness, the aid of the benevolent may supply all their wants, and furnish everything requisite for their comfort and recovery in their own humble abodes. It is not so, however, with insanity; for while all cases need not leave home, the universal experience is, that a large majority of them can be treated most successfully among strangers, and . . . only in institutions specially provided for the management of this class of diseases. It is among the most painful features of insanity, that in its treatment, so many are compelled to leave their families.[12]

Kirkbride here attempted to legitimate a distinction between the insane, who he claimed required institutionalization, and those suffering from "ordinary sickness," or medical disorders, who he believed could be treated perfectly well at home. In fact, short-term and long-term, mild and severe cases were sometimes treated by general doctors in the patient's home, under the daily watch of a family member.[13] Buttolph avowed that the home contributed to the patient's illness: "[T]he removal of a person from home and the associations with which their excited, depressed or perverted feelings have arisen, is often nearly all that is required to restore the healthy balance of the faculties."[14] In Buttolph's view, the family's refusal to commit a relative would lead to an incurable state. Kirkbride's and Buttolph's protestations must be understood in light of the supposedly high rate of curability, which was claimed to be as high as 90 percent during these optimistic years.

The necessary monumentality of an asylum for 250 people created a paradox for psychiatrists, who frequently referred to home and family as central to their therapeutic ideals. The superintendent and his wife lived in the central building as surrogate parents; doctors often referred to themselves as "fathers," the asylum as "the house," the patients collectively as "the family." The furnishings in the common rooms recalled the parlors of upper-class homes; occasionally, local philanthropists would donate pianos, for example. The recreational activities, too, inclined toward the supposedly refined: reading, playing and listening to music, and watching magic lantern shows. Christine Stevenson has noted that eighteenth-century asylums mimicked the social structure of the English manor house, with the doctor as philanthropic noble, the attendants as servants, and the patients as serflike dependents. One hesitates to extend this precise metaphor to mid-nineteenth-century America, but the imagery of an extended patriarchal family certainly applies. William Tuke could reasonably claim a fatherly presence among his thirty patients at the York Retreat; but the figures of speech become less believable when an asylum sheltered 250 and, later, 600 or more inmates. Asylums strove for domesticity they could not possibly achieve.

The rhetoric of the annual reports and other official documents repeats an almost absurd mythology of the mental institution as a home away from home; Andrew Scull has referred to an attempted "domestication of madness," an effort on the part of doctors to transform the company of the deranged into a reflection of family life.[15] Extending this interpretation, we can argue that as asylums grew in size, the references to home became more important to maintain the pretense of family. Yet another interpretation, equally valid, is that the exterior projected civic identity through its grandness, while the interiors were broken up into smaller rooms that provided a facsimile of domestic space. There is little question that doctors faced a paradox, wanting to promote the asylum in the public eye as a serious and stable institution, and at the same time calm the family's fears with domestic allusions and spaces.

Dr. Buttolph at Trenton faced a serious problem: his metaphorical family kept growing. Within two years of the completion of the Trenton hospital, Buttolph asked the legislators for more state funds. A few years later he succeeded in his efforts, and the state contributed funds to extend the building by adding a pavilion to each end (Figure 2.4). There was no question about where to place the new wings—they were anticipated by the principles of the Kirkbride plan. Samuel Sloan, architect of Kirkbride's Pennsylvania Hospital, managed the expansion. Superintendents valued the fact that the linear plan, with its discrete wards, made the means of expansion obvious and construction easy. Entire wings could be built without disrupting the life of the existing building. The addition of the wings may have seemed innocent enough at the time, but in retrospect it portended demise. The building was already full after just two years—overcrowding would eventually lead to the decline of these buildings, and, by extension, the collapse of the profession of asylum medicine.

The natural environment was thought to be essential to the cure, and thus the site of an insane hospital was crucial to its success: from the point of view of

reformers, state legislators, and doctors, there was simply no reason to spend state funds on a building that was not in a winsome location (Figures 2.5 and 2.6). A rural location offered better chances for full and cleansing ventilation, and therefore both asylums and medical hospitals needed country or suburban sites. As architectural historian Jeanne Kisacky explains, "'Approved' knowledge in mid-nineteenth-century hospital design . . . inevitably included the distinct requirement of a pastoral rather than an urban site."[16] The New Jersey site, unlike the one at Utica where Buttolph was first employed, was naturally hilly and had plenty of fresh water. Buttolph boasted about the Trenton hospital's attractive location:

> Reposing in the midst of the most beautiful scenery in the valley of the Delaware, combining all the influences which human art and skill can command to bless, soothe, and restore the wandering intellects that are gathered in its bosom, the state may proudly

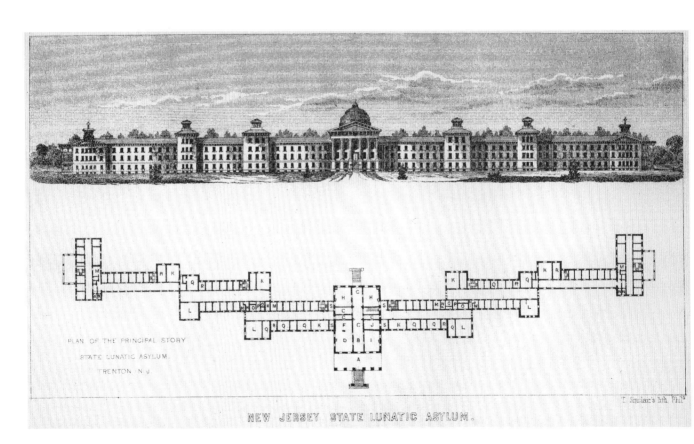

NEW JERSEY STATE LUNATIC ASYLUM.

Figure 2.4. Notman, New Jersey State Lunatic Asylum, plan of modifications (from 1850). This later plan shows wards added to both ends. Samuel Sloan was the architect in charge of the expansion. Courtesy of Oskar Diethelm Library.

Figure 2.5. A. J. Downing, landscape of New Jersey State Lunatic Asylum, photograph from 1907. This view looks past the pond and offers a glimpse of Notman's portico and dome. Courtesy of Oskar Diethelm Library.

Figure 2.6. Downing, landscape of New Jersey State Lunatic Asylum, photograph from 1907. This photograph shows the opposite view from the previous illustration. The photographer stood on the front porch looking down the slope of the lawn to the pond. The Delaware River is visible in the distance. Courtesy of Oskar Diethelm Library.

point to this asylum, as a noble illustration of that charity, which, borne from above, diffuses itself in blessings of the poor and unfortunate.[17]

The New Jersey State Lunatic Asylum was set at the crest of a hill, a site that was considered especially advantageous because it encouraged inmates to take uplifting walks and offered more exciting views than a flat site: "If [an asylum] occupy a dead insipid flat, . . . the horizon is limited and the scenery tame. Patients are not, in such a situation, so easily induced to take exercise, nor so much benefited by it, as when the ground is irregular, the landscape varied, and the necessity for exertion and exhilaration which attend it, greater."[18] W. A. F. Browne, a British doctor, here echoed Romantic theorists like William Gilpin, who favored irregularity over symmetry and roughness over smoothness. Browne exalted the knoll and disparaged the plain: "If the building be placed upon a summit or the slope of a rising ground, the advantages are incalculable. To many of those whose intellectual avenues to pleasure are forever closed, the mere extent of a country affords delight."[19]

Buttolph compared the views from the shallow-V form to those of other possible arrangements, such as the radial plan, the H plan, and the quadrangle, and he concluded that good views were most accessible from the Trenton design: "From a building of this form, also, the principal landscape view is visible to patients in all parts of the house, which is not the case to the same extent, in the other forms mentioned."[20] This emphasis on the view of the surrounding landscape drove the specific V shape of the American asylum.

British asylum doctor and hospital expert Sir Henry C. Burdett's four-volume 1891–93 publication on hospitals and asylums of the world lists not one medical hospital that takes the V shape. (Jeremy Taylor calls Burdett's book "unrivalled.")[21] Among the 150 medical hospitals, maternity hospitals, cancer hospitals, infectious disease departments, and dispensaries that Burdett illustrated, we can find pavilions arrayed in a staggering variety of patterns, including rows, crosses, and quadrangles. But none takes the precise form of the land-gobbling V. The most concise explanation for the distinctive V comes from Buttolph, who valued the "principal landscape view" for patients in "all parts of the house."[22]

To see why the landscape was so important for moral treatment, one need only think back to the imagery of an eighteenth-century madman, fettered to the wall and thus unable to go out-of-doors, ever. The Delaware River valley near Trenton was naturally lovely, but the actual site received significant human intervention from A. J. Downing, who designed the parklike surroundings for the New Jersey State Lunatic Asylum in 1848. His national reputation had grown considerably in the intervening years since he worked on the grounds for Utica, where Buttolph had served as assistant physician. Furthermore, Downing had known Notman since 1842. "Design IX," an "Italian or Tuscan" cottage, was Notman's contribution to Downing's *Cottage Residences*.[23] In his extensive writings, Downing promoted the simplicity of the rural life, and he sympathized with the plight of the insane, assuming that the pressures of capitalism led to the demise of the afflicted. As he observed in 1848, "Many a fine intellect, overtasked and wrecked in the too ardent pursuit of power or wealth, is fondly courted back to reason, and more quiet joys, by the dusky, cool walks of the asylum, where peace and rural beauty do not refuse to dwell."[24] Downing's mechanism is unclear: the patient is courted back to reason just by coming in contact with "cool walks" and "rural beauty." Many doctors also asserted that the rise in insanity was caused by the stresses of modern life. Mental illness was seen as the thorny underside of civilization, a steep but necessary price to pay for progress.

Downing's love of rural land—and distrust of the city—perfectly matched the values of asylum personnel. He might have disliked the way the boxy symmetrical building contradicted the curving walkways that meandered through his landscape. He disdained "Grecian architecture" for rural residences, complaining that it was "greatly inferior to the Gothic, [and] from the prevalence of horizontal lines and plain surfaces, it is not found to harmonize with picturesque scenery so happily as a style affording more bold and varied outlines."[25] On the other hand, the renowned landscape theorist could at least commend Notman's building for being made of rough local stone, thus clearly connected to its site.

One Anglican reverend disparaged the hustle and bustle of city life in a sermon titled "Made Whole: A Parting Address to Convalescents on Leaving an

Asylum," in which he noted the difference between asylum life and "the crowded street or lane." The minister told the recently recovered mental patients:

> Let me now suggest a few plain rules for the preservation of your health. . . . Pure water and fresh air are great friends of health. Living, as perhaps you do, in a crowded street or lane, you may not be able to get much of either. Anyhow, let into your house as much air as you can, and use water freely.[26]

Lunacy reformers and park enthusiasts shared many beliefs: that human behavior could be explained by environmental factors, nature was curative, exercise therapeutic, and cities a drain on the psyche.

Kirkbride's Book and the Alabama Insane Hospital

The Alabama Insane Hospital appears in Kirkbride's influential book, *On the Construction, Organization, and General Arrangements of Hospitals for the Insane*, published in 1854. Two illustrations are simply titled "Hospital on the Linear Plan" (Figures 2.7 and 2.8). Sloan made these drawings based on his design of the Alabama Insane Hospital, commissioned in November 1852.[27] The Alabama Insane Hospital was among the first hospitals constructed after the 1851 propositions, thus enhancing its profile. Although the building still stands, only one remaining photograph shows the original

ELEVATION OF A HOSPITAL ON THE LINEAR PLAN.

Figure 2.7. Samuel Sloan, hospital on the linear plan, 1854, as illustrated in Thomas Kirkbride, *On the Construction, Organization, and General Arrangements of Hospitals for the Insane* (Philadelphia, 1854; 2nd edition, 1880). This drawing illustrates the main principles of the Kirkbride, or linear, plan, which included short wards for ventilation and classification, a central pavilion for superintendent's dwelling, and division of men and women. The ideal hospital was set within a landscape garden and limited to 250 patients.

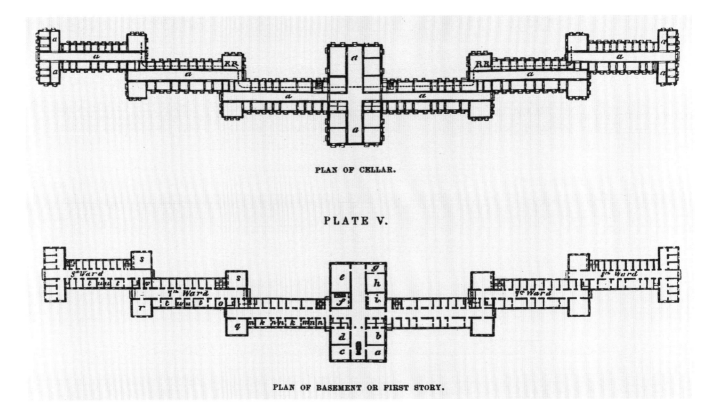

PLAN OF CELLAR.

PLATE V.

PLAN OF BASEMENT OR FIRST STORY.

Figure 2.8. Sloan, hospital on the linear plan, as illustrated in Kirkbride, *On the Construction, Organization, and General Arrangements of Hospitals for the Insane.* Plan of cellar (above) and basement or first floor.

cast-iron porch (Figure 2.9). This modest front was later replaced with a colossal order colonnade (Figure 2.10), which makes it appear to be quite different from the ideal hospital in Kirkbride's book, but, in fact, in its original form it was identical to Kirkbride's sample asylum except for the number of windows on the transverse wings.[28]

Kirkbride's book offered much advice on heating, flue design, and sewage removal, and he firmly recommended the use of stone or brick to prevent fires. He promoted the characteristics seen at Trenton: the bilaterally symmetrical plan, consisting of a central building with flanking pavilions arranged in the echelon fashion, like a row of birds in flight. Pavilions were to be no more than three stories and needed to be short enough that a breeze would carry fresh air through the wards. These wards would be used to categorize patients by severity of disease, with the noisiest patients farthest away from the center.

The massive Alabama hospital, like the one at Trenton, commanded its site (Figure 2.11). The *Tuscaloosa*

Independent Monitor noted in 1857 that the building was "imposing." Visitors would have entered the main building at ground level and immediately faced a spacious iron stairway leading up to the second story, which housed business offices and reception rooms. The third story was home to the chapel, and this placement became standard. The center main contained two dining rooms for the use of recovering or well-behaved patients.[29] The outer refractory wards were for the "most noisy or violent or those whom, for any reason, it is desirable to have secluded."[30] As we have seen, the outermost wards had single-loaded corridors, which made surveillance easier—the attendant never had to turn his or her back on a patient. Double-loaded corridors were standard for all the wards except the refractory ones, but if money had been no object, nineteenth-century doctors would have used single-loaded corridors throughout their hospitals. Hallways with rooms on one side only used space extravagantly, but Dr. Isaac Ray endorsed them in 1854: "The gallery . . . should have but one range of rooms opening upon it. On the other side,

Figure 2.9. Samuel Sloan, Alabama Insane Hospital, Tuscaloosa, 1852–60 (now Bryce's Hospital). This photograph shows the hospital before later alterations. Courtesy of W. S. Hoole Special Collections, University of Alabama, Tuscaloosa.

Figure 2.10. Sloan, Alabama Insane Hospital. This photograph shows the center main in the 1880s, with its renovated colossal order facade. Courtesy of W. S. Hoole Special Collections, University of Alabama, Tuscaloosa.

Figure 2.11. Sloan, Alabama Insane Hospital. Photograph by Mark Yanni.

the light should be admitted through spacious windows, and thus the inmates should have constantly before their eyes the surrounding country, which is, certainly, a more agreeable object to behold than a monotonous range of doors in a dreary expanse of brick wall." He went on to say that he and other Americans had wrongly abandoned the single-loaded corridor "solely from considerations of economy."[31]

In Victorian parlance, a ward was one floor of one pavilion; a pavilion or wing was usually three stories high, comprising three wards. A ward included a parlor, dining room, clothes room, bathtub room, water closet, laundry chute, and rooms for two attendants. The Lunatic Asylum in Utica, the New Jersey State Hospital for the Insane, and the Alabama Insane Hospital all included a mix of single bedrooms and associated dormitories; at Alabama the associated dormitories housed between four and six patients.[32] A photograph of a hallway at the Tuscaloosa asylum illustrates typical ward appearance, showing rooms on both sides of the hall (Figure 2.12). Medical treatments took place on the ward or in the bathing room. The daily life of patients was controlled and simple: early to bed and early to rise was an asylum rule. They awoke around 5 AM, ate breakfast on the ward at 6 o'clock, and awaited the superintendent's rounds at 8 AM. In the morning

they spent a few hours outside with attendants, whenever the weather allowed.[33] In the afternoon after lunch, middle-class patients (such as lawyers and businessmen) read and played games, while working-class patients worked on the farm or in the print shop.[34] They ate dinner in the early evening and retired to bed at 9:30 PM. Medicines and hydrotherapy were issued in the morning after breakfast or at night after dinner.[35] Patients spent daytime hours in the dayrooms or the ward hallways, but never in their bedrooms (Figures 2.13 and 2.14).

One British critic of typical ward design noted that the "torpid, indolent, and melancholic," who tend to want to sleep all day, would be better off farther away from their bedrooms: "If you make a rule that they cannot go in their bedrooms during the day . . . [,] the doors, close at hand, will ever create the desire to indulge in the withheld gratification of entering them."[36] When family or friends visited, they did not meet patients on the wards, but rather in public parlors in the center main. Thus the experience of the building was very different for patients (who stayed on the wards, except for visits), visitors (who remained primarily in the middle building), and the superintendent and matron, who moved freely throughout the spaces of the linear plan. In addition to the center main, visitors were allowed access to one model ward, close to the center

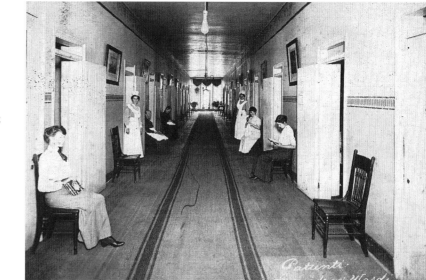

Figure 2.12. Sloan, Alabama Insane Hospital, patients' corridor and ward. This photograph shows the length of a typical ward. Patients spent most of their time in common rooms and hallways, not in bedrooms, which were used for sleeping exclusively. Courtesy of W. S. Hoole Special Collections, University of Alabama, Tuscaloosa.

Figure 2.13. Sloan, Alabama Insane Hospital, patients' dayroom. Courtesy of W. S. Hoole Special Collections, University of Alabama, Tuscaloosa.

Figure 2.14. Sloan, Alabama Insane Hospital, woman's bedroom. Courtesy of W. S. Hoole Special Collections, University of Alabama, Tuscaloosa.

main, which was kept tidy and well furnished. The short wards made it easier for doctors to divide patients into groups by type of behavior, from mild to violent. One reason for categorizing patients was to keep the noisy from disturbing the docile. But the classification system was also a management device—a transfer to a nicer ward was a reward for a well-behaved patient. Relocation to a lower ward was a punishment. Many accounts note that the central building and one or two nearby wards were better cleaned and furnished, and they contrasted vastly with the rest of the asylum.

There were also harsh contrasts between the accommodations for whites and blacks. In hospitals, as elsewhere, racial segregation manifested itself in physical space. At the Alabama Insane Hospital, African Americans amounted to 18 percent of admissions, but they did not live aboveground as whites did. Superintendent Dr. Peter Bryce noted in 1872 that blacks had been "assigned to the extreme lower wards." In other words, they lived in the basement; Bryce considered this an unacceptable arrangement, and thus he called for the construction of separate facilities.[37] Gerald Grob has observed that although southern superintendents believed state funds should be used to treat all the insane regardless of race, they deemed segregation necessary.[38]

Like many early asylums, the Alabama Insane Hospital was a technological wonder. In a time when few private houses had central heat, gaslight, or toilets, this hospital came fully loaded. The cupola over the main pavilion contained iron tanks that stored the water that had been pumped in from a spring one thousand feet away. From these lofty tanks, water flowed through pipes to every part of the building. Patients extracted coal from a mine on-site, and it was used both for heating the hospital and for manufacturing gas for the lighting system.[39] Each room was furnished with built-in gas lamps. Boilers in the basement heated air, and a steam-driven fan puffed air into flues for each room. A sturdy building was particularly important for a population that was unusually tough on the physical plant. Bryce noted later that mentally ill patients were "destructive of all kinds of bedding, clothing, and every species of property to an extent which is hardly conceivable by those who have no knowledge of their habits."[40] According to American superintendent D. Tilden Brown, European and British physicians were entirely too blasé

when it came to heating and ventilation. The English and Scottish county asylums he visited did not have centralized heat—just fireplaces. Brown was appalled that one British alienist had worked in the same institution for fifteen years without ever inspecting the heating apparatus in the cellar.[41] This failure to keep tabs on the water heater was a dereliction of duty. Samuel Sloan took such matters seriously and perhaps was well suited to asylum work because of his engineering competence. His primary biographer, Harold Cooledge, explained that Sloan's contributions were "functional rather than aesthetic," noting especially his devotion to "clarification of circulation in hospitals, schools, and commercial buildings; . . . modular, repetitive, construction; particular attention to fire safety; improvement of mechanical equipment."[42] All of these qualities are evident in the Alabama Insane Hospital.

Patients and the Reception of Asylum Buildings: An Interlude

Patients' accounts of their experiences of architecture are not widely available, but there are three stories of unfair incarceration that allow us a hint of how asylum architecture shaped their daily lives. Ebenezer Haskell, who believed he was incarcerated by greedy sons, escaped from the Pennsylvania Hospital for the Insane, and Elizabeth Packard, who was committed by her husband, lived in the Illinois State hospital in Jacksonville. Francis Delilez's description of an asylum in Wisconsin helps us envision the hard work done behind closed doors.

Haskell was over sixty years old when his son, terrorized by threats and Haskell's wielding a large knife, summoned the police. On the night of his commitment, the elder Haskell's insanity was certified by a local dentist, based largely on the word of his son. The son took his father to Kirkbride's hospital in west Philadelphia. He was released by his wife's order but then recommitted; he escaped. After this escape—his first—he was committed for an additional four months. He made his second escape in April 1867 but broke his leg vaulting the wall. Afterward, Haskell sought a jury trial to prove that he was in fact sane and to demonstrate that he had been wrongly incarcerated. At the trial, his sons disclosed the following symptoms: their father frequently spoke of starting a tub factory and a steamship line, tore up the carpet, put the furniture outside the house, imagined he had been poisoned, and claimed he owned the whole street. His daughter said his condition deteriorated to a point where he threatened violence to her and to the U.S. president, and "was hostile to his sons and his family."[43] Haskell wrote a book about his travails, from which it is possible to discern few hard facts but many fascinating perceptions of the spaces of the insane hospital.

A newspaper reporter following Haskell's story called Kirkbride's hospital "a great suburban palace prison."[44] Perhaps the classical portico gave this reporter the idea of a palace, as it has suggested grandeur to many observers. But Haskell recounted a macabre event that took place on that very portico. A distraught patient arrived on Haskell's ward; he was terrified of the attendants, and he expressed his wish to be killed. When his sister came to visit, she prepared to meet him in a family parlor in the center main. Somehow, during the visit, the patient "snuck up to the second floor, through a room, and out onto the portico over the front entrance, and leaped down . . . striking his head on the granite steps. He died later that night."[45] The portico, the public face of the asylum, was on that night the site of its disgrace.

Haskell also tells of Kirkbride's skills at self-promotion and the doctor's good relationship with the press. For example, Kirkbride escorted a newspaperman around the hospital, and during his private tour the reporter found "the floors well scrubbed, the parlors richly furnished, the grounds extensive, the ventilation good, and supper excellent." But as Haskell carped, "These things are exactly what are shown to every casual visitor."[46]

Francis Delilez, a mistreated patient in the Winnebago asylum in Wisconsin, also objected to the false presentation of the asylum to the families of the patients and the citizens of the state. Whenever his wife came to visit, the otherwise brutal attendants cleaned him up and dressed him in a new suit of clothes. He wrote: "Just what makes this state institution so awfully dangerous and mischievous is the diabolical craftiness of its managers to conceal the evil from visitors and investigators and to show them only what is clean, bright,

and beautiful."[47] For the historian, Delilez's remarks are tantalizing: because we have so much more documentation from the doctors than the patients, it is relatively easy to discern the doctors' intentions. Asylum doctors were talented self-promoters, and they left archives full of optimistic pamphlets and reports. It has been, unfortunately, very difficult to find out whether the asylum spaces were used in the way in which the doctors intended. Haskell and Delilez suggest that only a fraction of the asylum's interior spaces were kept in a presentable manner.

Scull explains that the hierarchy of wards created a tension in individual patients, who lived with the dread of being demoted and knew that placement on a clean, quiet ward was a concession that could be taken away at any moment: "Only by exhibiting a suitable willingness to control his disagreeable propensities was he allowed to obtain his former privileges, always with the implied threat that their grant was purely conditional and subject to revocation."[48] Haskell clearly felt this tension, and he reported that he liked Ward Two but disliked the crowded, filthy, and noisy Ward Seven. In Ward Seven, Haskell spent daytime hours with twenty-five other men and slept in a dungeonlike underground room; his basement neighbor howled and hurled his body against the door.[49] Soon Kirkbride decided Ward Seven was too rough for Haskell, and he was moved back to Ward Two. But Haskell reported that life was better for a while, until a new patient arrived who was "more excited and unpleasant" than anyone from Ward Seven. As if by way of explanation, Haskell noted that the troublemaker was "from Washington and had been in the employ of the government."[50] Delilez explained that a fellow inmate, an "amiable" and "gentle" young man, was transferred by cruel attendants who "help the devil in his work" to one of the bad wards. The young man eventually returned to the better wards, but his overall condition was worse than when he entered the asylum.[51] The interior space of the asylum was strictly hierarchical, and patients were constantly aware of their place within the numerical wards.

Elizabeth Packard, possibly the most recognized of asylum victims, also described the hierarchy of spaces within the Jacksonville, Illinois, asylum. Packard's memoir gives the reader a poignant sense of her movement through the building. She tells a spatial story of downward spiral, from the outside world to the asylum, from the spiffy bourgeois parlors of the center main to the spartan wards, and, finally, from good wards to ever worsening halls, more and more distant from the center main. Her husband delivered her to the asylum and stayed a few days to converse (or, as she later concluded, to conspire) with the doctors. Her positive outlook receded as she climbed the institution's steps:

> Now my last hope died within me and as the gloomy walls of my prison could be but indistinctly defined by the gray twilight of a summer evening. I held on to my husband's arm, as he guided my footsteps up the massive stone steps, into my dreary prison, where by lamplight he introduced me to Dr. Tenny, the Assistant Superintendent, to be conducted by him to my lonely, solitary cell.[52]

The first night they both ate dinner with the assistant superintendent; her husband slept on a "capacious, soft, luxurious bed," while she slept on a "narrow settee." The next morning she ate breakfast on the ward with the other ladies, who greeted her warmly. This was her first full day at the asylum. Her husband was still in nearby Jacksonville, and the couple met with the chief physician, Dr. McFarland, in a parlor in the center main. "I gladly accepted this invitation to be restored to the civilities of civilization, even temporarily. I seated myself upon the sofa by Mr. Packard's side, and the doctor took the big rocking chair, directly in front of us." She told the doctor she did not think of herself as insane, and said she felt more "out of her proper place" in the ward than in the reception room "with refined society."[53] By that evening, she realized her husband was retreating from her, both emotionally and spatially. Mr. Packard did not dine with his wife, but rather with the doctor. She was left to eat on the ward. He went for a carriage ride without her, but she could still see him. We know this because she described her feelings as she watched him drive away:

> After dinner I saw from the grated window of my cell, the Asylum carriage drive up in front of the steps. . . . Mr. Packard was politely handed in, and the carriage drove off. Upon inquiry, I found he had gone to ride, to see the beauties of the scenery about Jacksonville, and the buildings and handsome residences. "Oh," thought I, "Why could he not have invited me to ride with him . . . ?"[54]

Her husband left her at the asylum the next day. A few weeks later, he shipped to her an enormous trunk, which indicated to her and her fellow patients that her stay was not likely to be short.

Elizabeth Packard later claimed that she had never been insane but that her husband had objected to her unusual religious beliefs, especially her faith in spiritualism.[55] Her first few months at the asylum were better than the two years that followed. She wrote the doctor a letter complaining of injustices within the hospital, and after that affront, he harassed her by demoting her to a lesser ward where she was forced to sleep in a room with eight other patients. She was horrified by its bad smell and the washbasin shared by eighteen patients. Like Haskell, Packard noted the difference between the rooms on display for visitors and the reality of conditions at the back of the house. "This was not the visitor's ward. Seldom any, but the asylum occupants, found their entrance into this sink of human pollution."[56] The doctor claimed it was "all for her good." From the time the AMSAII organized in 1844, the alienists claimed that transparency was their goal—that the management of asylums could be freely inspected by all. They saw each new hospital as a model of both architecture and managerial openness, and this was especially true in the case of St. Elizabeths Hospital in Washington, D.C.

St. Elizabeths Hospital in Washington, D.C., the first and only federally funded asylum, was intended to be a model institution. The hospital was a pet project for Dorothea Dix, and thus the institution was particularly important in communicating the cause of lunacy reform (Figures 2.15 and 2.16). Dix proposed a nationwide federal system of charitable institutions for the mentally ill, funded by the sale of government land, and although she made progress with Millard Fillmore, she was stopped by his successor Franklin Pierce's presidential veto. Some historians have suggested that Pierce offered Dix funds for this one exemplary asylum as a kind of condolence prize after the failure of her national scheme. Dr. Charles H. Nichols, who was appointed to be its first superintendent, wrote to Dix in 1852:

> You, I have no doubt, think with me that a Hosp. for the Insane in or near the District of Columbia should by all means be a *model*

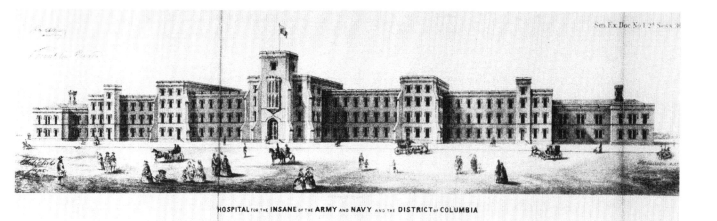

HOSPITAL for the INSANE of the ARMY and NAVY and the DISTRICT of COLUMBIA

Figure 2.15. Thomas U. Walter, Hospital for the Insane of the Army and Navy and the District of Columbia, now St. Elizabeths Hospital, Washington D.C., 1852–60, perspective. Courtesy of National Library of Medicine.

Figure 2.16. Walter, Hospital for the Insane of the Army and Navy and the District of Columbia, exterior of center main. Photograph by the author.

institution & that it may be so, it seems to me of paramount importance that the permanent *director* or med. Sup't be appointed before the site is selected (unless *you* choose it) who shall take the lead in choosing it, in selecting the most suitable material for building, in devising all plans & in superintending all the details of their execution.[57]

Dr. Luther Bell said it should be "a model in *regime* and detail, after which the hundreds of institutions to come may be wisely conformed."[58]

For the hospital, Dix had procured a spectacular site overlooking the Anacostia and Potomac rivers. At first she had trouble convincing the owner of the site (a tract of land historically known as St. Elizabeths) to part with his beloved farm, but eventually she persuaded him, because, he said, God chose her, and she chose the site. Addressing Dix directly, he wrote, "[You are an] instrument in the hands of God to secure this very spot for the unfortunates whose best earthly friend you are."[59]

When Nichols presented the plans to Congress, he proudly told the senators and representatives: "The institution itself will be one of the most conspicuous ornaments of the District, and will be visible to more people, and from more points, than any other structure, excepting perhaps the Capitol, and the Washington Monument when complete."[60] Nichols's enthusiasm notwithstanding, this perception of the capital city does not correspond very well to Pierre L'Enfant's vision, in which the Capitol, the Washington Monument, and the White House formed the three architectural foci of the urban plan, not the Capitol, the Washington Monument, and the lunatic asylum. Kirkbride approved of the choice of Nichols, saying in a letter to Dix that Nichols possessed "a taste for architectural arrangements and a practical knowledge of what is required in the planning, construction and general arrangements of a Hospital."[61]

Nichols may have had taste, but he also had his eye on the bottom line. He wrote to Dix that he had difficulty convincing the architect, Thomas U. Walter, to design "a cheap building," given that the well-respected architect was concerned about protecting his reputation for erudition and architectural refinement.[62] Walter had recently arrived in Washington, and he was nationally known for the elegant Greek Revival Girard College

in Philadelphia.[63] He was awarded the commission for the model asylum, variously titled, but originally known as the Government Asylum for the Insane Veterans of the Army and Navy and Residents of the District of Columbia, because he was already employed by the federal government. From the front of St. Elizabeths, he could see his more famous architectural contribution to the city, the dome of the Capitol (1851–65), under construction.

Walter designed the exterior of the redbrick asylum in a flat, fortresslike Gothic style in 1852. The structure was used as a military hospital during the Civil War and as a home for recuperating soldiers: these veterans did not want to be associated with the insane, and they began the practice of calling the institution St. Elizabeths.

The arrangement of spaces was the work of Nichols, who signed a site plan that also included an unambiguous printed citation: "Ground Plan designed by C.H. Nichols, Sup'." (Figure 2.17). Not only did the doctor devise this plan, he was evidently eager to get credit. Nichols invented a feature that was later copied widely: the wards farthest from the center were lower in height, thus the building tapered toward its outer ends. There were fewer members of the troublesome group that occupied the refractory wards, and the small, outer wards, which lacked parlors, housed the untidy, noisy, and violent patients. One can speculate that the seriously deranged patients did not interact successfully in the common rooms and that the omission of dayrooms allowed a saving of space at the building's ends.

The hospital employed an arrangement of double-loaded corridors with dayrooms and dining halls at the end of each ward. Connections between the wings were opened up more than in the New Jersey State Lunatic Asylum. Here, the wider linking hallways—almost as wide as the ward corridors—allowed doctors to move more easily through the right angle between wards. Iron doors blocked access from one ward to the next—not only to stop the spread of fire but also to keep patients from going from one pavilion to the next. Oddly, St. Elizabeths maintained the equal distribution of rooms for men and women on either side of the center main. Since most of the clients were veterans, there were many more men than women. In 1875, there were seven men for every two women.[64] The only women would have been residents of the District of Columbia. Thus

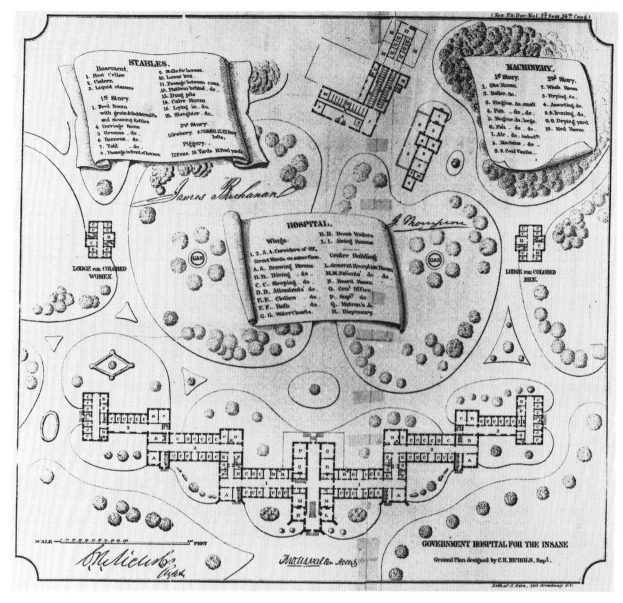

Figure 2.17. Walter, Hospital for the Insane of the Army and Navy and the District of Columbia, 1852, plan. The lodge for "colored women," on the left, and the lodge for "colored men," on the right, were separated from the main building. From Record Group 418, St. Elizabeths, item no. 20, United States National Archives and Record Administration.

the idealism of the builders—and the notion that this hospital was supposed to be a model—took precedence over practicality.

African American patients lived in the basement of the Tuscaloosa hospital, but at St. Elizabeths, they fared slightly better, as Walter designed two freestanding identical lodges, one for African American men and the other for African American women, a few hundred feet from the center main. The Government Asylum,

then, was the first to include separate accommodation for African Americans in its original plan.[65] Nichols specified that the distance should be "not less than 200 nor more than 400 feet" from the main edifice.[66] He imagined that they could be connected to the main building by ornamental covered walkways, but this never came to pass.[67] One of the redbrick lodges is still standing, and a plan labeled "Lodge for Colored Patients," from 1855 survives (Figures 2.18 and 2.19). It shows a

Figure 2.18. Walter, Hospital for the Insane of the Army and Navy and the District of Columbia, lodge for "colored women," 1855. The building was later used for nurses' housing, and it was also known as the East Lodge or Building 30. The lodge for "colored men" was demolished in the mid-1900s. Courtesy of Prints and Photographs, Library of Congress.

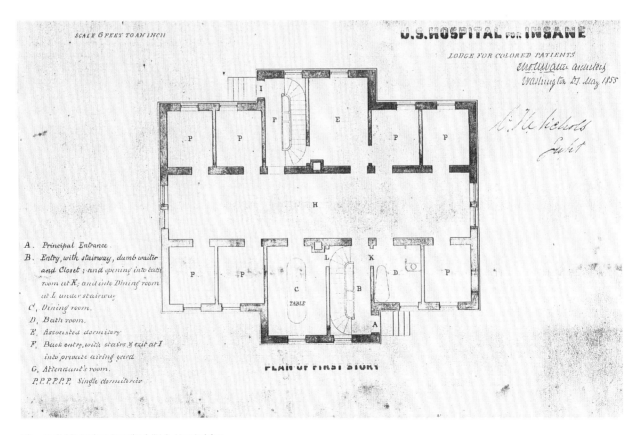

Figure 2.19. Walter, inscribed "U.S. Hospital for Insane, Lodge for Colored Patients," lower floor plan, 1855. From Record Group 418, St. Elizabeths, United States National Archives and Record Administration.

symmetrical building with entrances parallel to the facade and two staircases tucked in near the entrances. Eight cells and an associated dormitory, for between four and eight patients, opened onto a corridor. The dining room and bathing room were also accessible off this corridor. The two levels of the lodge were identical. The size of the rooms appears the same as in the main asylum. The stereotype of the happy slave emerged in Bucknill's account of what he called "the coloured lodge" at St. Elizabeths: "Separate from the main building is a smaller one, occupied by the insane patients of the coloured race. There was some boisterous and noisy talk, which was mostly merriment."[68] Nineteenth-century alienists claimed that slaves were less likely than free blacks or even free whites to become deranged, because they did not have to contend with "excessive mental action" or the strain of owning property.[69] As late as 1908, a psychiatrist in Virginia declared that slavery as a system prevented African Americans from becoming insane:

> [T]he regular simple life, the freedom from dissipation and excitement, steady and healthful employment, enforced self-restraint, the freedom from care and responsibility, . . . [the] nourishing food, comfortable clothing, the open air life of the plantation, the kindly care and treatment when sick, in those days, acted as preventive measures against mental breakdown in the negro.[70]

In this warped and nostalgic logic, white doctors alleged that living close to the land and conducting healthy outdoor labor staved off insanity. In so many ways, insane asylums were a microcosm of society, and St. Elizabeths was no exception.

The collaborative nature in the design of St. Elizabeths was characteristic of hospital construction, and although physicians saw asylum planning as a specialized task suited to medical experts, architects had important roles to play in refining the plans and designing the elevations. In 1891, Dr. Burdett restated a claim made by Kirkbride in 1854, that the future chief of any asylum should be hired in advance of its construction, that he should be charged with "the duty of advising on the plans, and of superintending the erection of the new buildings from start to finish."[71] For a linear plan hospital, the architect worked out the more complicated aspects of the plan, gave the exterior a coherent shape, applied appropriate details, and supervised the construction, all the while in consultation with a doctor.

Kirkbride's Second Hospital

After the New Jersey State Lunatic Asylum and St. Elizabeths were built, Kirkbride's own institution seemed, by comparison, to be a constricted building with a less-than-ideal plan. From his earliest years as superintendent, he shaped the public image of the asylum as a therapeutic place.[72] This message was communicated partly through architecture, and when his Pennsylvania hospital needed to expand—to relieve overcrowding—Kirkbride needed to continue to present a high standard of asylum architecture to his patients' families, his colleagues, and the public. Thus he commissioned Sloan in 1856 to design a second hospital, slightly larger than the first, on the same long, thin site in west Philadelphia (Figure 2.20). Men were moved to the new building in 1859, and women occupied the entire former building. The two hospitals were separated by Mill Creek and a deep vale; sheep grazed in a meadow between them; there was a deer park and flower and vegetable gardens (Figure 2.21). Kirkbride described the deer park as surrounded by a palisade fence, with "different animals in it [that] are in full view from the adjoining grounds."[73] Because of the narrow site, Sloan and Kirkbride altered the ideal plan as published in Kirkbride's book by creating courtyards toward the outside edges of the buildings for the most excitable patients (Figure 2.22). The plan thus appears less linear, in spite of the fact that Kirkbride used the term "linear" to describe it. (It is a further inconvenience of asylum history that Kirkbride's own institution does not demonstrate the ideal plan, whereas the hospitals in Trenton, Tuscaloosa, and Washington, D.C., do.) In an illustration from Ebenezer Haskell's book of 1869, we can see local people staring at the inmates, who are in the courtyard of the outermost ward, the dreaded Ward Seven (Figure 2.23). Gamwell and Tomes note that in an attempt to discourage the practice of gawking at patients, doctors inadvertently sanctioned it when they began to charge an entrance fee for visitors.[74] This type of tourism was not unusual in the nineteenth century, when upper-class ladies visited orphanages and

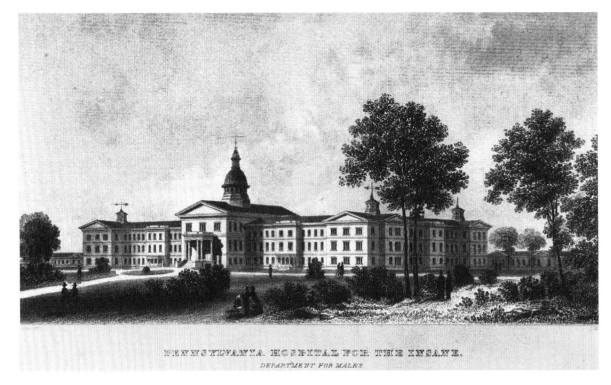

PENNSYLVANIA HOSPITAL FOR THE INSANE.
DEPARTMENT FOR MALES

Figure 2.20. Samuel Sloan with Thomas Kirkbride, Pennsylvania Hospital for the Insane, 1856, department for males. This was the second building constructed at Kirkbride's institution.

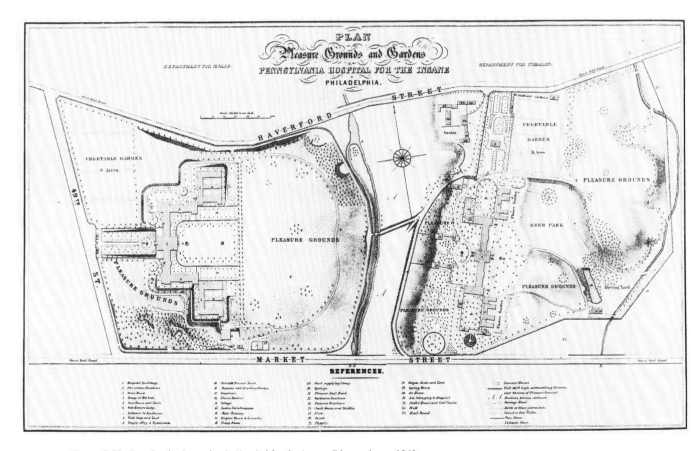

Figure 2.21. Site plan for Pennsylvania Hospital for the Insane, lithograph, ca. 1860. From left to right: the men's department (the second hospital on the site), the pleasure grounds, a creek, the women's department (the first hospital), a deer park, and other pleasure grounds. Courtesy of Archives of the Pennsylvania Hospital, Philadelphia.

schools for the deaf, and families strolled the grounds of picturesque cemeteries.

The site plan of the Pennsylvania Hospital for the Insane illustrates the close relationship between outdoor space and psychiatric therapy. All of the external areas, from the gardens to the deer park were considered essential for moral management. The doctors had little to manipulate other than the patient's environment, and they promoted the idea of walks in the grounds and carriage rides as part of a patient's daily regimen. A historical glance back at the simple wedge-shaped airing courts of Robert Mills's South Carolina Insane Asylum from 1828 (Figure 1.21) shows how far landscape design had come—both as a part of American architecture and as part of psychiatric treatment. In contrast to injured or contagious medical patients, who were confined to small spaces, asylum inmates were ambulatory; and prisoners in county jails and state prisons had no experience of the outdoors other than through tightly guarded exercise yards with no view of the surrounding countryside. Psychiatric patients had greater access to the out-of-doors than other institutionalized people.

Work and Recreation in the Midcentury Asylum

Nineteenth-century alienists promoted work in the gardens, an early form of what today might be called occupational therapy. Patients were expected to labor as much as they were physically able. Men, especially those with farming backgrounds, would tend the grounds. Women often possessed skills like cooking, cleaning, and sewing that were particularly useful to the asylum.[75] (There is no doubt that asylums benefited financially from having inmates mend the sheets, to pick one of many examples.) Labor inside the asylum was supposedly voluntary. As New Jersey's Horace Buttolph explained:

> We regard voluntary useful labor for the insane, where the state of their physical health will permit, as among the best curative means, though there is often a difficulty . . . in furnishing employment to insane men adapted to their taste, capacity and previous habits. With women it is different, for in addition to their being naturally more industrious than men, as appears to be the fact,

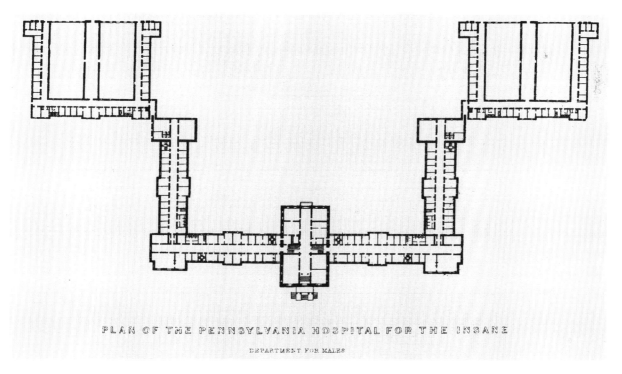

PLAN OF THE PENNSYLVANIA HOSPITAL FOR THE INSANE

DEPARTMENT FOR MALES

Figure 2.22. Sloan with Kirkbride, Pennsylvania Hospital for the Insane, department for males. Plan showing central pavilion, perpendicular wings, and courtyards. From Kirkbride, *On the Construction, Organization, and General Arrangements of Hospitals for the Insane.*

Figure 2.23. Sloan, Pennsylvania Hospital for the Insane, department for males. Courtyard facing pleasure grounds, rear of building, as illustrated in Ebenezer Haskell, *The Trial of Ebenezer Haskell* (Philadelphia, 1869). Courtesy of the New York Academy of Medicine Library.

there are a greater variety of pursuits in which they can engage within doors, at all seasons of the year.[76]

Psychiatrists argued for a balance between work and play, and many asylums—both private and public—offered recreational activities like billiards, ten-pins, sledding, skating, croquet, and golf (Figure 2.24). They encouraged indoor activities that today would be called arts and crafts, such as making baskets. The grounds of many hospitals included both naturalistic park areas and spots for organized games.

It is likely, however, that as the ratio of attendants to patients decreased, the patients were not allowed as much time out-of-doors as the rhetoric of doctors might indicate. Also, as the century wore on, patients were obligated to work. Delilez, in his account of his wrongful incarceration, alleged that three patients were forced to work on the Sabbath. He continued, mocking the typically rosy tone of the annual reports:

We read in a certain old report of this hospital: "Those of the inmates who are able and willing to assist in any of the departments of the farm, garden, kitchen or laundry, etc., are permitted to do so, care being taken that only a limited amount of work is permitted." That is not true, now at least. It is a lie. The truth is that they compel the patients in many cases to work against their will.[77]

Delilez further described the particularly difficult task of washing the asylum floors, which nearly killed one of the weakest patients.

The line between work and play could be blurry. Kirkbride thought of gardening, or the "improvement of the pleasure grounds," as "furnishing a variety of interesting employments" for the patients.[78] ("Improving" the pleasure grounds could mean anything from deadheading roses to moving a boulder.) Patients washed and dried dishes and returned them to their cupboards after breakfast, and thus helped the attendants put the ward in order before 10 AM, when the doctor or matron visited. Women sewed and mended bedding. At Trenton, two evenings a week were set aside for performing skits, representing characters by tableaux, and singing songs: the attention and effort the patients put into these performances were considered therapeutic, for the activity "withdrew the mind from morbid trains of thought."[79]

Parties and dances at both private and public asylums were commonplace and well known in their day. Both *Harper's Weekly* and *Frank Leslie's Illustrated Newspaper* (Figure 2.25) reported on a dance at the asylum on Blackwell's Island (now Roosevelt Island) in New York City. Titled "A Lunatic's Ball," the article in *Frank Leslie's* explained that it was held in

> honor of the completion of the first of a series of four frame buildings, recently commenced, in consequence of the overcrowded state of the institution. The structure being but slightly furnished afforded fine opportunity for the free exercise of "many tinkling feet." Not a few visitors were present to enjoy the novel spectacle

of a dance, in which nearly all the participants were among the most justly comiserated [*sic*] of the human species. Their delusions forgotten, many of the patients whirled about in glee, which, though wild, did not exceed the bounds of common-sense propriety.[80]

Victorian social dances consisted of either couples dances, such as the polka or the waltz, or a cotillion, which was more like a square dance. Either way, there were formal steps and expectations of decorum, so it is not surprising that one reporter took delight in noting how the dancers broke the rules yet remained within socially acceptable behavior. These reporters may not have known that attendance at the dances was used as a reward for good behavior. One doctor explained that dancing "is a favorite amusement among the patients wherever it is allowed; and we have been told by some of the Superintendents that patients will often control themselves for a whole week with a promise that they will be allowed the privilege of going to the next dance."[81]

G 21958 The Golf Links, State Lunatic Asylum, Taunton, Mass.

Figure 2.24. Postcard showing the golf links, State Lunatic Asylum, Taunton, Massachusetts. From collection of Robert H. Wozniak.

Figure 2.25. "Dancing by Lunatics," *Frank Leslie's Illustrated Newspaper*, December 9, 1865.

The "lunatic balls" vividly illustrate that insane patients were not isolated from one another. Such fraternizing among the inmates contrasted greatly with rules guiding prisons. Charles Dickens attended a similar dance in London, and when he visited the United States on his famous tour in 1842, he admired the Quakers' efforts to improve insane asylums far more than their attempts at prison reform. Dickens decried the solitary confinement he had witnessed at Eastern State Penitentiary, noting "very few men are capable of estimating the immense amount of torture and agony which this dreadful punishment . . . inflicts upon its sufferers."[82]

By all accounts, loneliness was not a problem in nineteenth-century asylums. In fact, privacy was in short supply. Given that Kirkbride's well-funded private hospital became quickly overpopulated, one can imagine the circumstances at St. Elizabeths after the Civil War, when the nation's only federal asylum was flooded with impoverished mentally ill veterans. Doctors and nurses could do little but watch their model hospital become a kind of human warehouse.

Sloan and Kirkbride collaborated on many asylums and both believed deeply in the value of architecture for the insane.[83] Sloan encouraged his fellow architects to take up the cause of the insane, "the great[est] suffering class of every community": "Nothing speaks more favorably for the true civilization of a community than the state of perfection in which its hospitals of every class are kept, and there is not one among these that requires the unbounded sympathy of our people, more than does the hospital for the insane; for, their patients are, in the fullest sense of the word, our protégés, and we, as Christians, their natural guardians."[84] He celebrated the easy expandability of the Kirkbride plan, claiming, "These sections may be increased in number . . . as the wants of the State may demand, and even extended to any number, this arrangement or composition cannot but prove harmonious as a whole."[85] His confident paternalistic tone served him well as he defended the importance of the asylum and his architectural specialty.

The peculiar shallow-V plan was common in American lunatic asylums because the AMSAII made it so. British asylum designers used similar but not identical plans. For example, the architect of the influential asylum known as Colney Hatch employed a plan commonly referred to as the corridor or linear plan, but which, in spite of the similar name, differed from the ideal Kirkbride plan (Figure 2.26). Opened in 1851, Colney Hatch was the second asylum for Middlesex County, near London; architect S. W. Daukes won a competition to design the 1,000-bed hospital, for which he used

an Italianate style in brick, featuring stone quoins, round-arched triple windows, square towers, and a tall thin dome over the center main.[86] A reformer in England, John Conolly, influenced American doctors with his philosophy of nonrestraint in the 1830s. Conolly had argued that to limit lofty stairwells, asylums should never be more than two stories tall, which led to sprawling constructions. Colney Hatch's four pavilions forming the front range were not set back—they were arrayed in a straight line from the center, obliterating the chance for ventilation. It is no wonder a contemporary report noted long cold corridors and huge wards.[87] At a juncture in the middle of the fourth pavilion, marked by an entrance porch, the building took a right-angle turn. Two more pavilions receded from the

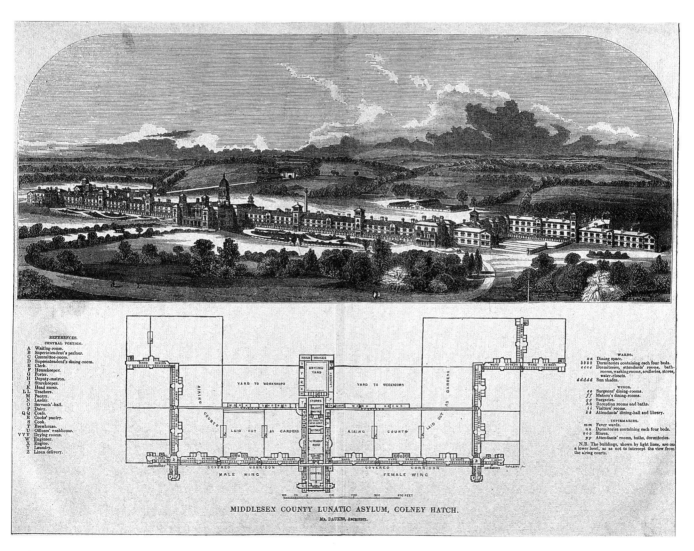

Figure 2.26. S. W. Daukes, Middlesex County Asylum, Colney Hatch, 1851, plan and bird's-eye view. Courtesy of Wellcome Library, London.

front range, and then the structure turned another right angle. Both the Colney Hatch plan and the Kirkbride layout were bilaterally symmetrical, with men on one side and women on the other; a central building held administrative offices; most rooms had views of the landscape. The major differences were in the patient population and the availability of fresh air inside—too many patients, and not enough air. Colney Hatch was designed for four times as many people as the AMSAII allowed in 1851. The site for Colney Hatch was adjacent to the Great Northern Railway, and the institution made a grand impression on passing rail passengers.

Kirkbride's book was quickly influential, spawning at least thirty similar asylums in the United States before 1866, and approximately seventy by 1890.[88] The architecture of American insane hospitals up to 1866 was especially directed toward 250 supposedly curable patients. When the AMSAII allowed hospitals to increase their maximum capacity to 600 in 1866, as will be considered in chapter 4, most architects adjusted to this large scale while maintaining the Kirkbride plan. But other doctors and charity reformers turned to creating smaller therapeutic environments, such as farm colonies and cottages added adjacent to existing linear hospitals; some even hinted at caring for mentally ill people in the community. These alternatives to the Kirkbride plan will be examined in the following chapter.

3

Breaking Down

THE COTTAGE PLAN FOR ASYLUMS

Kill out the Lunatic Asylum and develop the Home!

:: Dr. John. S. Butler to Frederick Law Olmsted (1872) ::

Frederick Law Olmsted received a letter from family friend and influential asylum doctor John S. Butler on the occasion of the doctor's retirement from the Hartford Retreat for the Insane, a private hospital outside Hartford, Connecticut. Butler remembered fondly that he and Olmsted had conspired to temper the institutional character of mental hospitals by introducing smaller buildings and pastoral plantings. He wrote to Olmsted with dramatic flourish, claiming that their plans from the early 1860s had served to "kill out the Lunatic Asylum." Such anti-institutional sentiments increased steadily in the second half of the nineteenth century, and the architectural expressions of them will be explored in this chapter.

During the period after the Civil War, the linear plan, though dominant, was joined by other methods for housing the insane. At its most basic, Kirkbride's idea was to house all the patients under one roof—or perhaps under two roofs, one for men and one for women. This was often called the congregate system. The segregate system, also called the cottage plan, broke monolithic hospitals into smaller units and thus, it was claimed, created a freer and more sociable atmosphere. As Andrew Scull has pointed out, the cottage plan was not all that revolutionary, as it left "intact the essential structure of the existing system," while claiming an "absurd and self-contradictory endeavor to eliminate the institutional aspects of the institution."[1] Furthermore, Scull continues, it promoted "the illusion that

[it] represented an approach toward community care," when in fact the patients were still living in an institution. The cottage plan was a hybrid: it continued old practices in new buildings.

Even so, the advantages of the segregate plan were many: doctors could reuse old houses, use structures with a variety of plans, and cluster small buildings around preexisting linear hospitals. The shapes of cottages varied widely and were not prescribed. Wooden houses could be built less expensively than fireproof masonry hospitals, and small buildings did not require the complicated heating and water technologies of a linear asylum. In some cases, the segregate plan was the impetus for an entirely new asylum. At other locations, cottages housing between sixty and one hundred patients were added to existing campuses. From about 1860 to about 1900, grandiose hospitals were erected at some state institutions, but cottages were built as well. Asylum officials did not immediately replace linear hospitals with cottages. The segregate plan merely hinted at community-based care; it was really just a different form of institutional care. Doctors still claimed that treatment had to be supervised in residential facilities, and they did not turn away from environmental determinism entirely. Instead, they believed that architecture shaped behavior in a conditional way, and they promoted the cottage plan as an alternative, improving environment. Most advocates for the mentally ill today suggest that living among the community is the best possible arrangement, but in the nineteenth century, community care was a bridge too far.

Willard State Hospital in Ovid, New York, was based on the segregate system: it was a collection of smaller buildings, a hodgepodge of existing and new constructions for incurable patients; a discussion of its history offers an opportunity to explore the vexed subject of the incurable insane. Next we will consider the singular town of Gheel, Belgium, which intrigued doctors. An experimental farm was proposed for Worcester, in Massachusetts, but its promise was never fulfilled. Real innovation in planning, if not in program or treatment, came in Illinois at Kankakee, where a linear plan hospital and a series of cottages were built all at once in 1878. The founders and builders of colleges also weighed the merits of large communal buildings against more homelike cottages, and those debates will be reviewed here.

Care for the Incurable and the Willard State Hospital in New York State

The increase in the number of asylums is related in a complex way to the increase in the number of incurable (also called "chronic" or "unimproving") cases. The population already inside the hospitals was getting larger. If one hundred patients checked in each year, the same number did not check out. Young people tended to be released fairly quickly, but elderly patients lingered in state care, losing ties with their families as the years wore on. The condition today known as Alzheimer's disease accounted for many cases of physically healthy, albeit elderly, individuals who might live for years in an asylum. Patients suffering from depression might live for decades. Doctors suspected that elderly patients, those categorized as having senile dementia, were "objects of the utmost pity," unlikely to recover.[2] Consequently, state hospitals increasingly became houses for the aged.[3] Ever since the eighteenth century, at the time of their founding, state mental hospitals accepted many paupers as "transfers" from penal institutions and almshouses. Doctors perceived these people, whose disease was of long duration, to be incurable.[4] When these indigent

people were transferred to a new state hospital at a rate greater than the procurement of beds, the crowding problem worsened.

Although recent research by David Wright shows that between 40 percent and 60 percent of patients were released within one year of admission,[5] from the doctors' point of view, incurability was still a major concern. Medical men had at first focused on supposedly curable cases, because they saw themselves as healers, not as custodians. Chronic patients were seen as the cause of overcrowding: one incurable patient occupied the same amount of space as one curable patient, but occupied that space for a much longer period of time. The incurables were not a new category of patient. There had always been patients who did not improve in spite of the cold baths, warm baths, laxatives, laudanum, daily walks, and games of croquet. The asylum doctors usually claimed that the patient could have been cured if institutionalized closer to the onset of the disease, which allowed the doctors to shift responsibility back to the patient's family. But the very existence of patients who did not recover undermined the doctors' stature as healers.

One spatial and architectural solution presented itself, although the AMSAII was opposed: separate state-funded homes for the permanently ill. The first distinct institution dedicated to this group was the Willard State Hospital for the Insane in the rural town of Ovid in upstate New York, opened in 1869. By providing accommodation for the incurable insane, the Willard State Hospital recognized the existence of patients who would be dependent on the state until their death. (Historian Ellen Dwyer has estimated Willard's annual discharge rate at .005 percent.)[6] Statistically, it was unlikely that any of the inhabitants of Willard would ever live outside the burgeoning institution. The first residents at Willard were moved there from jails and almshouses, and another group was relocated from the state hospital in Utica. The removal of the incurable patients helped maintain a therapeutic environment at curative hospitals, and it alleviated, in a temporary and minimal way, the problem of overcrowding.

The establishment of Willard posed serious problems both in terms of public perception and in terms of morale. To some alienists, the separation of incurable from curable was a pragmatic recognition of the sad situation that existed in state hospitals. If the patients were not getting better, why have them take up space in expensive, curative hospitals? To other doctors, the segregation of the incurable population was an embarrassing public admission that moral and medical treatments had not succeeded; these psychiatrists feared that once incurable cases were confined together, conditions in the places designated for the chronic would sink to an inhumane level. And last, doctors worried that once patients were shipped to Willard, both patients and their families would give up hope.

New York State acquired the site for Willard from the Ovid Agricultural College, which had opened on the eve of the Civil War but failed to survive the national conflict. Dr. Sylvester Willard sponsored the establishment of an asylum for the incurable, and in 1865 state legislators passed the Willard Act to provide accommodations for the chronically insane, many of whom had spent years in poorhouses. (Willard died while

appearing before a group of legislators in 1865, and the institution was named for him shortly thereafter.) In the act that established it, the state of New York designated it the "state Asylum for the chronic insane, and for the better care of insane poor."[7] The act was intended to force the insane poor out of jails and almshouses, placing the curable ones in Utica and those suffering from long-term illnesses in Willard. Its capacity was initially set at twelve hundred inmates.[8]

Little is known of George Rowley, the contractor and probable architect, who worked at Willard from 1872 until 1900, but many building projects were carried out under his watch.[9] In 1869, when the first patient arrived, she was accommodated in Chapin House, a still-unfinished Second Empire Baroque–style building with three-story wings and a towered central block. It offered a charming view overlooking Seneca Lake and the rolling hills of the Finger Lakes region (Figure 3.1). Willard did not follow the Kirkbride plan, because

Figure 3.1. Willard Asylum for the Insane, Ovid, New York, 1869, main building, also known as Chapin House. This institution was intended for insane patients whose illness was of long duration or who were deemed incurable by doctors. From *Public Service of New York*, 1:259. Reproduced by permission of the Buffalo and Erie County Public Library.

curing patients was not its mission. The main building was asymmetrical, resembling an irregular letter E. Later buildings took on many shapes and sizes.[10] The state added four groups of block housing, each one consisting of five end-to-end structures, just behind the new main building during the 1870s and 1880s. In 1870, with Chapin House, the main building, already filled, the institution's officials renovated the old college building.[11] The fact that they reused a collegiate building suggests an affinity between the two types of buildings. A visitor in 1875 commented wryly on the change of occupancy from college boys to maniacs: "The halls of Ovid College, where young men were full of study and joy, are now given over to the unmeaning chatter and grimaces of . . . the insane. . . . It is a most inviting walk up the grove. Here are squirrels and birds—all happy. But I hear other sounds—snatches of song, loud shouts, profane and vile words, calls for 'help' . . ."[12] Numerous buildings of various sizes had been added by 1878 (Figures 3.2 and 3.3). In the 1930s, Richard Dewey, the longtime superintendent at Kankakee remembered Willard's buildings for being a "noteworthy demonstration of less expensive construction" but little else.[13]

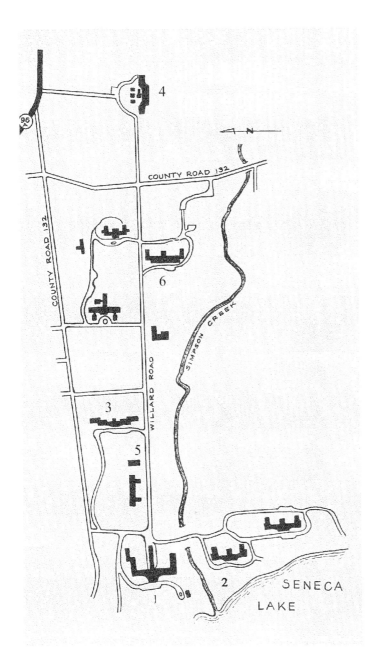

Figure 3.2. Willard Asylum for the Insane, begun 1869, site plan. 1 = main building, also known as Chapin House, 1869; 2 = block for men, also known as Pines; 3 = block for men, also known as Maples (in the 1878 annual report, these appear as three closely spaced but detached buildings); 4 = agricultural college building, renovated for chronic patients in 1870, also known as Grandview; 5 = Hadley Hall, auditorium, 1893; 6 = Sunnycroft, 1872. Reconstructed by the author based on Hilda R. Watrous, *The County between the Lakes*, 302.

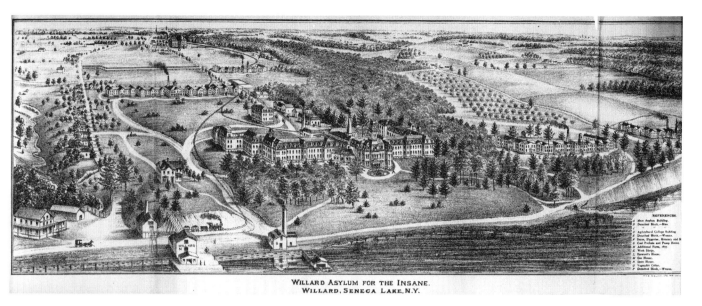

WILLARD ASYLUM FOR THE INSANE.
WILLARD, SENECA LAKE, N.Y.

Figure 3.3. Willard Asylum for the Insane, bird's-eye view, begun 1869 with several buildings added later. North is left of this drawing. Main asylum building (Chapin House) is in center of illustration; detached block for men (Pines) is south of center, at right of illustration; detached block for men (Maples) is east of center, at left of illustration; agricultural college building (Grandview) is east, toward top of illustration. From illustration in *Annual Report* (Ovid), 1878, 10. Courtesy of National Library of Medicine.

The effect of segregating these patients was both good and bad for their day-to-day lives. People whose illnesses were of long duration had often been confined to back wards at other hospitals so that doctors could focus attention on the patients who were likely to improve. At Willard, all the patients were equally worthy of the doctors' attention, or equally worthy of their inattention. In theory, every person at Willard was incurable, but what if someone had been misdiagnosed? Even though there had always been long-term patients in lunatic asylums, the establishment of Willard was a moment when an institution reified a cultural and medical category.

The foremost expert on hospital architecture, Henry C. Burdett, looked back in 1891 at random complexes like Willard and called them "heaps of buildings" and, less insultingly, "irregular." Burdett remarked that "it would be useless to give plans or detailed descriptions of irregular . . . asylums. No one would think of imitating them in the erection of new institutions, and little can be learned from them but what to avoid."[14] The pattern of development at Willard was a result

of haphazard attempts to serve its population. The state took the opportunity to experiment with different types of housing, sizes of buildings, and renovation projects. Ever present in the minds of reformers was the fact that almshouses and jails were unsanitary and publicly disgraceful homes for unfortunates; any new structure, especially one like Chapin House at Willard, offered improvement over locally run receptacles where the mentally ill were mixed in with thieves and hoboes.

Although Willard did not represent any great advance in architectural design or in program, the institution made it obvious that some percentage of lunatics could not be cured. The doctors pulled back from earlier rhetoric about the curing power of architecture, but they did write wishfully about the charming views, just as they enthused that boat rides on the lake lifted the patients' spirits. The program at Willard was not significantly different from the program of other asylums; vague notions of fresh air, rest, and recreation still held sway. Willard did project strongly the value that nature could soothe even the most deranged minds.

The Problem of Care for the Incurable as Related to Segregate Schemes

The deliberations about segregate versus congregate schemes were related to the question of care for the incurable, but the relationship was not clear-cut. Some physicians believed that insanity was curable at high rates (70 to 80 percent), and they, for the most part, were the same doctors who believed that linear plan hospitals were the best.[15] The younger generation of medical men, believing that only one-third of patients were curable, demanded reconsideration of the Kirkbride system, which had been devised specifically for curable cases. Some patients were considered chronic before they arrived in state care; for example, a person who had survived in a county jail and who was known to have been insane for several years would be assumed incurable. Such a patient might live for decades inside the state hospital, adding to that facility's already large population of nonimproving cases.

The issue of curability came to an embarrassing low point in the 1870s when the superintendents' carefully kept statistics were revealed to be seriously flawed. In 1877, Pliny Earle published a condemnation of Samuel Woodward's statistics on cures. Woodward, the director of Worcester State Hospital, was known for his success in curing patients who had been ill for a year or less. According to Earle, Woodward had counted each patient who left the hospital in better condition as "released as cured." Woodward did not distinguish between newly admitted patients and those who had relapsed. Thus, if the same person were committed three times and relapsed three times, he or she would count as three persons cured. Earle also noted that when a patient died in the asylum, Woodward simply eliminated him or her from the statistics. There was no category for those who died uncured.[16]

The cottage plan offered a solution to the increasing population problem, because any institution could add sixty-person wood-framed houses to an existing hospital campus. One needs to recall how seriously the alienists considered fireproofing, ventilation, and heating in their big buildings in order to understand how much they disliked the cottages. A leading superintendent in 1877 defended the practice of constructing large-scale hospitals, noting that the administrative cost per patient, plus the cost of food and clothing, would remain the same in cottages as in traditional buildings. He chided those who intended to crowd chronic patients into bedrooms, limit their fresh air, and cheapen their clothing.[17] The older generation of psychiatrists had always maintained that incurable patients deserved the same quality of care, and they were convinced that if the chronic were placed in separate quarters, "degeneration, neglect, and abuse of the inmates" would ensue.[18] A divided standard of care was the opposite of the principles of moral management; it might as well have been a return to Bedlam.

Gheel: Freedom for the Lunatic or Cemetery for the Living?

American doctor John M. Galt, superintendent of the Eastern State Hospital in Virginia, the successor to the Public Hospital in Williamsburg, was much impressed by European approaches in which lunatics enjoyed greater freedom than in the typical U.S. linear plan asylum. In an article in the *American Journal of Insanity* in 1855, Galt proposed that every asylum include a farm so that patients of quiet demeanor could live with the farmers and work the land. His immediate model was the Farm of St. Anne, which was established in connection with the Bicêtre hospital; it allowed much greater liberty to the patients, an approach that improved their health and outlook.

Galt particularly romanticized the medieval town of Gheel (also Geel) offering freedom to those besieged by mental derangement:

> At the village of Gheel, in Belgium, situated thirty-five miles from Antwerp . . . it was well-known that the insane, amounting to many hundreds, have been placed under the management of the villagers, instead of having them in one large building, as elsewhere. These lunatics have nearly the same freedom as the citizens of the commune, going everywhere at large.[19]

Galt described how some of them went to bars for a smoke or a glass of beer, and yet "their presence does not excite attention." Another American visited Gheel in 1867 and was impressed by the field-laboring patients, who attained a level of self-respect by exercising their personal freedom.[20] The key term in the pro-Gheel rhetoric held within it a deliberate irony: when madmen were given their freedom, they no longer tried to run away.

Gheel was an inspiration and a threat to nineteenth-century asylum builders, depending on one's point of view. It was widely described in medical journals and many doctors visited the town. Its special circumstances date from the late sixth century. According to one account, Dymphna, an Irish princess separated from her parents shortly after birth, lived the life of a devout Christian girl under the tutelage of a priest. When she was grown, her father, the king, attempted to force her to submit to an unholy marriage with him. She and the priest escaped from Ireland to what is now Belgium, but her father chased her down and decapitated her in front of the villagers of Gheel. The brutality shocked some witnesses, who happened to be crazy, back to their senses, and the martyred Dymphna became the patron saint of the mad.[21] Citizens of Gheel founded a church in her honor in 1349, but the mid-sixteenth century marked the height of clerical interventions at the site (Figure 3.4).[22] Although the clergy obliged pilgrims with the latest exorcisms, most afflicted visitors never found their way out of town. The few cells in the church basement overflowed with pilgrim-lunatics, and so the townspeople took them home.[23] This integration of insane patients into the community continued through the nineteenth century; today the town is home to a typical state-run psychiatric center.

A British woman who visited Gheel in 1869 described the physical attributes of the town, emphasizing its small scale and its ordinariness (Figures 3.5, 3.6, and 3.7):

Gheel has that quaint Dutch toy-like character which marks, more or less, all Flemish villages, none of the houses have more

Figure 3.4. Church of St. Dymphna, Gheel, Belgium. The congregation was founded in 1349, and the church was built in stages over several centuries. Photograph by Bill Winfrey, 2003.

Figure 3.5. Street scene in Gheel, as illustrated in G. Janssens, *Gheel in Beeld en Schrift* (Turnhout: Joseph Splichal, 1900), 248. Nineteenth-century doctors viewed the town of Gheel, where mentally ill persons lived among the towns-people, as a potential model for community-based care. Copyright British Library.

Figure 3.6. View of Gheel. From Janssens, *Gheel in Beeld en Schrift*. Copyright British Library.

than two stories, many no more than one; as for shop fronts, there are few to distinguish the place of business from an ordinary dwelling. . . . The village consists principally of one straggling street. . . . There is a calm, reposeful air about the spot.[24]

Gheel was a quiet, historically evocative town of one- and two-story buildings. It was the sort of place a twentieth-century observer might call humanly scaled. Indeed, the physical fabric of the town contrasted strikingly with the eight-hundred-bed institutions to which it was usually compared. It was small, old, and picturesque; institutions were big, new, and portentous.

Although lunatics had gamboled along Gheel's streets for centuries, their care did not become a matter of official Belgian state concern until the 1850s. In 1856, the central government hired a medical superintendent to manage the insane and their familial hosts. The town was divided into six districts, each with an assistant physician, an apothecary, and a guard.[25] One building, small by American standards, housed sixty patients and served as an intake station and infirmary. Here, the superintendent and his staff evaluated new patients and placed them with *nourriciers*, the villagers who were paid by the government to house, feed, and look after lunatics. The most tranquil patients lived at the center of the village, and the most dangerous lived in a series of isolated farmhouses outside of town.[26] The spatial implications of this system are complex. On the one hand, the inmates were not confined—not captured within four walls. On the other hand, the pattern of their dispersal was the same as in a linear hospital, with the most presentable at the center and the most disturbed at the periphery. Those who were suicidal or homicidal were not permitted to stay in the town at all and were transferred to a traditional asylum. The guards were "carefully trained by the head physician, appointed to take the surveillance of [each of the] sections, visiting the whole, each day, so that, by night, every house and every patient [had] been seen."[27] Linear hospitals did not need both roaming guards and caretakers, because the attendants did both tasks. At Gheel, guards had to pass from house to house, thus making surveillance inconvenient and obvious to any onlooker.

Galt, who recognized the limits to the Gheel situation, identified just two types of American lunatics who would be adaptable to life in detached structures within an asylum campus. First, there were tranquil incurable patients whose disease was of long duration, yet who were physically hearty enough for farmwork. These people, he imagined, would do well in cottages. The second class of potential beneficiaries would be those whose "unsoundness of mind . . . had not yielded through the operation of the various constituent influences of an asylum; in whom the monotony of an institution seems indeed to tally with the character of their derangement, actually giving it a fixedness instead of affording relief."[28] Galt here holds fast to the notion of environmental determinism, although it seems to work differently on different patients. He saw the linear plan hospital as "giving a fixedness" to insanity for some sufferers, rather than "affording relief." Galt believed that those patients, the ones whose illness the linear hospital made worse rather than better, would benefit from a cottage or farmhouse environment.

Members of the AMSAII thought Gheel was not a valid model because its historical circumstances could not be duplicated, it did not suit all classes of lunatics, and it was open to abuse. Pliny Earle visited the Belgian town just before Galt, in 1849, and he was appalled. He determined that of the one thousand lunatics, a high proportion roamed the streets aimlessly, which defied his medical opinion that lunatics should be kept busy. Another critic said that as many as one in ten patients were in restraints, because they were managed by nonspecialists who had other things to do all day.[29] Earle also observed one person who was covered with sores and "fettered with leg irons."[30] Leg irons were a symbol of the past; that restraints were visible to townsfolk seemed an unwelcome return to pre-Enlightenment malfeasance. Other visitors noted that the farmhouses were dirty and cold. Lacking the running water, flushing toilets, and roaring furnaces of large-scale lunatic asylums in the United States, the simple apparatuses in a Belgian house were technologically backward. Earle recognized that since the families were paid very little for the board and care of each lunatic, accommodations were not luxurious: many "are placed in garrets, lofts, out-houses, and other out-of-the-way nooks and corners where their accommodations can hardly be accurately described by that expressive word—'comfortable.'"[31] Many Protestant authors, revealing their aversion to Catholicism, objected that the town was mired in the myth of St. Dymphna.[32] Religious fervor, however, is probably what had led generation after generation of Gheel residents to take up the burden of caring for their insane fellows. Although Earle found no signs of ill treatment, he thought the system as a whole was unstable. An essay in the *American Journal of Insanity* decried the situation of the imbeciles, idiots, and senile elderly people who lived in the hamlet. Its author said Gheel was "a warning, not an example." The town had "no historical predecessor . . . no competitor, nor imitator, for a thousand years. . . . It has answered a purpose for chronic cases amongst a people unwilling of change even by way of improvement. . . . It is a cemetery for the living."[33]

In addition to Gheel, a model for community-based care could be found in the Scottish system. Scotland had not enacted a lunacy law as early as England had, but it innovatively adopted a policy of "boarding out" some patients with families. Some families, strangers to the patients, were paid for taking care of mentally ill people. In other cases, lunatics were allowed to continue living with their own families, but the lunacy board sent doctors and inspectors to the family homes. Studies at the time showed that mortality rates were lower for the patients who lived among families, not a surprising outcome since the crowded conditions of asylums hastened the spread of disease.

What did superintendents do, if not supervise? It is to be expected that they objected to community-based care, which made supervision difficult and called into question the very heart of their profession. The *American Journal of Insanity* mocked the romanticism of both cottages and care in the community:

> There is something attractive and romantic about cottages and cottage life. We associate with them domestic love, roses, woodbine and luxuriant ivy running over thatched roofs; larks and nightingales; lowing cows, bleating lambs, and browsing goats . . . and all sorts of pastoral delights sung by poets. . . . But the reality is apt to be very rugged prose.[34]

The British doctor J. B. Tuke was disappointed by a visit to the experimental situation in the Scottish town of Kennoway, where lunatics lived with the townsfolk. Any romantic notion of treatment in the open air was crushed by his visit to the small town in Fife, where he located a curable woman who had been "too troublesome for her guardians to manage" and who had "gone away far worse than when she came." He was dismayed by the conditions of the dwellings:

> The tenements in which we found the patients were of the class inhabited by the poorest of agricultural laborers and weavers, many were evidently damp and indifferently ventilated . . . and open drains stood or ran before the doors. As a rule, the aesthetic name of "Cottage" as applied to these dwellings is an utter misnomer—for certain of them the term "hovel" would be more appropriate.[35]

Care in the community presented "difficulties of supervision, of food supply, prevention of escapes, and prevention of improper communication between the sexes."[36] By "improper communication" obviously the doctor meant sex. This particular kind of recreation was not recommended under moral management, and worse, it led to offspring. And since psychiatrists held that insanity was heritable, "improper communication between the sexes" might bring about another generation of mentally ill persons who would become a burden to the state. Care in the community faced serious

obstacles: it was not clear who would manage and inspect the households, and anyone needing regular medical attention would still require an institutional setting. Massachusetts enacted legislation in 1885 to place patients with foster families, who were then paid by the state; 2 percent of patients, those who were quiet and harmless, participated in the program.[37] But for the most part, community care remained an idea, not a practice, until after the rise of psychotropic drugs in the 1950s.

A Proposal for a Decentralized Hospital at Worcester

The key difference between community-based care and the cottage plan was that the cottage offered a *representation* of home and family, but the patients were very much inside an institution. Debates in the *American Journal of Insanity* indicate that the official medical community rejected both community-based care and cottages. Its members intimated to state officials that they would be neglecting their wards if they housed them in randomly assigned old farmhouses; they successfully discouraged the construction of cottage-planned asylums until the late 1870s.

One source for cottages built alongside an existing hospital was to be found in the Farm of St. Anne; another French example covered in the U.S. press was the colony at FitzJames, three-quarters of a mile from the main asylum at Clermont, where both male and female patients were allowed to work as farmhands. Anyone who misbehaved was returned to the central house. Run by four brothers, the institution held twelve hundred mostly impoverished lunatics in an array of ramshackle buildings. Dr. Brown found little in the architecture to admire: "[I]n the principal buildings there is absolutely nothing deserving notice."[38] The colony at FitzJames indicated that cottages could be added to existing hospitals, a solution that would be economical, because cottages were cheap to construct.[39]

The question of cottage living entangled Merrick Bemis, the director of the Worcester State Hospital in Massachusetts, in a career-ending battle. The Worcester State Hospital had opened in 1833 under the direction of Samuel Woodward, but by the 1850s, when Bemis stepped in, its physical plant was in disrepair.

Bemis, its superintendent from 1856 to 1872, visited Gheel in 1868 and was greatly impressed. He then reconsidered the basic patterns of hospital design. Bemis, who suffered from periodic depression, had actually been a patient of Kirkbride's in Philadelphia. In his opinion, one of the biggest problems in hospital design was the indiscriminate lumping together of so many different people under one roof—"all classes of patients and . . . every grade of disease." Some patients needed the full brunt of institutional "skill and strength" while others only "require[d] the comfort, rest, and peace of an asylum."[40]

Bemis believed that no citizen should be incarcerated if proper care could be administered outside an institution. Given that Worcester's facilities were in poor condition, its commissioners needed either to restore the existing structure or build anew. The commissioners (temporarily) gave permission to Bemis to experiment with a system that was intended to simulate a community of families.[41] Bemis arranged the purchase of a few houses near the hospital where convalescent patients were allowed to live. The state purchased the site and its houses, and thirty-six females and twenty-five males moved into the homes as a kind of pilot program. Galt had noted the "potent agency of the family" as a remedy for the suffering of the mentally ill, and the married couple, attendants at the main hospital, who oversaw these cottages brought the insane into an environment that mimicked a family.[42] Such vernacular houses were not purpose-built for the mentally ill—they were not designed for medical care at all. Bemis wished to construct not a colossus but a modest, two-story building for the type of patient (one-third of those in his hospital) who were considered to be the most ill. The other two-thirds of patients would live in houselike structures. His innovative scheme envisioned patients moving toward the edge of the campus as they improved; thus the spatial concept of the hospital was the opposite of Kirkbride's plan, in which as people got better, they moved toward the center.

Finally, Bemis hoped to reintegrate patients into society after their recovery. This amounted to a new level of state care, in which the state would take the full responsibility of caring for the insane, including those who lived *near* the hospital, as well as those who lived *in* it.[43] (Typically, states paid for care only when a patient was incarcerated. If an insane person was not in a hospital, he or she was not considered to be a ward of the state.) Indeed, Bemis promulgated a fluid system that included care for many types of patients, both in and outside the asylum's boundaries, which, if carried out, would have led to community-based care.

Bemis was admonished by the old guard, especially Kirkbride's close associates Isaac Ray and Pliny Earle, who claimed the cottage scheme made moral management and surveillance difficult. A physically decentralized hospital, they feared, would reduce the central power of the superintendent. Earle, remembering his journey to Gheel, remained skeptical that cottages afforded more freedom than linear hospitals—restrictions could be lifted for certain inmates in the big buildings, too. More important, he did not think recreating a home environment was necessarily good. After all, the patients had gone crazy while living at home.[44] Earle also doubted that attendants would use less restraint in the cottages; away from the doctors' supervisory gaze, the attendants might use restraints more often. Bemis resigned in 1872 in the midst of squabbles over his financial management of the Worcester State Hospital. The moment he resigned, the trustees discarded the plan for a decentralized hospital in favor of a linear one.[45] After his resignation, other medical professionals and charity reformers moved decidedly in the direction of cottage plan hospitals; thus, although Bemis's medical career came to an ignominious end, he should be remembered as an innovator in a world of entrenched practitioners.

The Illinois Eastern State Hospital: "A Village for the Insane"

By the 1860s, a wide range of critics from outside psychiatry—local and state politicians, medical doctors, lawyers, advocates for sick or disenfranchised people—encroached on the power of the AMSAII.[46] Frederick Wines, for example, a Presbyterian minister who worked as secretary of the Illinois State Board of Public Charities for thirty years, led the reform of prisons, mental hospitals, idiot asylums, and other confining institutions. He insisted that since the management and physical structure of mental hospitals involved many nonmedical issues, the superintendents could not continue to wield total authority.[47] Wines was the principal organizer of a national conference, "Charities and Correction," in 1869, which addressed the problem of segregate versus congregate systems. The delegates reached no clear verdict. Instead, the diverse group settled on a two-part compromise:

> *Resolved,* that in the judgment of this conference, so far as practicable, a combination, in insane asylums, of the cottage system with that at the present in vogue, is desirable.

> *Resolved,* that there are weighty reasons for the belief that such a combination is practicable, and that it would increase both the economy and efficiency of asylums for the insane.[48]

The conference offered official sanction, albeit somewhat tentatively, for detached buildings as part of larger institutions, and Wines took advantage of the opportunity, persuading the legislature in Illinois, over a period of many years, that a combined system with one large hospital for acute patients and cottages for the incurable cases would serve both groups well. Medical officers could keep a close watch on the patients in the main asylum, and other attendants would care for the docile men and women at state expense on the asylum grounds.

State officials established the dual system at the Illinois Eastern State Hospital for the Insane at Kankakee, which included purpose-built domestic-scale residences for long-term mild patients alongside a linear hospital—the first such dual system in the country.[49] Illinois Eastern at Kankakee had a deliberate, organized master plan, and thus it differs from the collections of buildings at Willard and Worcester. Irish-born Chicago architect and Civil War lieutenant colonel James Rowland Willett designed the extensive complex, which opened to patients in 1878. Having worked as an engineer and inspector of railroads and fortifications during the war, Willett conducted a study during Reconstruction of damaged government buildings in the former Confederate states.[50] He was an authority on heating and ventilation, expertise that would have suited an asylum commission, and he was particularly keen on safety. His favorite exhortation in the teaching of young architects was "to master the principles of good construction and not be content with picture-making alone."[51]

In preparation for the design of Kankakee, Willett visited the asylums in Jacksonville, Illinois; Kalamazoo, Michigan; and Utica, Ovid (Willard), and Buffalo, New York.[52] Willett worked at Kankakee for twenty-five years.

A bird's-eye perspective drawing shows the main building, a linear asylum with a tower (at the top left), and an axial road leading from the lower right toward the main building, cutting past the kitchen, laundry, and bakery, all marked by smokestacks (Figures 3.8 and 3.9). As at many asylums, a railroad facilitated delivery of coal, linen, and other goods: here a small train chugs toward the miniature industrial complex. To each side, Willett included several streets lined with cottages, each housing fifty to a hundred people. Burdett referred to these parallel avenues as "bordered by walks and shaded with trees. These avenues represent village streets."[53] Overall the site was planned as a grid. One street (at the right side of the bird's-eye view) formed a perpendicular edge for the site, and another bounded the site parallel to the main building. The cottages were modest, two- or three-story with pitched roofs, porches, and front steps, and they were not connected by covered corridors. Although they were too large to be mistaken for typical houses, they did resemble small college dormitories or fraternity houses (Figures 3.9 and 3.10). Two rows of cottages line what looks like a suburban street (Figures 3.11 and 3.12). As described in an annual report, the cottages "face each other on opposite sides of the street, and resemble to some extent, ordinary dwellings, with home-like surroundings, such as covered porticos in front, shrubbery and flowers, the design being to get rid, to the utmost possible extent, of the air of an institution or any resemblance to ordinary asylum grounds."[54] Construction of the cottages entailed traditional wood framing, rather than the complex masonry fireproofing of the linear hospitals.

The interiors featured some homelike decorations—one photograph shows a parlor with a piano, a painting on an easel, area rugs, wallpaper, and curtained windows (Figure 3.13). Plans for the upper stories of cottages show beds arranged in rows, without walls between them. Detached Ward 4 North, a cottage for thirty-seven men, had no single bedrooms (Figure 3.14). Although they had the benefit of living in smaller houses, these men had little privacy.

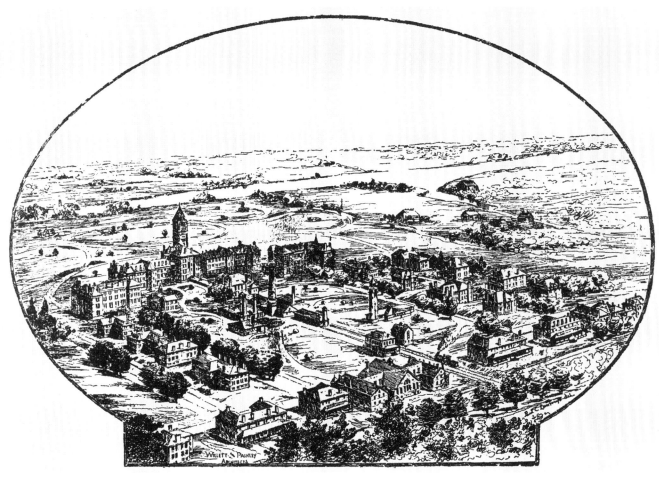

Figure 3.8. J. R. Willett, Illinois Eastern State Hospital for the Insane, Kankakee, Illinois, bird's-eye drawing signed "Willett and Pashley, Architects," as illustrated in *Fifth Biennial Report*, 1886.

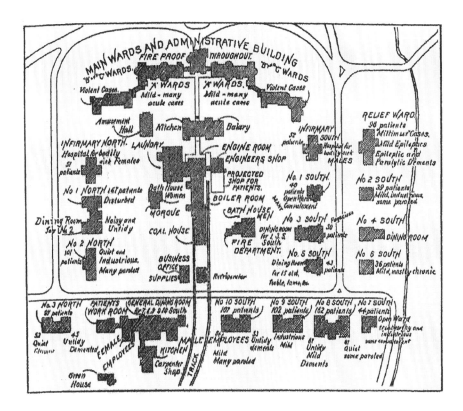

Figure 3.9. Willett, Illinois Eastern State Hospital for the Insane, 1878, plan, as illustrated in Richard Dewey, *Recollections of Richard Dewey, Pioneer in American Psychiatry: An Unfinished Autobiography with an Introduction by Clarence B. Farrar, M.D.* (Chicago: University of Chicago Press, 1936). Courtesy of Library of Congress.

Figure 3.10. Willett, Illinois Eastern State Hospital for the Insane, Cottage No. 10 South. Photograph by Mark Yanni.

Figure 3.11. Willett, Illinois Eastern State Hospital for the Insane (undated photograph). The main building is visible at far right, and cottages are arrayed in two rows perpendicular to the main building. Smokestacks mark the kitchen and bakery.

Figure 3.12. Willett, Illinois Eastern State Hospital for the Insane, cottages along street.

Figure 3.13. Willett, Illinois Eastern State Hospital for the Insane, parlor or communal room, interior of Cottage No. 5 North, ca. 1894. Courtesy of National Library of Medicine.

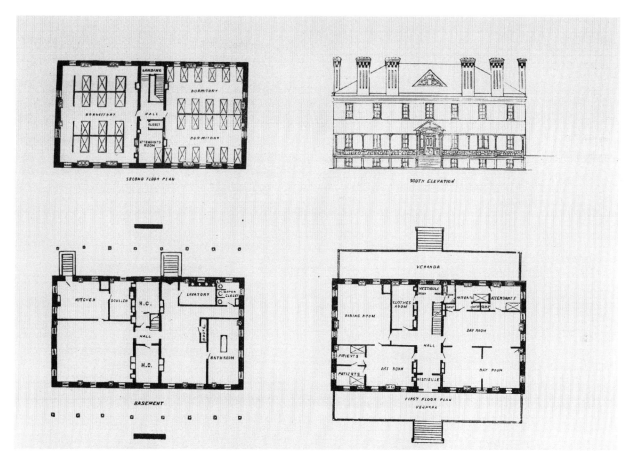

Figure 3.14. Willett, Illinois Eastern State Hospital for the Insane, Cottage or Detached Ward 4 North, plan of ground and upper floor, as illustrated in *Second Biennial Report* (1880), 100. This cottage housed thirty-seven patients.

The main hospital at Kankakee was a typical Kirkbride plan structure in the Romanesque style. Constructed in buff-colored stone with a tall clock tower, the building was easily visible in the flat prairie landscape surrounding the town. The linear plan hospital held the administrative offices and parlors. The wards housed people whose disease was recent in its onset, and who were therefore expected to improve (Figure 3.15). Kankakee's influence extended to Jamestown, North Dakota (in a state hospital designed by Willett), and also to Toledo, Ohio, Logansport, Indiana, and Mimico, Ontario. For certain asylum builders in the 1870s, Kankakee's campus plan was a model, with its large linear building for curable patients, its extensive naturalistic grounds, and, especially, its homey cottages that offered an alternative to the long wards and institutional scale of the center main.

Asylums and Colleges

Asylum builders were not the only nineteenth-century thinkers who debated the value of shared habitation of one large building as compared to family-style occupation of smaller dwellings. College builders also faced this problem. Although today casual observers tend to think of asylums as resembling prisons, in fact they more closely resemble colleges. Asylums and colleges were similar in that they projected a civic image through their architecture; the two types often housed large numbers of people in a single structure, attempted to subdue their populations through subtle surveillance, and operated out of a serious fear of fire and contagion. Colleges and asylums transformed the minds of their residents.

Many men's colleges founded in the colonial period contained several purposes in a single building. Usually

Figure 3.15. Willett, Illinois Eastern State Hospital for the Insane, postcard. From collection of the author.

a long, thin building with a central corridor, these early colleges embraced classrooms, teachers' apartments, student dormitories, offices, and a chapel. Familiar examples include Princeton's Nassau Hall, Old College at Harvard, Old Queen's at Rutgers, and Dartmouth Hall at Dartmouth.[55] At Pennsylvania State University, the "Old Main," hardly a linguistic leap to an asylum's "center main," contained classrooms, dormitories, laboratories, a chapel, and the president's quarters. Paul Turner has explored the scope of college planning in detail, and he suggests that colonial colleges rejected the traditional and closed quadrangle of English precedent in favor of "more open and domestic forms," which emphasized a goal of connecting the burgeoning universities to the community.[56]

Helen Horowitz has studied the relations between city and college by focusing on the social history of women's colleges, which vacillated between the congregate and cottage types. Vassar College, founded in 1861, was an architecturally distinct women's college. Matthew Vassar, a wealthy brewer who wished to give the world a useful, monumental building in order to memorialize himself, was inspired by Guy's Hospital in London. After some consideration, however, he decided against a hospital and chose instead to donate funds for an endowed women's college, with the intention of allowing women access to an education as fine as those offered young men at Yale and Harvard.[57] Andrew Jackson Downing and Calvert Vaux had built a gardener's cottage for Vassar in 1851, and Vassar had commissioned

(but never constructed) an entire country estate from Vaux, so he was familiar with the principles of the picturesque.[58] Educator Milo Jewett, Vassar's chief adviser, required that the new college be set in nature, "retired from the busy marts of commerce, from the hurrying multitudes": "protected by shady Avenues, the site would be in harmony with the modesty and delicacy which are always associated with the gentler sex."[59]

The founders of Vassar College determined that their college should be one large structure set in the landscape. James Renwick was awarded the commission in 1859, having already made a name for himself with Grace Church, St. Patrick's Cathedral, and the Smithsonian building. The design and construction took place in 1860–61 (Figure 3.16). The young women attended lectures, studied, conversed, worshipped, ate and slept in a handsome Second Empire Baroque–style building.[60] A single building made supervision easy, while removal from the city enhanced the intensity of the instruction. The picturesque grounds surrounding both colleges and asylums were open to ordinary citizens for Sunday afternoon promenades, and this openness may have elevated public opinion of the institutions.[61]

Vassar believed that at his college young women would be properly cosseted in one all-encompassing institutional building, but critics of his communal model thought the women were becoming too isolated in their Second Empire palace. The founders of Smith College in Northampton, Massachusetts, aimed to educate pragmatic wives and mothers for American society, not

Figure 3.16. James Renwick, Vassar College, Poughkeepsie, New York, 1860–66. Photograph by Slee Brothers, Poughkeepsie, New York, ca. 1865. Courtesy of Special Collections, Vassar College Libraries.

idealistic Protestant missionaries. Smith's founders built their school close to town with residential cottages in the 1870s (Figure 3.17). Classrooms, faculty offices, and the chapel were under separate roofs. Smith's homey dormitories, each of which held about thirty students, constituted a rejection of Vassar's previous model for all-female education. Furthermore, whereas the large expense for one massive building caused financial trouble for Vassar, the founders of Smith recognized, as did so many doctors, that it was easier and cheaper to begin small and expand a campus incrementally.

Horowitz has noted that insane asylums and women's colleges developed along parallel tracks. While the two institutional types were related, it would obviously be too reductive to conclude that lunatics were seen as feminine, or that college women were seen as insane. Rather, as Horowitz makes clear, the insane and college women were regarded as two different kinds of dependent classes.[62] Reformers in many fields recommended a sound daily regimen, healthy food, moderate study,

outdoor activity, all enveloped in the bosom of nature— what was considered a healthy lifestyle for normal people was used as treatment for the insane. In nineteenth-century rhetoric, mentally ill people needed to reeducate their deranged minds before they returned to society. This didacticism allied asylums to colleges as places of educational transformation.

Kalamazoo's Farm Colony

Cottages took on as many forms as the residential architecture of their day.[63] To describe the different architectural styles of all the cottages at insane hospitals would only duplicate what architectural historians already know about the wide range of architectural styles for houses. The cottages at Kankakee resembled one kind of domestic architecture—heavy stone, Romanesque buildings with porches. In Kalamazoo, Michigan, the cottages were derived from the Arts and Crafts movement and

Figure 3.17. Peabody and Stearns, Smith College, Northampton, Massachusetts, 1877–79. The Greek Revival house was already on the site. Courtesy of Smith College Archives.

incorporated cottage principles into an experimental farm colony. The physical plant at the Michigan State Hospital in Kalamazoo began as one linear plan hospital by Samuel Sloan, built in 1856, shortly after Trenton and Tuscaloosa (see chapter 2). The main building's original plan resembled that at Trenton, having two setback wings on either side of the center main. Following the pattern at Kirkbride's Pennsylvania Hospital, Kalamazoo's first structure became the Female Department when a new hospital for men was later constructed. (These were demolished in 1966 and 1975, respectively.) Additional buildings were added over time, including a freestanding chapel in 1872, and a round, redbrick crenellated water tower, now a local landmark, in 1895.[64] Kalamazoo's institution operated as a typical state mental hospital until 1885, when the board of trustees purchased an existing, two-hundred-acre farm for selected long-term patients. The land was

covered with elm and butternut trees that the hospital partly cleared, leaving eighty acres on which to cultivate what the chief doctor called "the celery that has made Kalamazoo more or less famous."[65]

In 1885, the Kalamazoo trustees built Trask Cottage, a two-story wooden house for forty-five quiet male patients on the periphery of the farm. The institution also constructed a cow barn, a silo, and other farm storage buildings, all to be overseen by the farmer and his wife—experienced attendants from the hospital who were selected for their background in agriculture. The *Annual Report* for 1895–96 boasted of the farm's success, saying "the patients living at this farm are of the agricultural class, are allowed the liberty of the entire premises and are healthy and apparently happy."[66] The patients, like the attendants, were farmers. The Annual Report observed that "in many cases there has been a marked improvement in mental and physical health after the transfer."[67] As time passed, the superintendents made less dramatic claims: instead of boasting of cures, they took credit for smaller physical and mental improvements.

The trustees eventually expanded their holdings by adding a tract of land large enough for a farm colony for 250 patients, plus one resident physician and twenty-two employees. Only mild patients whose illnesses were of long duration were eligible to live there. Four brick cottages were raised in 1888 at the edge of the farm; patients engaged in agrarian activities—raising corn, potatoes, fruit, and garden vegetables, cutting wood, clearing land, tending to livestock and poultry. The eighteenth-century airing court was followed by picturesque gardens, and now a working farm, a productive landscape, dominated the asylum dweller's access to nature.

To the patients who lived in cottages, the linear plan asylum built in 1856 was transformed into an exciting new destination. The asylum officials sent the "picnic wagon" out to the cottages to pick up patients for Sunday chapel services, and hardly a seat was ever empty.[68]

Palmer Cottage on the Kalamazoo campus (Figure 3.18) was a pitched roof house with some ties to Downing's earlier villa design, while the Van Deusen Cottage for women, opened in 1888, was a stocky Gothic Revival house with a generous veranda (Figure 3.19). It served as home to seventy-five female patients.[69] The arrangements of rooms imitated a typical house, with sitting rooms, dining room, and kitchen on the first floor. The second and third floors were used for single and associated bedrooms, and an extrawide hallway on the second floor doubled as a sitting room. Rare interior photographs of cottage bedrooms show a double room and an

Figure 3.18. Palmer Cottage for women, Michigan State Hospital for the Insane, Kalamazoo, Michigan, 1888 (photograph from 1892). Courtesy of Kalamazoo Public Library, Clarence L. Miller Family Local History Room.

Figure 3.19. Van Deusen Cottage for women, Michigan State Hospital for the Insane, ca. 1892. The house was designed for seventy-five women. Courtesy of Kalamazoo Public Library, Clarence L. Miller Family Local History Room.

associated bedroom for eight people; both rooms have narrow beds, overhanging gasoliers, and a few personal effects on the sturdy dressers (Figures 3.20 and 3.21). Overall, an Arts and Crafts spirit pervades the decorations. The Arts and Crafts movement endorsed simple forms, undecorated surfaces, truth to materials, and closeness to nature, and although the style tended to be used for domestic architecture rather than large institutions, it was suitable here. The tough interior furnishings in the asylum cottages were able to withstand heavy use, but they were also perfectly in keeping with the idealistic messages of housing reform that typified the 1890s. Michigan officials were pleased with their multifaceted accomplishment. The farm colony system offered "cheaper and quicker construction, more natural and homelike surroundings, the pleasing diversity to be obtained by change of locality, and . . . the opportunity for healthy, outdoor occupation."[70]

No Place Like Home, Redux

There is little doubt that the exteriors of the cottages at Kalamazoo resembled houses more than, say, the Alabama Insane Hospital. As discussed in chapter 2, alienists faced a paradox: they wanted their institutions to appear trustworthy and thus monumental, but also homelike. Dr. Galt agreed with his fellow psychiatrists in stating that it was generally wise to separate the patient from his or her actual home, because the home had been the source of morbid associations. On the other hand, the family, and by extension, the

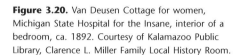

Figure 3.20. Van Deusen Cottage for women, Michigan State Hospital for the Insane, interior of a bedroom, ca. 1892. Courtesy of Kalamazoo Public Library, Clarence L. Miller Family Local History Room.

Figure 3.21. Van Deusen Cottage for women, Michigan State Hospital for the Insane, interior of an associated bedroom with eight beds, ca. 1892. Courtesy of Kalamazoo Public Library, Clarence L. Miller Family Local History Room.

family home, was the root of tender emotion and natural connectedness. Galt noted that moral management depended upon deviating as little as possible from ordinary life, and that therefore any mode of living that replicated the family home would be preferable to the linear plan. He specifically slandered "fanatical followers" of Charles Fourier and Robert Owen, both of whom advocated communal living.[71] Galt probably identified these collective societies as undermining to the nuclear family. No drastic changes to asylum architecture occurred on his watch, although he perceived the traditional family to be linked to the imagery of cottages.[72]

As the eight-bed room at Kalamazoo shows, cottages may have looked homey on the outside, but interiors were cramped. Cottage bedrooms typically offered their inmates precious little privacy, and some had as many as twenty beds per room on the upper floors. It was generally believed that curable patients needed privacy more than chronic patients did. Dr. Joseph M. Cleaveland, at the helm of the linear plan hospital for curable patients in Poughkeepsie, defended his expensive hospital because it had proportionately more single rooms, which he deemed necessary for curable patients. He had no qualms about ten or twelve chronic patients sharing a large bedroom, but his curable patients deserved more options.[73]

How does one make an institution seem like a home? Perhaps the privacy of single rooms, having a place within a building that one could call "my room," would have helped. Perhaps the avoidance of long ward hallways, almost never found in private homes, would also have assisted. These corridors, which functioned both as primary horizontal pathways and as indoor exercise areas, were abhorrent to John T. Arlidge, a British alienist who had served as medical officer at St. Luke's. Arlidge condemned the ward system for not allowing enough movement or exposure to different types of spaces:

> Within this curiously constructed and arranged place, [the patient] will discover his lot to be cast for all the purposes of life, excepting when outdoor exercise or employment in a workroom calls him away: within it he will have to take his meals, to find his private occupation or amusements, or join in intercourse with his fellow inmates, to take indoor exercise, and seek repose in sleep; he will breathe the same air, occupy the same space, and be surrounded by the same objects, night and day.[74]

To live one's life on a single hallway—ever to "breathe the same air"—was not what the founders of moral treatment had envisioned, but in many asylums it was the reality of daily life. In inclement weather, inmates stayed indoors, pacing back and forth along the corridors.[75]

Middle-class Americans in the nineteenth century did not travel much by comparison to present habits, but they experienced a wide variety of new building types and outdoor spaces. Beyond the limits of their own houses, they had access to homes of relatives and neighbors, churches, schools, parks, and streets; those who lived in cities might encounter museums, libraries, opera houses, railroad stations, medical hospitals. But mental patients, even at hospitals with large campuses, were fixed in a small physical area scattered with very similar building types.

The concept of the cottage plan contained within it the same antiurban bias that informed the siting of asylums at the edge of towns, in avoidance of the city, that harassing environment hostile to the peaceful recovery of madmen. Downing, who had designed picturesque grounds for linear hospitals at Utica and Trenton, had always believed that a modest laborer's cottage nestled in a garden was one of the advantages of the New World over the Old; therefore, the cottage idea resonated deeply with American concerns.[76] He presented this idea visually in numerous publications, as a cottage intimately set amid greenery (Figure 3.22). Galt knew Downing's works: a lightly sketched Gothic portico among his personal papers reads "Porch as in Downing's Cottages," a reference leaving no question that Downing offered a direct inspiration for the Virginia doctor.[77] Historian Francis Kowsky has shown, moreover, that Downing's ruralism was more than an aesthetic preference; it was a "vision of a new way of life for modern men and women."[78] As one reformer intoned, "[T]he essential elements of life, for an insane person, are the same which are essential for a man of perfect mental and bodily health."[79]

Architectural "Tinkering"

In the same article in 1855 in which Galt celebrated the Farm of St. Anne and joined the chorus of curiosity about Gheel, he accused his fellow physicians of being preoccupied with architectural matters, which he believed distracted them from the care of their patients. He predicted no advancement in the treatment of the mentally ill, so long as

> those entrusted with the supervision of the insane, and particularly those at the head of the most richly endowed asylums, shall deem the true interests of their afflicted charges not to consist in aught on their part but tinkering [with] gas-pipes and studying architecture.

Figure 3.22. A. J. Downing, "Cottage of S. E. Lyon, Esq. White Plains, N.Y.," as illustrated in *A Treatise on the Theory and Practice of Landscape Gardening* (1841).

Galt compared New England asylums to "prison-houses," although he acknowledged their "internal attributes of comfort and elegance."[80] He even invoked the name of John Ruskin in his diatribe, noting that all this dubious architectural know-how had been put to use "merely to erect costly and at the same time mostly unsightly edifices—erections at which Mr. Ruskin would shudder."[81]

Tinkering with gas pipes and causing Ruskin to shudder were not what the brethren of asylum medicine had set out to do. They had presented their propositions in 1851 as the central doctrine of their group. If patients could be helped by living in cottages, then the precious propositions were an evasion of the true task of their organization—the therapy and care of the mentally ill. The historical irony of this bitter debate is that the doctors were not arguing about the program: the therapeutic activities enacted in a Kirkbride hospital and a cottage-planned asylum were the same. The patients, for example, followed similar and strict daily regimes. The doctors were so enmeshed in debates about architecture that they continued along the path of arguing about buildings: they fought about cottage and linear hospitals without proposing detailed programmatic differences between the two forms.

The segregate plan eventually led to the demise of Kirkbride's linear plan, the ideal 250-bed hospitals, and the hierarchical control of the superintendent.[82] Scattered cottages eroded the power of the physician. Worse still, cottages did not in their architecture limit the overall population for the institution; asylum officials could add cottages as often as they wished. The restrictions the AMSAII placed on the overall number of patients in a given state hospital were easier to ignore when patients lived in an assortment of one- and two-story farmhouses. Proponents of the segregate plan devalued architecture as part of the treatment of insanity. Although they would not have posed the question in terms of vernacular building versus high-style architecture, the question hung in the air: if farmhouses could serve as homes for lunatics, then who needed obsessively planned, purpose-built linear hospitals? Today, institutional psychiatrists prefer the cottage plan.[83] But in the nineteenth century, congregate hospitals dominated; several of the most extravagant examples will be discussed in the following chapter.

4

Building Up

HOSPITALS FOR THE INSANE AFTER THE CIVIL WAR

Your hospitals are not our hospitals; your ways are not our ways;
you live out of range of critical shot.

:: Neurologist S. Wier Mitchell, addressing an assembly of asylum superintendents at the
Fiftieth Annual Meeting of the American Medico-Psychological Association, 1894 ::

After the Civil War, keeping pace with architectural taste in America, linear and cottage plan asylums became more adventurous, colorful, ornamented, and varied in silhouette. More significant, asylums ballooned in size (see Appendix D). Superintendents agreed to expand their institutions, because earlier hospitals, including the model hospitals in Trenton, New Jersey, and Washington, D.C., had become dreadfully crowded. In 1851, the AMSAII had stated that to fulfill their therapeutic role, asylums should house no more than 250 patients. At the annual meeting in April 1866, its members allowed hospitals to house 600 patients. The issue caused intense debate: the vote was eight to six in favor of expanding the size of institutions. Kirkbride dissented.[1]

Psychiatrists did not reject moral management (they continued to encourage patients to keep a daily schedule, eat healthy food, exercise, and play games), and they still intervened medically. But moral management was demanding of time and space: the staff's time, the space for a park or golf links. Even though the members of the AMSAII still claimed allegiance to the moral treatment, they could not practically carry it out after they increased the maximum capacity to 600.[2] Environmental determinism continued to direct alienists' thinking, too. Even when they conceded that some patients were not likely to be cured, they felt that

an orderly building and soothing landscape would ease suffering.

The institutions described in this chapter, the Hudson River State Hospital by Frederick Clarke Withers, Greystone by Samuel Sloan, and the Buffalo State Hospital by H. H. Richardson were congregate asylums: they housed more than 600 patients in a single large building, and each refined the linear plan, but the order in which they are presented here does not imply any teleology; one does not necessarily lead to the next. As state asylums expanded, criticism of them increased, too. After a while, these institutions came to symbolize the opposite of their intention. Their lavishness, instead of representing the generosity of the state, symbolized the wastefulness of Victorian psychiatry. A doctor looking back from a distance of forty years said, "In the state of New York, at Poughkeepsie and Buffalo, extravagant appropriations had been made," and added that Buffalo had "twin ornamental towers estimated to cost $70,000."[3] This chapter will first explain the lingering historical question of what caused the rise in the number of insane hospitals. Then it will briefly discuss private asylums before a longer analysis of selected hospitals constructed during psychiatry's building boom. It will end with a look at an ill-fated congregate hospital that was demolished to make way for a cottage plan hospital on the same site.

The Increase in Institutions for the Treatment of the Insane in the Nineteenth Century

Although the subject of the increase in the number of mental institutions is a controversial one in the historiography of madness, historians generally agree that such facilities developed at a rapid rate during the nineteenth century.[4] Why the increase in facilities? Was there an increase in mentally ill people or only in the institutions that provided their care?

The answers are complex. First, several scholars have pointed out that the very existence of hospitals inspired families to incarcerate their relatives and thus drove the need for still more hospitals. As Nancy Tomes has explained:

> The increasing number of hospitals [in the United States] that treated the insane, from 18 in 1800, to almost 140 in 1880, reflected not only population growth, but also a greater demand for the asylum's services. The ratio of hospital beds for the insane to the adult population grew dramatically, from 1 for every 6,000 persons over age fifteen in 1800 to 1 for every 750 persons in 1880.[5]

According to Tomes's reliable assessment, the number of beds increased, partly because the population was getting larger, and partly because it became socially acceptable to commit family members. Moral treatment was considered a novel and promising therapy, and families could potentially ensure a cure for their family member while at the same time relieving themselves of the daily trials of living with a severely mentally ill person.[6] There was a perceived greater need for these institutions, and the institutions, through their annual reports, promoted and legitimized the need. There are many contributing factors, but, generally, scholars agree that there were more institutionalized people and more hospital beds for the insane in 1900 than in 1800.[7]

Some have argued that the category of mental illness was expanding to include more of the general population, and, using this reasoning, scholars have claimed that asylums informed the structure of social categories. It might have been in the alienists' professional interest to expand the categories of the mentally ill. If doctors sincerely believed asylums were curative, they might accept new cases rather than turn people away.[8] Others believe that superintendents were peripheral agents in confining the insane.[9] (Many mentally ill people lived at home during this period, in spite of doctors' rhetoric claiming that a cure was thus impossible.) Andrew Scull has posited that the industrial-capitalist labor market of the eighteenth century forced families to incarcerate non-wage-earning members, which in turn freed healthy family members to participate in the market. He states more generally that "definitions [of madness], its boundaries, its meanings, are but a distorted mirror image of the shifting social order."[10] In my view, Roy Porter's elegant analysis of the British madhouse may also serve to elucidate the American scene: the expansion of the lunatic asylum may be understood as part of a growing commercial environment in which service industries of all types abounded. These quasi-professional occupations flourished in a society with "an economic surplus and pretensions to civilization."[11] In sum, the increase in the number of asylums was a result of the increased general population, the widening category of insanity, the perception that insanity was treatable, the doctors' penchant for empire building, and the increase in all manner of service professions during the nineteenth century.

Private Asylums

Historian Gerald Grob concludes that the overwhelming majority of people in the care of an asylum in the United States in the nineteenth century were housed in state-run rather than private institutions.[12] Even so, a brief review of private hospitals will shed some light on class issues and the range of architectural expressions available at the highest end of the market. As historian Peter McCandless has explained, insanity affected "rich, middling and poor, men and women, white and black," and while some were treated at home, others went to the asylum, in almost every case the care of an insane person was perceived to be a family responsibility.[13] Research indicates a wide range in expenditures between private and public asylums, although the superintendents of the state-run hospitals would claim there was no gap in basic comfort. In 1872, the average weekly expenditure per patient at private hospitals was $10.33, while public hospitals spent

$4.33 per patient.[14] The architecture of the private hospitals certainly afforded greater privacy; as Butler expounded:

> [D]ifferent classes require different styles of accommodation. . . . The State should provide for its indigent insane, liberally and abundantly, all the needful means of treatment, but in a plain and rigidly economical way. Other classes of more abundant means will require, with an increased expenditure, a corresponding increase of conveniences and comfort.[15]

Superintendents of private mental hospitals argued that since the well-to-do were accustomed to privacy and luxury in health, it was reasonable and proper to supply them with the same consolations while they were recovering. They also proposed that those of a higher social position needed familiar conditions, and thus recommended that the upper-class patient be surrounded by the comforts to which he or she had become accustomed. Patients' apartments at private hospitals often included a bedroom, sitting room, and bathroom.

Some wealthy families chose private hospitals so that their relatives would not have to mix with lower social ranks, but private asylums sometimes included a small percentage of poorer people. Bloomingdale Asylum, originally located in Morningside Heights on the present site of Columbia University, remained small and exclusive, in spite of being located in a major metropolitan area. Impoverished New Yorkers sought treatment at the city-run Blackwell's Island asylum, although its conditions were considered wretched. Bloomingdale had an obligation to treat some poor people because part of its funding came from the state, but treatment was offered only to "indigent persons of superior respectability," including teachers, clergymen, and their family members.[16] Overall, it remained an institution for the affluent. In spite of their well-off clientele, private asylums, like public ones, garnered criticism. One woman who had voluntarily committed herself to Bloomingdale complained of abuse in 1872, writing that that the shower-bath was used to torture rather than to clean, that the doctor always took the attendants' word over the patient's when one lodged a complaint, and that the food was "more suitable . . . for dogs and cats than human beings."[17] Private retreats were no more free from tension than public asylums.

McLean Hospital in Massachusetts and Hartford Retreat in Connecticut both accepted a few indigent lunatics. Dr. Butler, superintendent of the Hartford Retreat, sympathized with the "old and hopeless cases," those people who had come to his luxurious hospital to find a "quiet, kindly resting place." All the same, he knew that if he allowed all such incurable patients to live out their days at the Retreat, his hospital would become "a simple Receptacle," where "all recoveries would cease."[18]

The Hartford Retreat's first building, designed to house between forty and fifty persons, closely resembled its namesake, the York Retreat, both having central pavilions and flanking two-story wings. In contrast, the buildings at the McLean resembled a collection of large houses, irregularly dispersed across a pastoral landscape.[19] Private institutions could limit the number of patients, and therefore they did not face the overcrowding that plagued other hospitals. And calm patients enjoyed greater freedoms at private hospitals, coming and going as they liked.

Both public and non-state-run hospitals had lavish landscape gardens. The Hartford Retreat invested in landscape in order to attract elite patients. In 1861, Butler had invited Olmsted (whom he knew as the son of a longtime family friend) to renovate the grounds of the Hartford Retreat. The grounds were at that time run down: walks were muddy, trees were crowded, and the front lawn did not drain properly.[20] Olmsted's goal was to accentuate the generous meadow in front of the main building. Butler later wrote to Olmsted, "As I look forward to the completion of these plans I realise more and more the benefit they will confer upon these sufferers."[21] Landscape historian Kenneth Hawkins has interpreted the style for the Hartford Retreat as derived from the Beautiful rather than the Picturesque: the surfaces were smoothly undulating, with most of the acreage given over to greenswards, trees relegated to the perimeter, and screening plantations to dampen noise and thwart sight lines to the city (Figure 4.1).

Jacob Weidenmann, who later worked with Olmsted and was at the time engaged in City Park in Hartford, was the chief contractor for the renovations, conducted between June and November 1861, and he published the plan for the Hartford Retreat in *Beautifying Country Homes* (plate 18) in 1870.[22] The highly detailed plan locates a small greenhouse, to be used for growing plants and as a winter garden, a circular flower garden, an orchard, and a single-room octagonal natural history museum by Calvert Vaux, the co-designer of Central Park. The public drive served as a persuasive form of community relations, according to Butler:

> The drive which gives the public an opportunity of observing these pleasant [grounds] exert[s] a happy influence abroad, in making it evident that the externals of a lunatic asylum need not be repulsive, and may lead to the reflection that its inner life is not without its cheerful, home-like aspects.[23]

The landscape was varied enough so that patients would have different experiences with each walk through the grounds, and the renovations presumably cleared up the draining problems on the lawn. The superintendent wrote in 1864 that "it is now easy to rally a party for a ramble or rest upon the lawn."[24] The elaborate landscape contrasted with the building, which was at this stage rather plain.

Connecticut was late in establishing a public hospital, and from the 1820s through the 1860s, the private Hartford Retreat took in state-subsidized patients. In

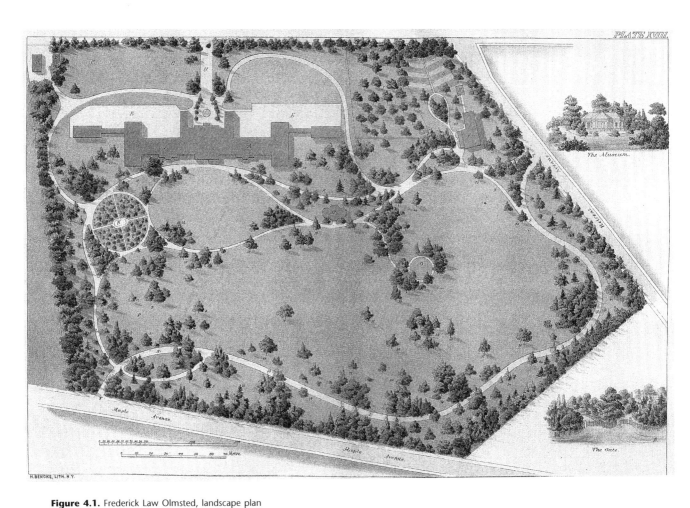

Figure 4.1. Frederick Law Olmsted, landscape plan for the Hartford Retreat, Hartford, Connecticut, 1860. Work supervised by Jacob Weidenmann in 1861, as illustrated in Jacob Weidenmann, *Beautifying Country Homes* (1870). A = retreat buildings; B = barn; C = drying yard; D = ice house; E = patients' yard; F = superintendent's dwelling; G = superintendent's vegetable garden; H = superintendent's barn; J = orchard; K = patients' flower garden and conservatory; M = museum; O = green; P = playground; R = patients' drives; S = public drive; T = main entrance. Vaux designed the retreat's own museum of natural history (M), shown in the vignette at the upper right.

1868, when the Connecticut State Hospital for the Insane in Middletown finally opened, state officials shifted the poor patients out of the Retreat and over to the state hospital, and the Retreat ceased to accept the poor. Using the momentum from the landscape renovation, Butler took the opportunity to upgrade the Retreat's existing buildings, which he disparaged by comparing them to factories. Historian Lawrence Goodheart has pointed out that by adding turrets, porches, and surface ornament, Butler, an outstanding administrator, "reinvented" the Hartford Retreat in order to make it a profitable venture with solely well-paying patients (Figure 4.2).[25] Goodheart further explains that for four decades, rich and poor were cared for alongside one another, with the only difference being in the variable size and cost of rooms. But when the state hospital opened, a two-tiered system of care went into effect

statewide. Connecticut's elite sought care among their equals at the Hartford Retreat, while middle-class and poor residents headed for Middletown.

Outside Baltimore, Olmsted's former partner Vaux designed a private hospital that served a wealthy clientele. Trustees of Sheppard Asylum, founded by a prosperous Quaker merchant, held an architectural competition in 1859 but selected none of the finalists, although the group included Samuel Sloan and Richard Upjohn.[26] Instead, Sheppard's architectural committee paid for Dr. Brown of the Bloomingdale Asylum to explore the most up-to-date asylum architecture in Europe. Upon Brown's return, the doctor asked Vaux to prepare sketches for the new hospital, and the trustees hired Vaux directly. Although the institution was wealthy, it had to survive on the interest earned from the trust, as specified in Sheppard's will. The institution, therefore,

Figure 4.2. Vaux, Withers, and Company, renovation of the Hartford Retreat, exterior after renovations, 1868, as illustrated in *Annual Report* (Hartford), 1875. Courtesy of Oskar Diethelm Library.

had to be constructed in stages.[27] Vaux's design dates from 1861, but no patient was admitted for thirty years, because of the slow release of interest on the endowment. On opening day in 1891, a visitor expressed the now familiar Romantic adulation for nature: "We can see on all hands the wooded hills, the flowing springs and streams, the undulating uplands, and the flower meadows. In fact the situation and the landscape look . . . like an English park."[28]

Architectural historian Francis Kowsky notes that Sheppard's "humane injunction" urging that the hospital resemble domestic architecture influenced Vaux in the design of these two redbrick and marble villas, which resemble those that can be found in the illustrations of Downing's books. Villas, in contrast to more modest cottages, suggest that Vaux anticipated the wealth of the patients (Figures 4.3 and 4.4).[29] Gabled roofs, reaching chimneys, delicate dormers, and prominent Rhenish towers created picturesque silhouettes that served to break down the size of the buildings. Porches at the end of the longer halls offered a sheltered outdoor recreation area. These paying patients had single rooms, and the original concept was for each patient to alight with his or her live-in servant. The communal rooms, especially the dining halls, were meant to

imitate a "well-conducted hotel."[30] These two domiciles, set on a hill, overlooked a grassy slope dotted with tall trees. A sunken lawn, at the foot of the hill, led to a shingled casino, a multiuse playroom and workshop with a low overhanging roof. Later photographs show the lawn scattered with umbrella-wielding ladies, Adirondack chairs, and round tables. Since the hotel-like Sheppard Asylum took thirty years to build, it did not have an immediate influence on the architecture of other asylums. Its mere existence and its elaborate architecture, however, suggested the growing trend toward separation by social class. Indeed, when Dr. Brown wrote to Olmsted in 1868 about plans for the grounds of the Bloomingdale Asylum on its new site in White Plains, New York, the doctor enthused, "Our future asylum will be the Chatsworth of Lunatic palaces and Domains." Brown's manor house reference indicates his aspirations for the new building and its grounds, and his enthusiasm reveals, perhaps unwittingly, the class divisions in the world of asylums.

Kirkbride briefly experimented with a small house for wealthier patients on the grounds of the private Pennsylvania Hospital, but he decided that supervision was too difficult among a scattering of small buildings. In 1851, Kirkbride reported that cottages were an

Figure 4.3. Calvert Vaux, Sheppard Asylum, Male Department, building B, begun 1861. The Female Department was a mirror twin of this building and was sited on a parallel line. Photograph by the author.

Figure 4.4. Vaux, Sheppard Asylum, view, begun 1861. Courtesy of Collection of the Sheppard and Enoch Pratt Hospital.

impractical luxury, "desirable for a certain number of those who do or ought to resort to our Hospitals for the Insane, [but] it is also quite certain, that such an arrangement is not important, nor would it prove useful for the great majority of patients."[31] He greatly underestimated cottages, as revealed in the previous chapter.

The Hudson River State Hospital at Poughkeepsie

The second half of the nineteenth century witnessed an increase in institutions for the insane, and in addition to the upsurge in the number of asylums, the hospitals themselves increased dramatically in size. The Hudson River State Hospital in Poughkeepsie was among the first new designs to accommodate six hundred people (Figures 4.5 and 4.6). It was a publicly funded institution intended to care for curable cases. It attempted to communicate philanthropic ideals to the state's inhabitants.

Poughkeepsie had vied with Newburgh for the right to donate land for the new hospital.[32] Towns often competed for the privilege of being home to the latest mental hospital. Local historians tell a story of a blizzard that nearly prevented Poughkeepsie's representatives from attending a meeting in Newburgh about the site selection for the new state hospital. Despite the snow that blocked the train lines, the delegates, intent

on their purpose, took a sleigh and a late-night ferry over the ice-ridden Hudson to present their bid at the meeting.[33] In a small town like Newburgh or Poughkeepsie, an asylum would bring with it short-term construction jobs and an immediate economic jolt. The long-term benefits were also considerable. At state hospitals, patients did some of the day-to-day maintenance, but a new state-funded institution would be a permanent source of jobs (attendants, handymen, janitors, and so on)—a boon to small-town residents. Its arrival set in motion a series of ongoing relationships with the community, and in the time before formal social welfare spending, the employment of local voters was key.[34]

Poughkeepsie won the commission by raising funds through the sale of bonds for the site, augmented by a gift of 260 acres from Dutchess County in 1867. It was an excellent site, one mile north of the city, offering lovely views of the Hudson River valley. James Roosevelt, father of Franklin Delano Roosevelt, had previously owned part of it. A quarry on the site provided for many construction projects throughout the institution's history.

Having observed the confusion over the competition for a new state Capitol at Albany, Poughkeepsie's commissioners decided to hire the firm of Vaux and Withers directly.[35] Frederick Clarke Withers had come to the United States in 1852 to work with Andrew Jackson Downing, but was forced to begin anew when Downing died in a steamboat accident shortly afterward. He found work with fellow countryman Vaux,

who had already designed the Sheppard Asylum prior to joining Withers, but given its different program and slow construction schedule, Sheppard probably did not serve as a direct model for the Hudson River State Hospital. On the other hand, these two men were working on the asylum building type within five years—Vaux in 1860–61 and Withers in 1866. Olmsted consulted for Butler in 1861 about the Hartford Retreat and, with Vaux, had designed the grounds for Poughkeepsie in 1867. Mental illness was a familiar subject for these men; when Vaux suffered some sort of emotional breakdown in 1862, he sought help from Brown to relieve his delusional state.[36] Brown himself suffered

from depression and eventually committed suicide.[37] Olmsted died in 1903 at the McLean Hospital, where he had once submitted landscape designs; he complained about his penultimate resting place: "They didn't carry out my plans, confound them!"[38] This close-knit circle of artists would have had many opportunities to discuss the environmental needs of the mentally ill.

Withers served as the chief architect of this hospital for six hundred men and women. The exterior of the Hudson River State Hospital typified the High Victorian Gothic style, with its mixture of French and Venetian detail, structural polychromy, and detailed surface treatments, including pressed brick, decorative

Figure 4.5. Frederick Clarke Withers, Hudson River State Hospital for the Insane, Poughkeepsie, New York, 1867, view showing one-half of the edifice, as illustrated in Paul Chadbourne and Paul Ansel, eds., *The Public Service of the State of New York. Historical, Statistical, Descriptive, and Biographical* (New York: The Photo-gravure Company, 1882), 1:362. Courtesy of Library of Congress.

ironwork, and voussoirs of blue and white stone. The colorful facade and lively window treatments went a long way toward relieving the monotony that might arise in a building of this mass. In spite of the rich exterior, Withers claimed that the "general character of the elevation is simple, the lines following strictly the necessities of plan."[39] The "interior plan of arrangements," however, as annual reports make clear, had been "most carefully prepared by the medical superintendent," Joseph M. Cleaveland, "acting on his own knowledge of the necessities of such an institution, with the counsel and approval of eminent men employed in the care of hospitals for the insane."[40] Although the center

main still held the superintendent's quarters and the chapel and acted as the dividing point between male and female departments, the plan differed from those of earlier linear hospitals.

Most obviously, the setbacks were more complex than in Kirkbride's 1854 publication, with return wings of almost equal length to those parallel to the facade, rather than the tightly compressed pavilions as seen in the shallow-V plan (Figures 4.7 and 4.8). The building was composed of a central structure and six linear pavilions set in a parallel plane with the facade of the center main. There were three pavilions to either side of the center, each with its own entrance. Withers

HUDSON RIVER, STATE HOSPITAL FOR THE INSANE, POUGHKEEPSIE, N. Y. *1906*

Figure 4.6. Withers, Hudson River State Hospital, postcard.

used a different type of connection between each two pavilions. One-story connecting passages with delicate polyhedronal roofs offered a charming pathway from the main block to the first flanking wings, the ones adjacent to the center main.[41] On the exterior, these resemble those at Willard, but here they are angular rather than curved (Figure 4.9). The architect and doctor imagined these passages as plant conservatories, and Withers proposed to "present a pleasant general effect to patients and visitors" by decorating these little structures with "shrubs and plants of a somewhat hardy character."[42] By installing plants in the passages, he would have brought the beneficial effects of nature inside.

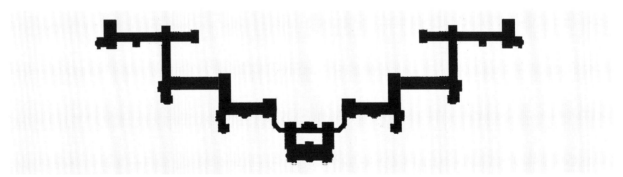

Figure 4.7. Withers, Hudson River State Hospital, diagrammatic plan reconstructed by the author based on the plan of center main, published in *American Architecture and Building News*, August 24, 1878, and the plan of two pavilions published in *American Architect and Building News*, March 30, 1878.

HUDSON·RIVER·STATE·HOSPITAL·FOR·THE·INSANE·POUGHKEEPSIE·N·Y·PORTION OF SOUTH WING· F.C.WITHERS: Archt.

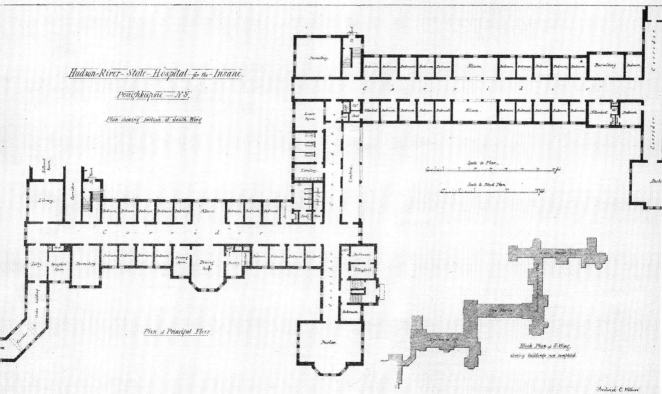

Figure 4.8. Withers, Hudson River State Hospital, plan and view of two pavilions published in *American Architect and Building News*, March 30, 1878.

The pavilions closest to the center main were three stories tall, and the next two pavilions, moving away from the center, were two stories tall. Withers explained that the chapel was placed between the wings at the rear of the main building so that male and female patients could not see one another from their respective wards. Fireproofing remained a major concern. The asylum was constructed entirely of masonry, although the technology for iron floors and ceilings was certainly available. As the *American Architect and Building News* described it, "All the partition walls are twelve inches thick, except those in which the ventilating flues are carried up, which are sixteen inches thick. Every room has at least one of these flues carried up to a ventilating ridge in the roof."[43]

The architect celebrated the return wings in this asylum by introducing three-tiered loggias, each of which he called an "ombra," meaning *shadow* in Italian. The ombras were described in the annual reports and the architectural press as "open spaces . . . for light and circulation of air marked OMBRA on the plans, [and] are intended to be used by patients in mild weather for open air exercise, in immediate connection with the wards to which they are attached"[44] (Figure 4.10). Behind these loggias, in the return wings, were "living rooms,

lavatories, etc., arranged on one side only of a separate corridor that runs at right angles to a bedroom section."[45]

The bedroom section contained both single rooms and associated dormitories, with a predominance of single bedrooms. As the superintendent, Dr. Cleaveland, explained, "The hospital which, like ours, is intended for the treatment of acute insanity, must consist principally of small separate bedrooms."[46] American asylums usually had a mix of single and shared bedrooms, but as hospitals for curable patients sought to distinguish themselves, they argued more stridently for single rooms. According to Cleaveland, people whose illness was recent in its onset, although more likely to be cured, tended to be noisy, highly delusional, destructive, and even homicidal. To create single bedrooms for such people that were "comfortable and pleasant," and "perfectly secure against all attempts at escape or injury," was "no cheap or easy achievement."[47] On the other hand, one asylum inmate wrote that he preferred company: "Strange and startling as were my eleven companions, with whom I was securely locked in, I was glad not to be put to sleep alone; for, had I been put into a single room, and locked in, it would have been unendurable to me."[48] Hudson River State Hospital was an accomplishment in design and engineering; from its

Figure 4.9. Withers, Hudson River State Hospital, passage between administrative block and pavilion. Photograph by the author.

Figure 4.10. Withers, Hudson River State Hospital, return wing, showing triple-story "ombra," as illustrated in Paul Chadbourne and Paul Ansel, eds., *The Public Service of the State of New York*, 1:362 (detail). Courtesy of Library of Congress.

mechanical systems to the ornate exterior, the state hospital in Poughkeepsie garnered the attention of contemporary observers.

Greystone, the New Jersey State Hospital in Morristown

Samuel Sloan's New Jersey State Hospital for the Insane in northern New Jersey restated the basic principles of the Kirkbride plan (Figures 4.11 and 4.12). It acquired the sobriquet "Greystone" for its material. It was intended to alleviate overcrowding in the New Jersey system. It opened its doors for its first residents in August 1876, when 292 patients were transferred from the asylum in Trenton "without the slightest accident, escape, or other difficulty."[49] The hospital was designed for eight hundred inhabitants—two hundred patients over the limit set by AMSAII in 1866.[50]

To choose an architect, the new asylum's commissioners held a limited competition, judged by Kirkbride and Brown, and they published their account of the competition and site selection in 1872, four years before opening day.[51] Greystone presented another case, as at Poughkeepsie and Buffalo, in which a county generously gave land to the state for the privilege of hosting the hospital. Horace Buttolph served as first superintendent of Greystone, having moved there from the once-vaunted but now crowded and decrepit Trenton. Greystone's site was particularly fine, offering a stone quarry, a freshwater spring, and enough material to manufacture bricks for the interior walls.[52] Surrounding forests were dappled with chestnut, maple, oak, and hickory trees, forming a varied natural backdrop. The landscape design at Greystone, completed in 1895, recalled the formality of Utica, rather than the picturesque winding paths of Poughkeepsie or Buffalo. A wide boulevard lined with trees led straight to the front door (Figure

STATE ASYLUM FOR THE INSANE, AT MORRISTOWN, N. J.

(PERSPECTIVE VIEW.)

Figure 4.11. Samuel Sloan, New Jersey State Hospital for the Insane at Morristown, also known as Greystone, begun 1872, view. From *Report of the Commissioners Appointed to Select a Site and Build an Asylum for the Insane of the State of New Jersey* (1872), opposite 17. The administration block at Greystone was five stories high, and the three wards to either side of the center were originally three stories plus an attic. An additional story was added in 1881. Courtesy of Oskar Diethelm Library.

Figure 4.12. Sloan, Greystone, main administrative building. Photograph by Joseph Schembri.

4.13). This unflinching axial approach emphasized, or certainly did nothing to diminish, the building's size.

The flanking pavilions maintained a constant height, and the outermost U-shaped wards for the most violent patients were just one story (Figure 4.14). Turned ninety degrees to the rest of the building, the U shape allowed attendants to monitor patients easily in their outdoor exercise yard. Sloan had used this arrangement at the 1856 hospital for Kirkbride in Philadelphia. Greystone's wards were long hallways with a mix of private rooms and shared bedrooms on long corridors; this is the same combination of singles and associated bedrooms that could be found in Kirkbride asylums going back to the 1840s. There were no elaborate passages, but rather return wings that contained dayrooms and dining rooms. These return wings also included porches like the ombras at Poughkeepsie, but here facing the rear of the structure. The center building was in two parts, the forward section isolated from the remainder of the asylum except for one connecting corridor perpendicular to its facade.[53] The annual reports evinced the usual pride in the fireproof construction: the stone was gneiss over concrete foundations, with interior and lining walls of brick, and the ceilings were iron beams with brick vaults between them.[54]

Sloan and Buttolph incorporated a dual-use room on the third floor of the main building that included an amusement room and a nicely decorated chapel. An amusement room or theater was common in asylums. This example boasted a raised stage and scenery for theatrical productions on one end and a screen for magic lantern shows at the opposite end.[55] The theater's

Figure 4.13. Sloan, Greystone, showing axial approach. Photograph by Joseph Schembri.

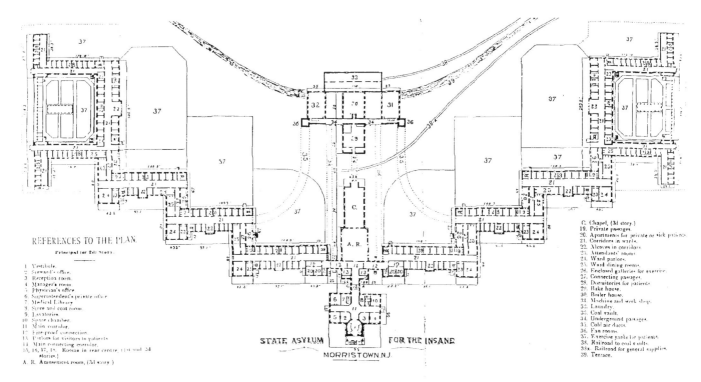

Figure 4.14. Sloan, Greystone, plan.

seats were designed with reversible backs so that patients could face either end. The only snag was that to get to the chapel, one had to walk through the amusement room, hardly a decorous transition.[56] The chapel was charmingly painted and stenciled in earthy tones, in a gentle, American neo-Gothic style. The placement of the chapel at the center of the asylum symbolized the fact that religion was at the center of an improved life; God was a beacon, a source of steadying influence (Figure 4.15). A typical sentiment was that "no class of mankind more truly needs the influence of religion than the insane."[57]

Nineteenth-century state mental hospitals were nondenominational, with local clergymen offering services on Sunday afternoons on a rotating basis. At St. Elizabeths hospital in Washington, D.C., religious services were "conducted in turn by six associate chaplains, representing the six leading denominations of the District. Each chaplain preached in the afternoon on each Sunday for two months of the year . . . and attended the funerals of such as died and were buried in the hospital's cemetery."[58] At other asylums, the superintendent conducted a modest service in the chapel that consisted of reading scripture, and in the evening the patients

gathered again in the chapel to sing religious tunes. Tomes has observed that "asylum therapy might be regarded as a secularized version of the conversion experience," and that "nineteenth-century physicians such as Kirkbride essentially had only a religious model of personality change to draw upon."[59] Kirkbride, Pliny Earle, and Charles Nichols, all Quakers, were deeply religious men who felt a calling to public service. Generally, the superintendents viewed religion as a healing influence, and although many of them were lured to asylum medicine by a Quaker call for social justice, they did not force their religious beliefs on others, or build specifically Quaker spaces into the fabric of their hospitals. Protestantism dominated the lives of most Americans, and therefore a chapel, rather than a Friends' meeting room, marks the midpoint of these linear plan hospitals.

The center main, or administrative block, was the heart of any asylum. As patients improved, they were relocated toward the middle of the building, because the luxurious wards were gathered in close to the center main, which contained the superintendent's home and the chapel. In linear plan hospitals, the wards progressed from quieter environments in the middle to noisier and more chaotic zones at the outer edges. The chapel gave the patients something to strive for metaphysically, and to move toward physically. The superintendents and the second-ranked doctor had offices in the center main, and parlors for visiting families were located in this grandest of spots. Sometimes the center main contained a library, the matron's office, and an officers' dining hall, in addition to the chapel and auditorium. Our British visitor Charles Bucknill, in his 1875 tour of the United States, noted Greystone's "mansard roof now in so much favour" and the surprisingly large administrative block. He found Sloan's Second Empire Baroque edifice to be somewhat overdone: "The Americans think much, perhaps too much, of the architectural appearance of their new asylums."[60] Perhaps it seemed imprudent that while the wards of public asylums were jammed with patients, the administrators were rattling around in five floors. But the center main, with its chapel, was literally the center of asylum life.

Bucknill worried about this new asylum, saying it included too many ambiguous spaces that might lead to "possible overcrowding of inmates into parts of the building not originally intended for occupation."[61] Although he had been assured by the authorities that the basement and attic would not be used for patients, he was frankly dubious: "Perhaps not at first, but we know from dire experience in our own country what this intention comes to in the long run, when the increase of population presses upon supply of asylum accommodation. . . . [I have seen] a great number of lunatics crowded . . . into miserable attics."[62] The British alienist with a keen eye for architecture here identified the problem of functionally ambiguous spaces; he foresaw beds placed in every available nook. Sadly, his prediction about Greystone was correct. Dining rooms and

Figure 4.15. Sloan, Greystone, chapel interior.
Photograph by Joseph Schembri.

hallways were soon converted into sleeping areas. The mansard roof was raised in 1881 to transform the attic into a fourth floor. In 1887, the exercise rooms were also converted into dormitories. This was a big asylum, but bigness was not universally praised.

In the view of Hervey Backus Wilbur, a contemporary critic of asylums, ostentatious asylums were evidence of architectural faddishness and vanity on the part of the commissioners and doctors. Wilbur calculated that the Poughkeepsie hospital ($2,000,000) and Greystone ($2,500,000) were among the most expensive ever built, snarling that the cost per patient was even higher than at the most expensive hotels in America: the "stupendous folly of such expenditure of public money" may be calculated at "$2,600 per bed, while the most expensive hotels in the USA would not exceed $1,500 a guest" (Appendix C).[63] The true test of good design, he said, "shall be the test of fitness of structure and not some assumed standard, based upon what is becoming in point of style or architectural adornment" or "what will subserve the pride of building commissioners."[64] Cleaveland of the Hudson River State Hospital responded indignantly to such criticism. He was particularly outraged at comparisons between the Willard Asylum for the chronically insane and his own state hospital, because the two complexes served entirely different patients. The people he dealt with required costlier buildings—they were violent, destructive, and "regardless of decency"—and usually they had more severe symptoms than the docile, elderly population at Willard.[65] He remarked that charity reformers had no more business designing mental hospitals than farmers had designing warships.[66] Cleaveland's annual reports have a self-protective tone, as he defends the cost, size, and highly specialized character of his hospital. Cleaveland at Poughkeepsie and Buttolph at Greystone were not alone. The state hospitals in Danvers, Massachusetts, Napa, California, Traverse City, Michigan, and Buffalo, New York, demonstrated similar grandiosity.

Asylums and Medical Hospitals

While Greystone was under construction in New Jersey, another institutional building with a high public profile was going up in Baltimore. A comparison of Greystone to Johns Hopkins illustrates key similarities in the care of medical and mental patients: both types of hospitals were intended to cure patients, both created a public and civic presence, and both controlled large populations. Like colleges, both kinds of hospitals required ease of surveillance and good ventilation. The chief differences lay in the fact that medical hospitals tended to employ detached pavilions and wide, open wards, whereas Kirkbride asylums, as we have seen, used setback pavilions and corridors.

Johns Hopkins, the founder of the hospital and medical school, left funds in 1873 to build a hospital that would compare favorably to the best hospitals in the world. To understand its plan, it will be helpful to review the tenets of the pavilion plan, which dates back to the mid-eighteenth-century hospital at Plymouth and which remained the central concept for medical hospitals up to World War I. As architectural historian Jeremy Taylor has explained, both clients and architects took to the pavilion idea, and "its overriding orthodoxy was well established within the 1860s."[67] Taylor effectively explains how architects from 1850 to 1914 manipulated the basic concept of the pavilion hospital, and he concludes that the basic form of the pavilion hospital lasted beyond the rejection of the miasma theory of disease. Although the depth of his research on the pavilion hospital cannot be replicated here, the main ideas of the pavilion hospital bear repeating.

Florence Nightingale's *Notes on Hospitals* from 1863 firmly established the importance of naturally ventilated pavilions, and architects repeated her rhetoric in the pages of professional journals. Thirty years later, hospital expert Dr. Henry C. Burdett decreed, "The cross-ventilated single ward is the perfect form of a pavilion ward."[68] Nightingale lauded the design of Lariboisière in Paris for its two parallel rows of pavilions, with plenty of light and air coursing through the structures, and rectilinear connecting corridors to shelter doctors as they moved among pavilions. Pavilions prevented cross-infections—after all, it rather defeated the purpose of a hospital to admit a person with a broken arm and have him contract smallpox.

In Nightingale's system it was necessary for the main area of a medical ward to be one long narrow room with beds placed on opposite walls, leaving enough space between the beds for nurses to tend to patients; an imaginary chamber of fresh air surrounded each patient's bed (Figure 4.16). Nightingale preferred wards that housed between twenty and fifty patients. Each bed needed to be placed between windows, so that a freshening cross-breeze could sweep the room. An efficient hospital ward was one in which the nurse could supervise all the patients, many of whom were bedridden until the final stages of their treatment, when they were considered "convalescent" and were allowed to walk in restricted areas.[69] Medical hospitals did not usually feature cells off a corridor, because such an arrangement would not allow proper surveillance. The large open ward of a medical hospital, in which patients were confined to their beds, was thus antithetical to the Kirkbride plan asylum. Mental and medical patients had fundamentally dissimilar daily habits.

The theory that "bad air" caused disease continued to rule Nightingale's century. Effluvia, vitiated breath, waste, and all the other putrid excrescences of human beings (especially sick ones) were dangerous sources of corruption. Too many patients in a small room degraded the internal atmosphere of that room, and the hospital environment became a further source of disease.[70] Nurses helped to establish a properly curative environment, in the sense that they maintained the air flow, monitored heat and cold, and kept the ward quiet. If patients closed the windows, as they often did if they were cold, no ventilating breezes would break up clouds of bad air. So keeping the windows open was part of the nurse's job.[71] The best pavilions would have windows that let in rural air, not citified air, with its coal dust, its odors of horse manure, and the exhalations of

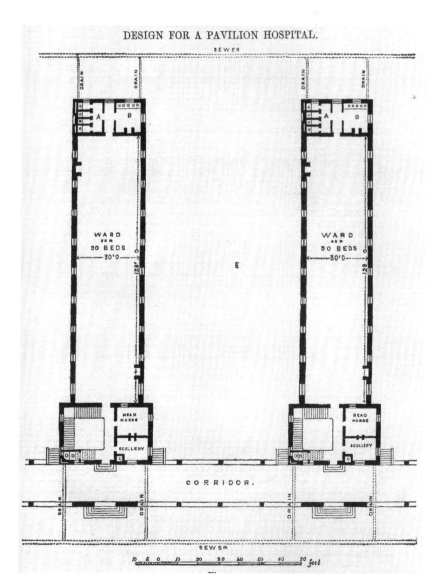

Figure 4.16. Florence Nightingale, "Hospital Construction—Wards," *The Builder*, September 25, 1858. This was Nightingale's plan for two ideal medical hospital wards, each serving fifty patients. Beds would have been located perpendicular to the walls, between the windows, to allow cross-ventilation and room for the nurses to maneuver.

an entire metropolitan populace. In Nightingale's view, the only really fresh air came from natural surroundings, because such air was believed to be self-purifying. Air that traveled across built-up city surfaces would be corrupted before it even entered the hospital.[72] Therefore, the ideal medical hospital, like the ideal mental hospital, had to be in the country.

One might wonder, then, why Greystone was built in the ideal locale, the country, while Johns Hopkins was located in the city. Architectural historian Jeanne Kisacky explains that although medical doctors claimed that they required pastoral sites, the actual daily work of a medical hospital in the second half of the nineteenth century had to accommodate emergencies that arose from injuries, fires, and industrial accidents. For a hospital to serve as an effective acute care facility, it needed to be in close vicinity to a density of people.[73]

While Nightingale and others endorsed rural settings, hospitals were actually almost always found in cities.[74] This directly contrasted with the siting of mental hospitals, which had no need for emergency rooms and could be located outside the city on less costly real estate braced by fresh air.

Both Johns Hopkins and Greystone were massive complexes, and each individual building was meant to be fireproof.[75] Although similar in size and monumentality, Johns Hopkins strikes the viewer as an orderly grouping of buildings arranged in subservience to the domed administration building (Figures 4.17 and 4.18), whereas Greystone appears as an unrelieved cliff. Mr. Hopkins allowed the trustees to choose a plan; led by eminent physician John Shaw Billings, they selected pavilions for their scheme. Five parallel pavilions in a row allowed for plenty of air to circulate around them;

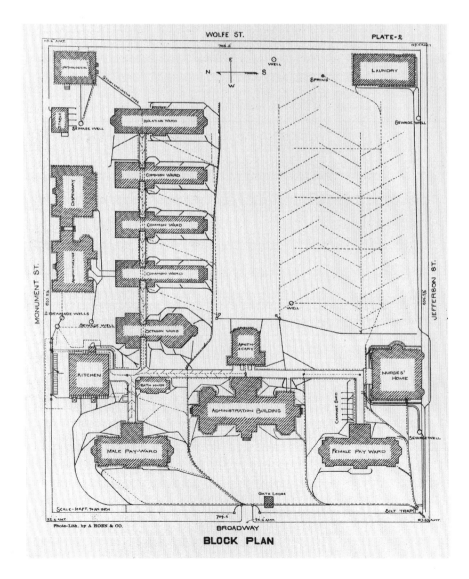

Figure 4.17. Cabot and Chandler, Johns Hopkins Hospital, Baltimore, Maryland, 1773–1889, plan. Courtesy of National Library of Medicine.

Figure 4.18. Cabot and Chandler, Johns Hopkins Hospital, exterior view looking west past common ward blocks toward administration. Courtesy of National Library of Medicine.

these pavilions contained wards that were linked on the ground level by straight, covered walkways. The physical form of the Johns Hopkins hospital differed from Kirkbride asylums in that the pavilions were not arrayed *en echelon* but rather in parallel rows. As built, most of the structures were along Monument Street, while the T-shaped grand administration building and two buildings for paying patients faced Broadway around the corner. Walking east on Monument Street, a pedestrian would have passed the kitchen, the amphitheater, the dispensary, the stable (necessary for horse-drawn ambulances), and the pathology building.[76] Johns Hopkins was used for "clinical teaching to the medical classes of the university," and therefore its architecture included an operating theater, a room for watching autopsies, and apartments for thirty medical students.[77] This urban, university-based hospital accommodated 310 patients,

most of whom would not be allowed to walk around the grounds until the final stages of their recovery. This contrasts with Greystone's grounds for its 800 patients, many of whom were encouraged to stroll.

The term "ward" was used in both medical hospitals and mental hospitals, but it referred to different types of spaces in each context. In a medical hospital like Johns Hopkins, the word ward referred to one, large open room with beds exposed. Most patients at Johns Hopkins spent their days and nights on open wards with twenty-four beds laid out in two rows (Figure 4.19), whereas patients at Greystone slept in dormitory rooms and spent their days in corridors or day-rooms. In a mental hospital, a ward referred to a hallway plus the bedrooms on either side of it, a dining room, day-room, and the attendant's room. The corridor acted as a shared public space within the asylum's ward.

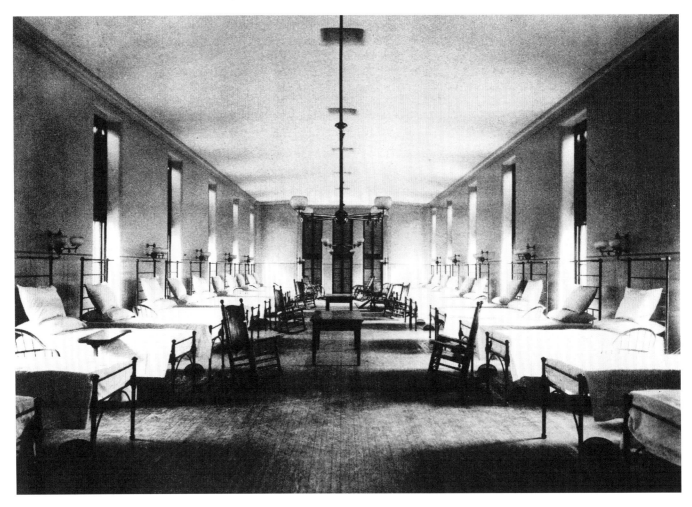

Figure 4.19. Cabot and Chandler, Johns Hopkins Hospital, interior of common ward. Courtesy of National Library of Medicine.

Single bedrooms were more commonly found in asylums than in medical hospitals. Asylums usually had some singles and some associated dormitories on each hall, although refractory wards would often have only single rooms. (In another example, Buffalo's wards included sixteen private rooms and three associated bedrooms, each with four beds, for a total of twenty-eight patients per ward.) Asylum patients had more privacy than medical patients, at least at night, because they could retreat to their bedrooms. This added privacy would have made the asylum seem slightly more home-like than a medical hospital, but neither could be mistaken for a house.

To complicate the definition of ward even further, Hopkins boasted several different types of wards, each with technically advanced ventilation. First, the common

ward blocks extended toward the south, and on each of these common wards, the northern end of each rectangular building was reserved for services such as the dining room, bathing rooms, and kitchen, and the toilets on the common ward were ventilated by "extraction shafts."[78] The octagon ward maintained the same north-south division, with the northern end holding services and the southern portion exposed to sunlight and fresh air.[79] Johns Hopkins included another type of ward called the isolating block for the most contagious people. (Mental illness was frightening to many, but at least it wasn't contagious.)[80] This consisted of double-loaded corridors, lined with special private rooms, each with its own water closet, a novelty at that time. The WCs were lined with metal walls for easy cleaning, and their walls did not reach the floor or ceiling to ensure swift movement of air. The ends of the isolating ward were open to the out-of-doors, the floors were perforated, and the air swooped upward toward a lantern with louvers, leaving the patient "in a condition of being out of doors in a very gentle current of air."[81] The currents of air inside Greystone would have been far less likely to blow up a lady's skirt. Ventilation, although always a concern for asylum builders, was less important than in medical hospitals.

The detached wards allowed professors to study various diseases apart from one another. In a university hospital, where new knowledge was produced by doctors studying patients on the wards, segregation by type of disease was an added benefit. As historian Adrian Forty has explained:

> [I]n a hospital concerned with effective cure and the acquisition of knowledge, the segregation of patients with different conditions was important. The probability of cross-infection in an unsegregated ward reduced chances of recovery and made it difficult to give effective treatment or to isolate and study the development of a particular case.[82]

The parallel pavilions at Johns Hopkins were separated by small green spaces, and its rooms did not offer views out toward the extensive park landscape. Greystone was one entirely connected building, with the ventilation coming only from the offset of the ward blocks. Underground tunnels did allow staff to bypass the wards as they walked from one end of the long structure to the other. At Hopkins, corridors abounded. The passages made it possible for a doctor or medical student to greet a family member in the administration building, visit a long-term patient on a ward, stop by the dispensary (a type of outpatient clinic for those who did not need a bed), or pick up medicine at the pharmacy, all somewhat protected from the weather. At times, the passages ducked, tunnel-like, underground. Separate blocks made categorization of patients easy, but required passages and corridors.

The designers and doctors at both Hopkins and Greystone were eager to present a forceful, positive public image by making the administration building larger than the rest of the ensemble. Buildings funded by taxpayers' dollars, like Greystone, were supposed to avoid appearing too grand, but they could not look too

cheap, either. Bucknill concluded his remarks on Greystone with tempered praise for its magnificence: "The new asylum for New Jersey is indeed a magnificent building, and very creditable to the liberality of the State authorities, but I should have liked it better if it had been decreased two stories."[83] Bucknill was not alone in his concerns about the architectural grandeur of American asylums. Charity boards in many states questioned the legitimacy of the purpose-built mental hospital, with its architectural pretension and elaborate landscape. Cost cutters in the state government began by eliminating the various amusements such as dancing and billiards, which had been deemed so important to moral treatment. One critic observed that working-class inmates were not going to appreciate the games and luxuries anyway: "Billiards, . . . battle-doors, and bagatelle are well enough for some, but most of the patients never saw such things before they came to the hospital, and will not be likely to get a taste for them any more than they will for olives or for the fine arts" (Figure 4.20).[84] Again the paradox between magnanimity and parsimony, seen back in the days of Bethlem, was evident here.

The Buffalo State Hospital for the Insane

Designed by H. H. Richardson, the imposing Buffalo State Hospital for the Insane has received more scholarly attention than any other asylum because of its famous architect. But it stands tall in the history of psychiatry, too, for it was designed with the assistance of a leading doctor, and it was at the center of the debate about the extent and expense of state hospitals. A Romanesque building in dark stone with a triple-arched portal, paired towers suggestive of pilgrimage churches, and set within an extensive park, the hospital was intended for curable insane patients, and it was visible from the main avenues of the city (Figure 4.21). This extended discussion of the design development will indicate how Richardson nodded toward the cottage plan while coming into conformity with established linear plan practices, and, as such, it serves as an excellent example of an architect working within the constraints of this highly prescriptive building type.

Figure 4.20. Withers, Hudson River State Hospital, billiard room (date of photograph unknown).

Figure 4.21. H. H. Richardson, Buffalo State Hospital for the Insane, Buffalo, New York, begun 1871. Postcard, ca. 1910. From collection of the author.

A state-appointed commission chose the site in May 1870.[85] The structure was approximately 2,200 feet long when it was finally completed in 1895, and its long construction kept a steady flow of income streaming into Richardson's office during the economic depression of the early 1870s.[86] The center administrative building and eastern wards were begun in 1871 but not completed until 1878, and the western wards were finished between 1891 and 1895, after the architect's death. Richardson's office received its last state payment in 1876, but the building was still not finished when Richardson died in 1886.[87]

Two more major nineteenth-century designers, Olmsted and Vaux, were involved in this creative, expensive, and expansive project. Olmsted and Vaux sited the hospital at a southeast angle diagonal to Forest Avenue, thus ensuring that the building would be approached from an angle, thus seemingly diminishing its size upon approach (Figure 4.22).[88] Olmsted first visited Buffalo in 1868, and he and Vaux formulated their master plan for the city's park system in 1870; construction began in September of that year. Olmsted was duly proud of the city plan: upon submitting it to the 1876 Centennial Committee, he had immodestly called Buffalo "the best

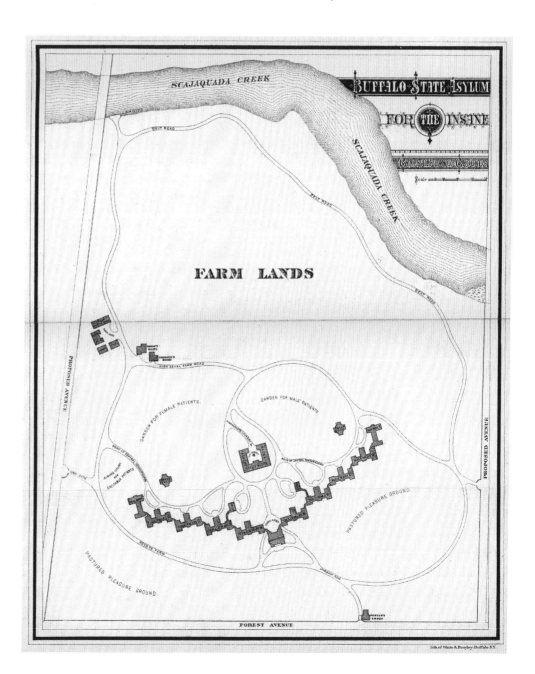

Figure 4.22. Richardson, Buffalo State Hospital for the Insane, site plan. From *American Journal of Insanity* 29 (July 1872): 4–5. Courtesy of Oskar Diethelm Library.

planned city, as to its streets, public places and grounds, in the United States if not in the entire world."[89]

Through Olmsted, Richardson met William Dorsheimer, a lawyer, politician, and park advocate who had hired him in 1868 to construct a mansard-roofed house on posh Delaware Avenue. The building committee for the Buffalo hospital included Asher P. Nichols, an attorney and state senator, who was another client of Richardson's.[90] Dr. James Platt White, whom Richardson probably knew from a failed bid to design Christ Episcopal Church in Buffalo, also served on the asylum's building committee. White, Nichols, and Dorsheimer were all on the committee to select the site. The city of Buffalo competed with Lockport, Warsaw, Westfield, Mayville, and Batavia for the opportunity to host these dependents of the state.[91] White was a local physician who did much to found the institution, but the better-known Dr. John P. Gray was the guiding force.[92] In 1869, Richardson's wife mentioned a meeting between her husband and Dr. Gray.[93]

As was by now the accepted procedure for this building type, the chief doctor, in this case Gray, devised the original plan. Annual reports and the newspapers leave little room for interpretation on this point: "The ground plan of the asylum was originally designed by Dr. Gray, Superintendent of the State Lunatic asylum at Utica, [and] was adopted by the Board of Managers."[94] (Gray had served on the site selection committee.)[95] As a doctor, Gray accepted without reservation the premise that insanity was a physical disease, and therefore, as a later historian noted, "the medical care of the patients assumed the highest importance, and the institution became more completely than ever before a hospital for the care of sick people."[96] His patronage at Buffalo shows how much asylum architecture had changed since 1841, when Utica opened its doors.

From a penciled note in Richardson's autograph sketchbook (Figure 4.23), we know he admired Gray's idea for pavilions connected by walkways:

> I prefer Dr Grays system—that is large wards connecting with iron corridors or galleries, it is more economical—the classification is as select & privacy as great & the promenading galleries or loggias ~~in~~ of D^r. Gray are incomparably superior to the parlors of 1st floor as in D^r. Bemis' ~~plan~~ [words crossed out in original].[97]

Bemis and Gray were known adversaries. Bemis was recognized by his contemporaries for his radical innovations at Worcester State Hospital, where he instituted a farm colony (discussed in chapter 3).[98] Unlike Gray, Bemis was preoccupied with breaking up large-scale asylums into smaller units to create homelike environments. But one of the drawbacks of detached houses, as Richardson suggested, was that the only communal spaces would have been parlors on the first floors ("parlors of 1st floor"). These were likely to be small rooms that did not allow patients to stroll. A striking benefit of the linear plan hospital, after all, was its *linearity*—it offered "promenading galleries" so that patients could walk indoors in winter. Richardson jotted his note beneath sketches of an institution with small pavilions placed around a rectangular courtyard, possibly connected by walkways. The sketch resembles a college or medical hospital complex rather than an American mental hospital.

This quadrangle sketch by Richardson never found fruition in Buffalo. The next important drawing, illustrated by Henry-Russell Hitchcock but now lost, apparently dates from 1870. It shows a large rose window surmounting a double door (Figure 4.24). Above the rose window, a small arcade, like a king's gallery on a Gothic cathedral, spans the width between two finials. The rose window appears to enclose a grand double-height interior.[99] A spire would have crowned the center main. This ecclesiastical imagery was highly unusual for an American insane hospital. Although almost all insane hospitals had chapels, they were not usually identifiable as religious spaces in the facade. The religious overtones of this drawing must have surprised the doctors. Richardson brought the École des Beaux-Arts lesson of *architecture parlante* to the world of asylums, but, for the doctors, this drawing was saying the wrong thing, and too loudly. This 1870 elevation drawing shows remarkable curved, double-height, unglazed, iron passages connecting the administrative building to its flanking pavilions. In a plan from 1870, these passages are visible as quarter circles on the front of the building (Figure 4.25). Staircases climbed from the garden up to the corridor and back down the other side, connecting to paths in the landscape design. (A building of this length needed a convenient route from front to back so that workers and visitors would not

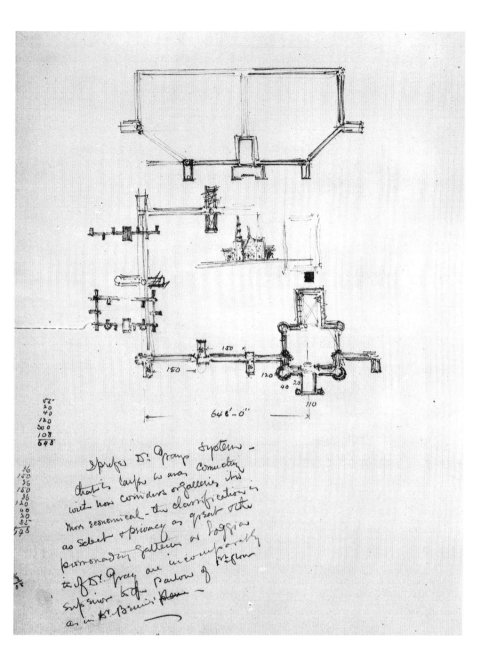

Figure 4.23. H. H. Richardson, folio 17R, sketchbook page, H. H. Richardson Additional Drawings and Papers, 75M 7(50), Department of Printing and Graphic Arts, Houghton Library, Harvard College Library.

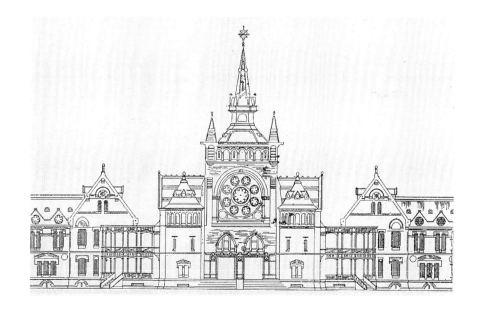

Figure 4.24. Richardson, preliminary drawing for Buffalo State Hospital for the Insane, showing rose window, spire, and iron-and-glass passages on the front of the building, ca. 1870. Published by Henry-Russell Hitchcock, *The Architecture of H. H. Richardson and His Times*, 1935 (presumed lost).

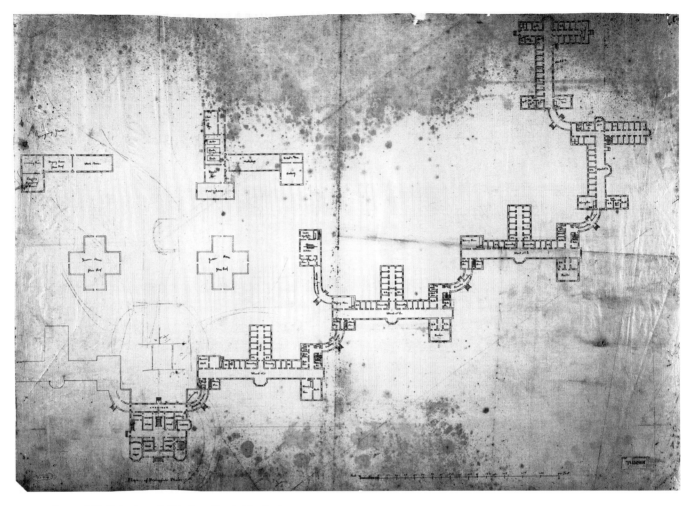

Figure 4.25. Richardson, Buffalo State Hospital for the Insane, early plan corresponding to elevation drawing from 1870. The curved glass passages were placed at the front of the building and show staircases that conveyed visitors up and through the rounded hyphens. In the final design, the passages were moved to the rear, and the outermost pavilions were not turned back on themselves as they are here. Courtesy of H. H. Richardson Papers, BLA A28, Department of Printing and Graphic Arts, Houghton Library, Harvard College Library.

have to circle the far end.) Delicate and graceful, the iron passages might have worked in a more merciful climate than Buffalo's, but as it was, they would have been cold in winter, difficult to keep clean, and too visible to passersby. This arrangement would have produced an extremely unusual facade, alternating between curving lightweight projections and heavy rectangular blocks. Gray probably knew the Willard Asylum for the insane (see chapter 3), which had semicircular passages of masonry on its front that connected the administration building to the ward blocks to either side of it. It did not, however, have curved passages

along the entire facade. Another source for the design may have been the plant conservatories on either side of the center main at Poughkeepsie, although these were angular, not curved. The well-educated Richardson could have seen many examples of curved *barchesse* in Palladio's *Four Books;* additionally, Colin Campbell's *Vitruvius Britannicus* illustrated many curved hyphens connecting manor houses to their ancillary structures.[100]

In 1871, the center main began taking on the lithic qualities later considered characteristic of Richardson's signature style (Figure 4.26). Two unmatched towers flanked a steeply pitched roof. Beneath the level of the tower windows, the administrative block was symmetrical. The only vestige of the rose window appeared as a small round window of a forward-facing dormer, and the portal was triple-arched, as in the final design. The fenestration of the main block tells us that the floor heights are regularized—no more double-height interiors. Richardson also shifted the curved corridors, now constructed of stone, to the rear. This was their final placement. In Hitchcock's teleological vision, these drawings show Richardson moving toward his distinctive style, becoming identifiably Richardsonian.[101] Richardson had rejected fussy Victorian motifs, eliminated the historically imitative rose window, and arrived at a simpler solution.[102]

Olmsted and Vaux produced an unusual landscape plan for Buffalo, accompanied by a descriptive report in July 1871 that defended the placement of all the doors except the main one on the north of the building and the use of airing courts on the south of the building (Figure 4.27). At most asylums, such confining airing courts had gone out of fashion. They had once been used for the most disruptive patients, those who could not be allowed to wander an asylum's grounds, and the idea that an approaching visitor would immediately lay eyes on inmates behind bars goes against decades of asylum planning. However, Olmsted suggested the airing courts could be tucked in next to the structure, with a "a terrace slope with a light iron fence around it," thus creating a sunken fence (and making the patients slightly

less like animals at the zoo than with a ground-level iron fence). Also, the south front of the asylum would have been "treated in a very simple park like way, that is, to say, with groups of trees and large open spaces of turf."[103] The key to understanding this peculiar arrangement lies in the purposeful omission of doors and walkways at the front of the structure, giving the asylum a public face. Olmsted and Vaux placed all the doors on the rear of the building, assuming that all visitors would enter the main block through the portal. Patients would be screened, categorized, and taken to their assigned ward by exiting the rear of the administrative block and following paths. Visitors would arrive at the center main, meet the doctor or his assistants, and be escorted to wards via the rear pathways. But it is no surprise that this plan was squelched, given that doctors had been attempting to diminish the prisonlike appearance of mental hospitals since the 1820s.[104] As landscape historian Hawkins correctly observed, "This arrangement contradicted traditional efforts to counter the impression of covert confinement."[105] In the end, Olmsted and Vaux's conception of the landscaping for Buffalo was to provide a gentle parklike appearance, with softly curving, open spaces and rounded clumps of trees. A curving internal carriageway was provided for those who could not leave the premises but who could take a spin around the grounds.[106] In 1876, Olmsted, who was no longer associated with Vaux, returned to the Buffalo State Hospital project with more specific planting instructions.[107]

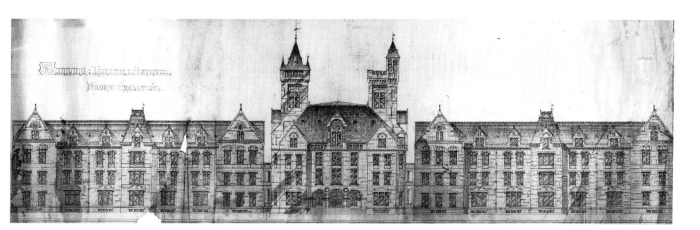

Figure 4.26. Richardson, preliminary drawing for Buffalo State Hospital for the Insane, second phase, showing more institutional and less ecclesiastical appearance, ca. 1871. Redrawn by Mark Yanni.

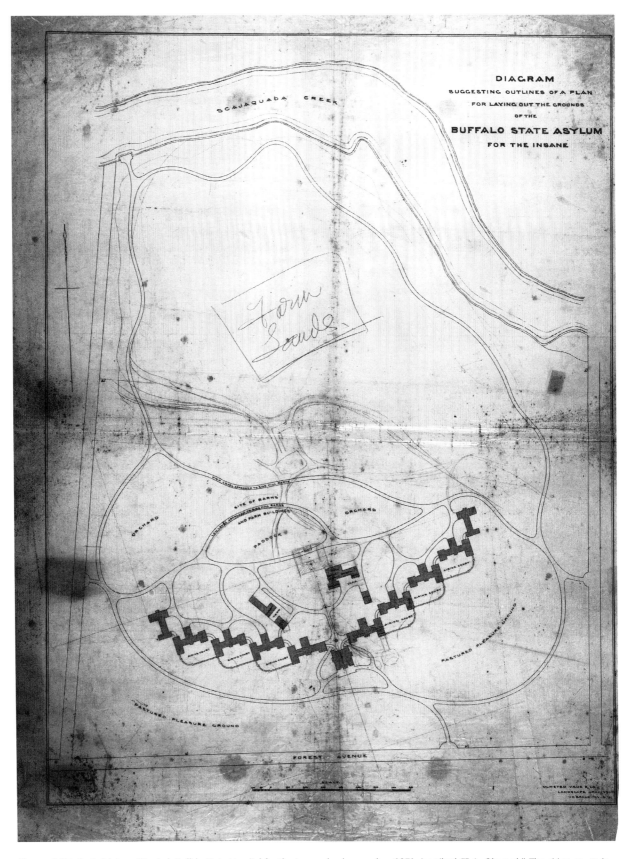

Figure 4.27. Frederick Law Olmsted, Buffalo State Hospital for the Insane, landscape plan, 1871, inscribed "F. L. Olmsted." The airing courts in front of the pavilions correspond to a written description from July 7, 1871. The curved corridors have been moved to the rear. There are no paths or entrances on the front of the building. Patients and visitors would enter the center main from the front but continue their path by exiting at the rear, following walkways to the desired destination. This plan shows the final placement of the refractory wards (the outermost pavilions) at a ninety-degree angle from the ward blocks. Courtesy of H. H. Richardson Papers, BLA F3, Department of Printing and Graphic Arts, Houghton Library, Harvard College Library.

The building committee turned to yet another plan for the building in 1872. Richardson and Gray managed to maintain one of Gray's innovations—the use of single-loaded corridors along the facade—although such an arrangement was expensive. These wide open spaces on the south side, almost too wide to be called hallways, acted as communal rooms and promenades. Cost-saving double-loaded corridors were used at the back of each pavilion, forming the stem of a T. The partition walls were brick throughout, with floors a combination of iron beams and small, brick arches and iron stairs.[108] The committee intended to construct all of the exterior walls in dark red Medina sandstone, but around 1876, the hospital officials decided instead to complete the building using common brick with stone trim for the three outer wards on either side. In the 1872 facade design, Richardson retained the quarter-circle external passages behind the pavilions, added triple dormers, and adjusted the details on the towers, now with much steeper roofs (Figure 4.28).

Figure 4.28. Richardson, Buffalo State Hospital for the Insane, facade of administrative block, 1872. From Folio 13R, Photograph Album, 75 M–7 (51), Department of Printing and Graphic Arts, Houghton Library, Harvard College Library.

The Buffalo State Hospital, especially when compared to Vaux's Sheppard Asylum, Withers's Hudson River State Hospital, and Sloan's Greystone, projects a newly dignified style, a "quiet and monumental treatment of wall surfaces," to use Richardson's own phrase.[109] Contemporary critics noticed this powerful, somber quality and lack of applied ornamentation as well. The *Buffalo Daily Courier* reported in 1872 that "the construction of the building so far as it has progressed, is extremely substantial and durable, but there will be no attempt at an effect in the exterior beyond what the extent and massiveness of the building itself will produce."[110] Another reporter wrote that it was built with the "solidity and care of a cathedral."[111]

The newspaper reporters also noted that, in the final plan, the sharply recessed setbacks allowed sunlight to fall upon "a greater portion of the buildings" (Figure 4.29). The added distance between the buildings effected an increased separation of the disturbed patients from the quiet ones, and thus the "convalescents do not hear the maniacal," and prevented fires spreading from block to block.[112] The breadth and placement of the

connecting corridors were clear improvements, but their curvature was mostly aesthetic. The round hyphens lent a graceful appearance to the long facade, and their big windows allowed for easy surveillance of staff comings and goings. The connecting corridors were an attempt to solve a long-standing design problem that came from Kirkbride's 1854 guide. For the doctors who traversed them, the connecting links between ward blocks had always been the most awkward part of the linear plan, because the links were no more than right-angle turns through closet-sized openings. (Nurses and patients, who stayed on their individual wards, would not have been bothered.) In contrast, the plan at Buffalo facilitated doctors' hikes from ward to ward. The *Buffalo Morning Express* stated specifically that *officers*—but not attendants or patients—could move with ease through the lofty curves (Figure 4.30). The doctors saw the attendants as potentially difficult to manage, little better than the patients, and one annual report explained that the plan "increases the efficiency of discipline among attendants and employees by preventing their going so readily from ward to ward."[113] This remark constitutes

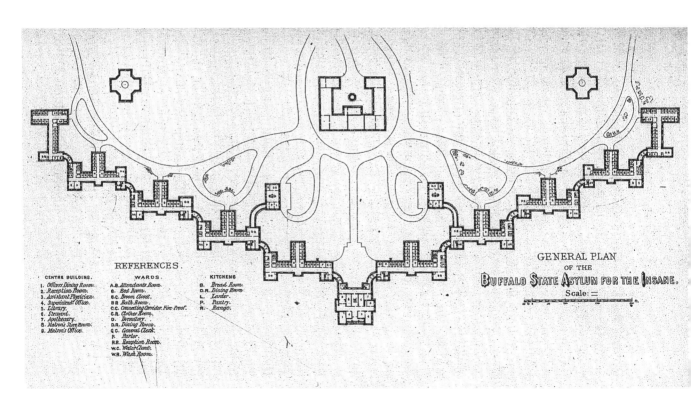

Figure 4.29. Richardson, Buffalo State Hospital for the Insane, final plan, 1872, as illustrated in *Annual Report* (1872) and the *American Journal of Insanity* 29 (July 1872): 6–7. Courtesy of Oskar Diethelm Library.

an unusually clear statement of the superintendents' desire for surveillance over the attendants as well as the patients.

Bucknill admired the Buffalo State Hospital greatly. When the British doctor arrived in 1875, the hospital was still under construction: "At Buffalo a third asylum for the state of New York is being erected on plans which pleased me extremely. The building is of three, two, and one stories, and the different wards fall back rapidly *en echelon*, leaving the central offices prominently in advance."[114] Bucknill approved of the pavilions of different heights, which made the building's considerable mass taper toward its outer limits. (Nichols and Walter introduced this tapering at St. Elizabeths in Washington, D.C., in 1852.) The outermost pavilions, as was by then standard in psychiatric hospitals, housed the most violent patients. Bucknill further noticed that Buffalo's overall V shape was more pronounced than in other asylums, with each pavilion set wholly behind its neighbor, permitting the full extent of ventilation. He observed: "The wards are connected with each other by semicircular glass-covered passages only fit for use as passages, not for occupation."[115] Here, Bucknill made

a subtle architectural observation regarding the multifunctionality of spaces. The glassy, curved corridors were such an unusual shape, they were cold, and they offered little privacy—thus they could not be turned into dormitories.

The curved passages at Buffalo gave the British doctor hope that there could be an architectural solution to the looming problem of crowded wards. Their uncommon design would help to stave off the overcrowding Bucknill had predicted for Greystone. Burdett complained that "overcrowding is a distinguishing feature of American asylums," and he accused his American counterparts of hypocrisy: "If it be true that individual treatment is absolutely necessary in the treatment of insanity, as a competent American doctor declares, it follows, that in one vital point the institutions in his country are diametrically opposed to the cause they were intended to further."[116] Burdett recognized that overcrowding would cause the demise of the moral treatment (Figure 4.31), and while there was nothing an architect could do to *prevent* future doctors from overfilling their hospital wards, he could at least design spaces that *made it more difficult*. Richardson's and

Figure 4.30. Richardson, Buffalo State Hospital for the Insane, curved connecting corridors. Photograph by the author.

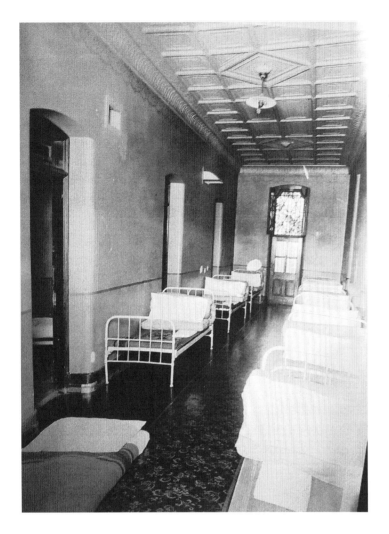

Figure 4.31. Withers, Hudson River State Hospital for the Insane (date of photograph unknown). Beds in ward corridor and on the floor are the result of overcrowding.

Gray's curved passages were not just elegant, they were an architectural response to a medical and bureaucratic problem.

The Buffalo State Hospital "combine[d] all the advantages of the cottage and pavilion plans without their disadvantages," according to the *Annual Report* of 1871. The cottage plan, described in chapter 3, was a competing mode of asylum design whose advocates objected to the unhomelike quality of mental institutions. As Buffalo's annual report explained, "[C]onnecting corridors promote ease of Administration; officers could visit the wards and transport patients in any weather."[117] A comparison of Sloan's Greystone, which was 1,243 feet long, to Buffalo State's 2,200 feet, suggests that Sloan did little to diminish the apparent size of the hospital, while Richardson divided the facade of each block with three forward projections, each of these topped with a domestic-looking gable (Figure 4.32). Richardson's accomplishment at Buffalo, it could be

argued, was the tempering of the visual monotony of such a large building. The cascading gables were not gratuitous picturesque additions but thoughtful responses to the cottage plan. It was, however, imagery unaccompanied by significant changes in program, and therefore still a kind of public relations device that served the state, the doctors, and the families. In the face of the state charity reformers who were arguing for cheaper buildings, Richardson and Gray built one of the grandest hospitals of the period.[118]

Peoria: A Short-lived Congregate Asylum and Its Cottage Plan Replacement

The Hospital for the Incurable Insane in Peoria, Illinois, began as a congregate asylum and then adopted the segregate system: first the state erected a large unified structure; then state officials had it demolished and replaced with cottages. This turn of events would not have been so remarkable had it not happened in a span of just seven years. In 1895, the state spent $50,000 on the first phase of a structure designed by Lonsdale Green, a Chicago architect (Figure 4.33). The institution, intended to house eight hundred incurable lunatics, was designed to be roughly cruciform in plan.[119] The central building was a square with chamfered corners; attached to each of these cut-off corners would have been four octagonal towers, and four two-story ward blocks would have extended outward from the towers. Only one ward extension, one tower, and the central building were constructed. Above its stone foundation, the exterior walls were brick, and the asylum met the sky with foreboding crenellations. Blank brick walls show the location of future corridors visible as blind fenestration. Where the ward blocks met the towers, corner turrets emphasized the castle keep motif. A later superintendent described the overall impression:

Figure 4.32. Richardson, Buffalo State Hospital for the Insane, gabled ends of pavilions northeast of administration building. From *Buffalo Illustrated: Commerce, Trade, and Industries of Buffalo* (Buffalo: Anderson & Gillette, 1890), 54. Reprinted by permission of the Buffalo and Erie County Public Library, Buffalo, New York.

Figure 4.33. Lonsdale Green, Asylum for the Incurable Insane, Bartonville, Illinois (outside Peoria), original building as partially constructed in 1897, showing octagonal center and one of four proposed wings (demolished). From H. W. Lewis, *Glimpses of Peoria: A Volume Devoted to the Interests of the Second City of Illinois* (Peoria: J. W. Franks & Sons, 1898), 18.

The building was large and showy, without being extravagant in ornamentation, the chief dependence for architectural effect being placed upon the brick battlements with stone caps which adorned the exterior walls. . . . The wing which had been constructed was in effect a barrack, and presented a barn-like appearance of cold discomfort.[120]

Later assessors deemed the towers, as designed, to be unfit for the patients' use. "There was no staircase, except the one in the tower . . . which was cheaply and poorly built of iron, with spiral treads with a low balustrade, so that this stairway was in fact, dangerous for use by the insane; neither were there any entries to the wings except by a door in the tower, and in case of fire the lives of the unfortunate inmates would have certainly been in great peril."[121] The central building was thus stripped of its usual function as it did not contain the costly superintendent's apartments, parlors, or offices of the institution's leaders. The ventilation system consisted of little beyond opening and closing the windows. The patients had no privacy in the barracklike rooms for fifty patients each. These rooms (two on the ground level, two above) were divided by an unlit corridor. "A worse plan for an institution for the care of the insane was never devised," complained one doctor.[122]

The partially built asylum had yet more troubles. It was set above a coal mine. Its foundations cracked and its walls crumbled, even while it was under construction. When the cracks were discovered, expert engineers (including Dankmar Adler) assessed the situation and concluded that the building was unstable. An advisory team of charity reformers and state politicians recommended demolition. It was torn down—before ever having been inhabited. In the intervening years, the segregate system had attained high status, and state officials now recommended a new set of buildings based on the cottage model. Some of the construction materials from the old building were reused, and the new cottages were placed reasonably far away from the disused mine. Thus the ill-fated single building was replaced with scattered houses set along both straight and curving streets. Four cottages, much like the ones at Kankakee in plan and outward appearance, rested on the crest of a hill overlooking a lake (Figure 4.34).

As a measure of the preference for cottages over large institutions, we have Peoria's Dr. George Zeller roundly

condemning the castlelike structure in public remarks made in 1925. Zeller claimed that the first Peoria insane asylum was an ominous image, wrong for a charitable institution:

> The first building, a frowning fortress with battlements and turrets, was erected on the brow of a hill in 1895. . . . The building, though a magnificent example of medieval architecture, was wholly unsuited to the purpose it was to serve, and before its completion the walls showed wide cracks and it was conveniently found that it was built over an abandoned coal mine.[123]

Looking back from a distance of twenty-five years, it seemed a lucky accident that the big building had

Figure 4.34. Reeves and Baillie, cottages at the Illinois General Hospital for the Insane, Bartonville, Illinois, 1902 (originally Illinois Asylum for the Incurable Insane). These cottages replaced the congregate hospital. *Fifth Biennial Report of the Illinois Asylum for the Incurable Insane (1904)*, opposite p. 8. Courtesy of the Oskar Diethelm Library.

self-destructed. Zeller, like most doctors in the 1920s, declared that the cottage plan was far superior to the "usual four-story 'center,' right and left wing, annex and other stereotyped architectural monstrosities."[124]

Kirkbride lived until 1883, just long enough to see his linear plan decline in prestige as cottages rose to the fore. To the end of his life, he continued to reject the segregate system because it made surveillance difficult, and he especially objected to the use of cottages to separate chronic from curable patients,[125] imagining that if hospitals ceased even trying to be curative, they would revert to the madhouses of the eighteenth century— the very horror he spent his career trying to overcome. His life's work was tied to the linear plan, an attachment most evident in his last major accomplishment, the second edition of *The Construction, Organization, and Arrangement of Hospitals for the Insane*, revised from his sickbed in 1880. By this time, all of his major concepts (wards set back for ventilation, easy views of the landscape, the superintendent's apartments in the main building) had begun to fall out of favor.

In 1893, a pamphlet produced for the World's Columbian Exposition described Kirkbride's outdated principles as impediments to progress: "It was apparent to many friends of the insane that those propositions, admirably adapted as they were to the small curative hospitals to which they were meant to apply, had proven a cast-iron fetter upon any real advance in hospital construction, and that the country had outgrown them. But they were regarded with reverence which almost savored superstition, and dissent from them in any particular was regarded in the specialty as heresy."[126] Kirkbride's shallow V was uniquely suited to what he believed were the needs of the curable insane when he devised the plan in 1847; in fact, the plan was so highly specialized that linear plan hospitals could not be reconfigured for other uses. To anti–linear plan thinkers, if all the patients were housed under one big roof, then they were much too limited in their spatial experiences. In the 1930s, Kankakee's first superintendent, Richard Dewey, recalled the inflexibility of Kirkbride plans as compared to the many different options in Europe: "In the U.S. we had this inflexible plan for all the varying classes of patients, acute and chronic, quiet and disturbed, able-bodied and infirm, alert and impassive, industrious and idle."[127]

Moral treatment depended on an attendant/patient ratio of about 1:15, but the pace of hiring attendants never kept up with the overall increase in the number of patients.[128] With the steady rise of the mentally ill population, state hospitals attempted, but failed, to administer the care that reformers in the 1840s upheld. The doctor and matron could not visit every patient in a 600- or 800-bed hospital, and nurses were too busy to supervise those much-touted strolls in the grounds. One patient described a walk in a Wisconsin asylum in 1886 as being "led out between two keepers as a herd of cattle."[129] The reporter Nellie Bly, who faked her own insanity to embed herself inside the Blackwell's Island Asylum, similarly described the contradiction between the appearance of the gardens and their actual use:

> I looked at the pretty lawn, which I had once thought was such a comfort to the poor creatures confined on the island, and laughed at my own notions. What enjoyment is it to them? They are not allowed on the grass—it is only to look at. I saw some patients eagerly and caressingly lift a nut or a colored leaf that had fallen on the path. But they were not allowed to keep them. The nurses would always compel them to throw their little bit of God's comfort away.[130]

Bly was appalled by the manner in which the women traversed the grounds; they were not strolling, rambling, or promenading. Two attendants dragged patients along using a single rope and a series of belts: "A long cable rope fastened to wide leather belts, and these belts locked around the waists of fifty-two women."[131]

After Kirkbride's death, institutional psychiatrists favored the cottage plan, although they continued to use existing linear hospitals if they were already on campuses. At the start of the twentieth century, it was not just the linear plan that was under fire but also the entire enterprise of curative asylum medicine. Charity reformers such as Frederick Wines had deeply undermined the public trust in asylum doctors, recasting them as profligate, political operatives. The next wave of criticism—from neurologists—hit asylum doctors even harder. Neurologists sought biological causes for nervous disorders, and while they typically studied and attempted to cure milder conditions (hysteria and neurasthenia, for example, rather than schizophrenia), they maintained a secondary interest in the severely mentally ill. They envisioned a scientific world in which one could conduct serious medical research on mental illness, which contrasted the approach of asylum doctors, who concentrated their efforts on the prosaic management of their organizations. In 1879, Dr. William Hammond openly denied the basic concept of asylum medicine—that the insane had to be treated outside the home, saying, "[I]t is the commonly received opinion among physicians and the public generally that as soon as possible after an individual becomes insane, he or she must at once be placed under the restraint of a lunatic asylum . . . but these views are erroneous."[132]

In 1875, neurologist Edward Spitzka attacked asylum doctors for their misplaced interest in architecture and for their ignorance of medicine, particularly cerebral anatomy. To neurologists, the cure for mental illness lay in healing the body. The annual reports, which reward the architectural historian so nicely, revealed to Spitzka only that the superintendents were experts in all kinds of useless fields, like:

> gardening and farming (although the farm account frequently comes out on the wrong side of the ledger), tin roofing (although the roof and cupola are usually leaky), drain-pipe laying (although the grounds are often moist and unhealthy), engineering (though the wards are either too hot or too cold) . . . experts at everything except the diagnosis, pathology, and treatment of insanity.[133]

Clearly, architecture was seen as a frivolous distraction, not the purview of medical doctors.

S. Wier Mitchell was a prominent neurologist in Philadelphia whose condemnation of asylum practice has come to symbolize the end of the era. Mitchell held fast to the idea that "you cure the body and somehow find the mind is also cured."[134] He is best known to architectural and literary historians as the model for the menacing husband and doctor character in Charlotte Perkins Gilman's *The Yellow Wallpaper*, a vaguely autobiographical story about a woman writer who has been put on the rest cure—she is prevented from writing, she is infantilized, she is caged. The doctor-husband character did not commit her to an asylum. Typically, the rest cure required four to six weeks in bed, a nutritious diet, massage instead of exercise, and obedience to the doctor.[135] In *The Yellow Wallpaper*,

the doctor prevented the unnamed protagonist from writing, which was her most ardent desire. The novella ends with her obsessional break with reality, as she envisions an imaginary woman trapped in the yellow wallpaper of her room.

In 1894, Mitchell was asked to deliver an address to the organization that replaced the AMSAII, the American Medico-Psychological Association. It was the fiftieth anniversary of the AMSAII's formation by the superintendents Kirkbride, Gray, Ray, Butler, and others. Rather than congratulate the assembly, however, Mitchell berated them for their lack of research interest, their detachment from science, and their distance from medical doctors. He accused them of laziness, the result of not having up-and-coming medical students nipping at their heels: "Your hospitals are not our hospitals; your ways are not our ways; you live out of range of critical shot, you are not preceded and followed in your wards by clever rivals, or watched by able residents fresh with the learning of the schools."[136] And, after all this, the delegation of the American Medico-Psychological Association rather pitifully elected him an honorary member.

Mitchell's speech called attention to the diminished prestige of psychiatry practiced in the asylum, and simultaneously marked a diminution of the importance of all kinds of architecture for psychiatry. The autonomy of the superintendent himself also declined as research-oriented physicians took the lead in the changing field. The notion that a superintendent needed to have good taste in architecture, as Kirkbride had said of Charles Nichols years earlier, was at an end. The demise of architecture as part of the cure came from two directions. Charity reformers had already demanded that chronic patients be warehoused in state hospitals, and now, at the turn of the century, neurologists studied the nervous system in university labs and conducted body-centered therapies in private offices. Every state hospital, regardless of its lofty or optimistic beginning, was by 1900 a last-resort facility for a thousand or more mentally ill people. Most inmates were elderly, poor, and unlikely to improve, and they lived their days in rundown linear hospitals, or clusters of cottages, or campuses composed of some combination thereof. The asylum was not a site for the production of medical knowledge, nor was it the place for the reinforcement and legitimization of the psychiatric profession. Furthermore, when Poughkeepsie, Greystone, and Buffalo were constructed, the showcase linear plan hospitals from the 1840s were already decrepit. Many onlookers believed that behind the walls of Trenton or St. Elizabeths, all that remained of the moral treatment was regimentation. In 1866, when the AMSAII allowed the number of patients in each institution to rise to six hundred, the first strike was dealt to moral management in the purpose-built hospital. In 1888, the second blow fell. The AMSAII rejected the construction propositions that Kirkbride and the others had set down in 1851. The propositions, so intensely focused on architecture, seemed ludicrously out of touch in 1888, when the field of psychiatry was changing under pressure from research-oriented neurologists and belt-tightening charity reformers. As Butler once suggested to Olmsted, the lunatic asylum had been killed.

Conclusion

THE CHANGING SPACES OF MENTAL ILLNESS

Today, mental illness is generally considered to be treatable, but it cannot be prevented or cured. Many patients recover, but their path is not an easy one. There is no vaccine for mental illness, such as that which has led to the eradication of smallpox, nor is there a drug that purges mental illness from the body, in the way that a course of penicillin can conquer a staphylococcus infection. No cure has reduced insanity to a minor problem, the way vitamin C has made scurvy a mere medical nuisance. Mental illness remains, for many, shrouded in mystery, and that mystery creates further stigma for its sufferers. Those recovering from severe psychiatric illness must cope with this social stigma in addition to finding work and housing, and developing meaningful relationships. The difficulties faced by people in the nineteenth century have not disappeared at the start of the twenty-first century, but architecture plays a far less significant role in the practice of psychiatry than it once did. As Joseph Melling and Bill Forsythe explain, for the past three decades, "almost every developed country has abandoned the mass institutionalization of the mentally ill."[1]

Most practicing psychiatrists now see mental illness as an interaction of biology and environment, yet the precise role of the environment is still uncertain. Schizophrenia is one of several diseases that was probably common in Victorian asylums. Scientists currently estimate that 1 percent of the world's population is beset by schizophrenia.[2] Drugs stop all symptoms in 20 percent of cases; less encouragingly, two-thirds of recovering patients gain relief but remain symptomatic throughout their lives.[3] Modern pharmaceuticals decrease the suffering of schizophrenics, but the drugs are far from perfect. Research psychiatrists still do not know exactly what biochemical processes cause schizophrenia, and much research remains to be done. Doctors have studied heredity, but twin studies disprove an easy causal connection: "If the illness were dictated solely by genetic inheritance, the identical twin of a schizophrenic person would always be schizophrenic as well. In reality, however, when one twin has schizophrenia, the identical twin has about a 50 percent chance of also being afflicted."[4] A person might inherit biological conditions that strongly predispose him to schizophrenia, but "*environmental factors* [my emphasis] can nudge susceptible individuals into illness."[5] Environmental factors here refer to prenatal infections, malnutrition, birth complications, and brain injuries, not to improper architecture or a vice-filled city.

It is true that long-term stays, those stretching from years into decades, are far less common now than in the past. Do we still need psychiatric hospitals? Do drugs make psychiatric hospitals obsolete? The question is not easy to answer. Some psychiatrists envision that if drugs are properly prescribed and taken, then all psychiatric patients could be integrated into society. Other say that even with drugs, there will always be mentally ill people who require confinement because they are dangerous to themselves and to other people. A middle ground might be that short-term care is the one necessary form of confinement, and that such short-term hospitalization is required only for monitoring patients and establishing pharmaceutical regimens. Large hospitals where patients dwell for lifetimes are not a cherished or central part of the practice of psychiatric medicine, but they still exist.

Today we need regular medical hospitals more than ever, because, for all their faults, they offer lifesaving technologies. But we need psychiatric hospitals less than ever before. By 1920, the medical hospital was steeped in the "legitimating aura of science."[6] Physicians like those at prestigious Johns Hopkins associated themselves with universities, claiming higher status in society than previously and reinforcing their ranks with large, carefully organized, hygienic, technologically advanced hospitals. In this way, the status of the asylum and the medical hospital were at odds: as the medical hospital increased in eminence, the asylum declined. By comparison, state mental hospitals had lost status, drifting away from science and appearing to physicians as mere warehouses for humans: little or no research was conducted there, so neither the causes of mental disease nor potential cures were likely to issue forth from the state mental hospital. Even the cottages, which institutional psychiatrists saw as a massive reform, seemed yet another trifling architectural distraction to medical doctors, because they came without any serious change of program. Physicians had successfully aligned themselves with science (and all its socially constructed status), but asylum superintendents were still managing construction projects, repairing leaky roofs, fixing broken furnaces, and counting bales of hay. No new knowledge would ever come from a lunatic asylum.

Asylum medicine's focus on architecture was one of the signs of its failure. That alienists were once nearly obsessed with architecture was obvious in the 1851 propositions and in Kirkbride's 1854 book, but such architectural dedication had dissipated by 1900. Some critics accused traditional institutional doctors of claiming that the severely mentally ill needed to be institutionalized in order to keep their state hospitals open. These critics, again coming from the field of neurology, asserted that while public institutions were needed for the poor, any lunatic who had a family would be better off at home.[7] This attitude diverged from William Dean Fairless's assessment in 1861 that "the treatment of the insane is conducted not only *in*, but *by*, the asylum."[8] In 1900, creating a therapeutic environment was not the key goal of asylum doctors. Indeed, it had become somewhat embarrassing that the allegedly therapeutic environments of the preceding sixty years were crowded with the lingering unwell. The profession needed to disassociate itself from the once-grand claims of environmental determinism, because, quite evidently, the environment had not determined many cures. Some doctors held dearly to the claim that if the patients had been admitted sooner, the asylum could have saved them; but by the turn of the twentieth century, this special pleading was difficult to accept. State mental hospitals signified the times before psychiatry was serious medicine. Asylum doctors had managed the prosaic life of institutions, and this approach represented the past; the future of psychiatry would be to conduct research on diseases, rather than to manage institutions. The institutions themselves began to be neglected by both the doctors and the state, because they carried negative associations. They were filled with incurable people who reminded both doctors and the public of past failures.

The concept of environmental determinism subsided from psychiatric discourse, but did not retreat entirely; environmental arguments were still used to improve the lot of patients. The reasoning could be inverted: if treatment *inside* the asylum was not working, perhaps treatment *outside* would. In fact, during the last decades of the nineteenth century, outpatient care developed on several fronts. It offered a reasonable, quick, inexpensive option for treating the mentally ill. In 1885, Massachusetts attempted to place docile patients with foster families.[9] Reformers opened dispensaries, like the ones attached to the Pennsylvania Hospital in 1885 and, in 1897, the Boston Dispensary. These clinics treated patients outside the traditional asylum in hopes that if their diseases were caught early, the afflicted could be spared institutionalization altogether. Aftercare programs marked another innovation: these were programs for those recently released from state hospitals. (These types of care facilities exist in large numbers today and are a relative of the halfway house.) Another type of institution, the psychopathic hospital, began around 1912. Its mission was to assess patients' illnesses for a few days, give doctors a chance to observe acute cases, and then refer the most deranged patients to the state hospital while sending others home. George Kline, commissioner of the Massachusetts Department of Mental Health, wrote in 1927: "The past decade has witnessed a remarkable extension of the sphere of psychiatry *beyond the walls* of the mental hospital" (my emphasis).[10] The extension of psychiatry "beyond the walls" of the asylum was a bold step forward for the mentally ill because it allowed people to receive treatment without leaving their homes.

This would seem at first glance to be a welcome turn of events. But an insidious result ensued: the psychiatric profession gradually turned its attention away from the poorest, sickest patients, those who had no families, those who were forced by circumstances to live in institutions. The budding field of psychiatry in the 1840s, as measured by the pronouncements of asylum doctors and the poignant petitions of Dorothea Dix, once zealously attended to friendless and hopeless lunatics. By 1900, these lunatics were slipping from view. And today, the severely mentally ill are almost invisible. Few ambitious graduates of a prestigious medical school seek employment at a state mental hospital; few young psychiatrists choose to work with institutionalized, impoverished schizophrenics or bipolar patients. As the profession has shifted its attention to noninstitutionalized, milder cases, architecture has declined in importance to the field of psychiatry.

Freudian psychoanalysis is another factor that lessened the importance of architecture in the practice of psychiatry. Freud's major interest was neither a person's lesion-filled brain nor an adult's interaction with environmental factors. Rather, he searched for explanations for insanity in the subconscious mind, childhood trauma, past events of a sexual nature, and general intrapsychic experiences. The adult's environment ceased to seem so important—either as cause or as cure. Freud published *Studies in Hysteria* in 1895; his emphasis on the repression of childhood memories influenced many practitioners. Freudian psychoanalysis had a particularly strong influence on the care of middle-class neurotic cases in the United States from about 1930 to 1970. There are few strict Freudians working today, but there are many mental health professionals whose practices are founded on one-on-one therapy.

Historians of medicine hardly need be reminded that Freud had a greater impact on cultural and intellectual discourse than on medicine, or that his influence was little felt before 1920.[11] There is, however, much misunderstanding among art historians about the importance of Freud, and I am frequently asked about the influence of Freudianism on asylum architecture. The answer is that Freudian psychoanalysis had almost no effect on the architecture of American psychiatric hospitals. Initially, psychoanalysis appealed to bohemians, intellectuals, and artists; its processes were slow, labor-intensive, and not well suited to the institutional setting. Psychoanalysis worked best (and some say it did not work at all) on patients who were mildly neurotic, not severely psychotic. As sociologist Allan Horwitz has explained, "[A]sylum psychiatrists . . . tended to identify and treat distinct conditions such as schizophrenia and bipolar [disorder]." He continues, saying Freud's "theory of psychoanalysis and the dynamic psychiatry that stemmed from it expanded the field to take in a broad range of neurotic conditions rather than the small number of psychotic conditions that asylum psychiatry emphasized."[12] Even proponents of Freudian psychoanalysis found the techniques to be almost useless in institutional settings; doctors did not have the time for daily conversations, and the patients tended to have types of diseases not treatable by analysis.[13] For the most part, analysts trained in the Freudian tradition treated a "wide variety of neuroses or problems in living,"[14] rather than schizophrenia, bipolar disorder, or psychotic depression, the most common afflictions of asylum dwellers. The new psychoanalysts needed an office and a couch, not a hospital.

It is beyond the scope of this book to engage in an analysis of psychiatric hospital architecture in the twentieth century, although it is a subject worthy of further scholarship. Over the course of the twentieth century, the desire to keep patients *out* of institutions dominated policy making. Deinstitutionalization as a policy began just after World War II. (Without pushing the interpretation too far, one can see some aspects of deinstitutionalization in Gheel, in Scotland's boarding-out policy, or in Bemis's ill-fated scheme for a farm colony in Worcester.) The basic concept as it emerged in the United States in the 1950s was to limit the mentally ill in institutions to the most incompetent and the most dangerous. Doctors began to use short-term stays at regular hospitals to observe patients and decide where they should be sent. Only the most severe cases were committed to the state hospital; the goal in the 1950s was rather to observe patients, send them home, and continue treatment on an outpatient basis.[15] State policy makers eliminated certain categories of patients from state hospitals to keep costs down. Drug abusers, alcoholics, autistic children, and any voluntary self-commitments were not allowed into state hospitals. This left the institutions with inhabitants who were chronically psychotic and required highly structured settings, as well as people who had multiple handicaps and could not cope with daily life.[16] State hospitals did not become institutions of last resort by accident. Policy decisions made it so. State officials determined that the old lunatic asylums were among the most secure of state-owned structures, and they therefore used the old masonry heaps for locking away dangerous patients. This was a sad irony for the Kirkbride plan buildings, which were purposely designed to be distinct from prisons. Local entities—counties and cities, as opposed to states—incorporated the less serious mental cases into a range of welfare settings, leaving the state hospital as the lowest level of state-funded habitation in America.

The 1970s saw the height of deinstitutionalization, occasioned by cost cutting. Andrew Scull has argued that during that decade the drive to lower costs was the "primary factor" in what he calls "decarceration." The proponents of deinstitutionalization claimed that patients could be cared for in the community, where they could live in more comfortable, homelike environments; but Scull glumly concludes that "'community care' for many of its 'beneficiaries' frequently involves no more than a transfer from one institution to another institution or quasi-institutional setting."[17] Another reason for deinstitutionalization was the spread of psychoactive drugs. Historians and sociologists warn against a deterministic argument about drugs causing deinstitutionalization, however, because administrators had started the process of deinstitutionalization before the drugs became commonplace. The first antipsychotic drug, chlorpromazine, and the first antidepressant drug, imipramine, were discovered in 1952 and 1957, respectively. Psychiatrists also administered other drugs,

including tranquilizers and barbiturates, to mentally ill patients.[18] Indeed, it may be that monetary concerns rather than improved treatment drove deinstitutionalization, and that some policy makers overstated the effectiveness of drugs in order to legitimize their cutbacks.[19] Drugs could be administered anywhere: nursing homes, residential treatment facilities, halfway houses. To many observers, it seems as if the twentieth century's psychoactive drugs superseded the nineteenth century's asylum, just as the carefully planned asylum had replaced the eighteenth century's chains. The control function of the lunatic asylum was unnecessary post-1950, because drugs did the controlling. Of course, it is not that simple. Drugs cannot alleviate symptoms if patients don't take them, and it is well known that many people with schizophrenia and bipolar disorder do not like the side effects of drugs and refuse to take them.

As explained in the introduction, I follow those sociologists and historians who describe mental illness in the present (and in the past) as both biological and structured by culture. This dual depiction is markedly different from the definitions promoted by the antipsychiatry movement in the 1970s, whose proponents believed that mental illness was a fabrication of establishment thinkers. (Deinstitutionalization seemed like an excellent idea to such people: if mental illness did not exist, why lock people up?) That movement's leading proponents were R. D. Laing and Thomas Szasz, who both rejected psychiatry's oppressive demands for compliance and a sameness of human experience. The Scottish psychiatrist Laing viewed psychosis as a possible reflection of the patient's reality, but cast doubt on the very existence of mental illness as mainstream doctors perceived it. Szasz held that mental illness was a myth—that illnesses must by definition be physical, and therefore theories of disease could not be applied to psychological abnormalities where no physical pathology was detectable. Some theorists claimed that schizophrenia was a social construct and that society's thrust to incarcerate schizophrenics was an attempt to control deviance or stave off revolution. Followers of the antipsychiatry movement reasonably criticized the most abusive weapons in the state hospital's arsenal, psychosurgery, electroshock therapy, and involuntary hospitalization. The antipsychiatry movement also attacked psychopharmacology as a means of covertly controlling the patients: a kind of chemical version of shackles, chaining them without the chains. If the principles of moral treatment (good food, exercise, plenty of sleep, daily visits from doctors) had been carried out in giant hospitals, the institutions might not have lost so much credibility.

At the same time as the antipsychiatrists attacked mental institutions from the political *left*, the political *right* called for community care for entirely different reasons: politicians like Ronald Reagan (and Margaret Thatcher in Great Britain) were opposed to ever-growing welfare states and both hoped to cut government costs by eliminating beds for the mentally ill.[20] At the same time, the extreme poor in America plunged into a further abyss. In the 1970s and 1980s, homelessness became a crisis in America's cities. Estimates of the percentage of homeless people suffering from mental illness range from 25 to 40 percent.[21] It need hardly be stated that deinstitutionalization required no specialized architecture. The final architectural setting for a welfare-dependent schizophrenic or manic-depressive, after institutionalization, was not a building, it was the street.

Historic Preservation for Difficult Histories

This book has described sweeping changes from small structures like the Virginia Public Hospital that did not have specialized interiors, to complex linear plans set in picturesque landscapes, to the apparently anti-institutional segregate plans. But by the turn of the twentieth century, the public distrusted all asylums, whether they looked like cottages or castles. The overcrowded asylums were decrepit; they had become custodial, not curative. This building type—and asylum medicine, the profession that was intimately connected to it—were at the end of their legitimacy as early as 1900. Given this sad state of affairs, one might think that the buildings would by now have just disappeared. In fact, many were torn down in pieces or as a whole. But for much of the twentieth century, U.S. states actually needed these large buildings: where else would the underfunded mental health departments house

thousands of people, people who could not care for themselves; who had no one to speak for them; who had nowhere to go. And so even as the respectability of asylum medicine declined, the buildings lingered.

Victorian asylums present enormous challenges to historic preservation. The Public Hospital in Virginia was demolished and reconstructed as a tourist attraction in the 1980s—this is a singular case, imaginable only in the unique world of Colonial Williamsburg. More typical is the stunning Greek Revival New York State Hospital in Utica; it sits empty with trees growing from the sediment on its roof. Walter's St. Elizabeths is entirely boarded up, although it is currently under discussion as part of a renewal of the Anacostia neighborhood in Washington, D.C.; it is an extensive campus with dozens of buildings and will pose a significant challenge to developers.[22] Withers's Poughkeepsie is also mothballed, although its location along a major commercial highway is promising. There are no plans to renovate or adaptively reuse the Trenton Psychiatric Hospital. Notman's building has a few offices in the center main, and the rest of the building is empty except for groundhogs and feral cats, who tend not to get along. Bryce's Hospital in Tuscaloosa is in slightly better condition than Utica or Trenton, containing again offices in the center main but having no occupants in the outer wings. Richardson's Buffalo State Hospital was partly demolished, but the remainder of the building is a National Historic Landmark. The National Trust for Historic Preservation considers it important to the nation's heritage, and, overall, it stands a good chance of adaptive reuse. The building's chances of survival are enhanced by its location in a park near a university. Buffalo State College, the Buffalo Board of Education, the Buffalo Psychiatric Center, the city, and the state plan to cooperate in transforming the hospital into offices for educational programs, while maintaining inpatient and outpatient services at this location.[23] In February 2006, the state pledged $76 million to the reuse.[24] Greystone, in northern New Jersey, houses offices in the center main, but 90 percent of the structure is empty. Developers eyeing Greystone's land find the site enormously desirable, because it is within commuting distance from New York City and close to a likable midsize city, Morristown. Some are in favor of demolition, some have proposed luxury condominiums for the main buildings, and still others suggest a museum of medical history. In 2002, the mayor of the town of Parsippany supported its preservation, observing that "in Europe, they save places like that for thousands of years."[25] Kankakee, Illinois, now the Shapiro Developmental Center, is in very good condition, although much of the main building and many of the cottages are empty there, too. Architecturally sympathetic officials in Kankakee transformed a portion of the linear plan building into apartments for adults with developmental disabilities and other parts of the main house into offices. The caretakers at Kankakee recognize the historical importance of the institution and its architecture.

"It has long been axiomatic that the functional and technical success of hospitals depends on the ease with which they can grow and change," contend hospital experts Paul James and Tony Noakes.[26] The looser the original functional fit, the more likely a hospital is to survive over time. Kirkbride hospitals are the opposite of this flexible and survivable kind of architecture. Indeed, the linear asylums discussed in chapters 2 and 4 were designed with such a level of specificity that they cannot easily be modified to allow for other types of medical treatment. In fact, they cannot easily be adapted to any other purpose. With hundreds of rooms, all with load-bearing walls, these buildings stubbornly resist transformation. Buffalo State originally had about eight hundred rooms, all with walls made of eighteen-inch-thick brick. If the buildings had been less specialized in the arrangement of their interior spaces, they might have been more pliable. If they had open plans, like factories and warehouses, they could have been reused for dwellings, offices, or art studios.

Although it is probably not practical to save every one of these difficult asylums, some local communities are attempting to come to terms with these structures and their histories. The Northampton Lunatic Asylum in Massachusetts, built in 1858, was considered for development by Peter Calthorpe, the California-based neotraditionalist urban planner, who had drafted a master plan calling for 150,000 square feet of the original Kirkbride plan structure to be preserved. This structure was to become part of a "mixed-use village center with 207 units of housing, ample open space, and 400,000 square feet of office, light industrial, retail and institutional space."[27] Northampton's state hospital

resembled other Kirkbride institutions discussed in this book, especially Trenton, in its heavy institutional appearance. Artist Anna Schuleit organized a tribute to the building in November 2000; the installation artwork called Habeas Corpus attracted thousands of participants, including many former patients, who walked the grounds as Johann Sebastian Bach's "Magnificat" played through hundreds of speakers.[28] Schuleit astutely summarizes her approach as follows: "I want to shape my findings into a new form of memory, personal and collective, by opening up the dialogue about the anti-heroic, outsider history of institutions, of certain sites and places that have no master narrative, and that remain raw and untold to this day."[29] On the day of the event, visitors received a program on cream-colored paper that evoked nineteenth-century annual reports, the very documents so often cited in the endnotes of this book, that promised cures and oozed optimism. A film produced by David Petersen beautifully captured the aching sadness among the former patients and the lingering effects of the psychiatric hospital's confining and isolating techniques.

Although Schuleit has been asked to prepare memorials for other psychiatric hospitals, she believes her tribute to Northampton should remain unique. Her next installation, Bloom, packed the empty halls of a disused psychiatric center, the Massachusetts Mental Health Center in Boston, with rows of live flowers forming carpets of bright color. This intrusion of nature, however cultivated, into the institution recalled the claims of nineteenth-century doctors about the therapeutic qualities of horticulture. Schuleit's knowledgeable and sensitive installation pieces garnered much praise from critics, who viewed both works as funerals for the buildings and institutions. She neither promotes nor discourages the preservation of psychiatric hospitals, even historic ones. Rather, she hopes for sympathetic and honest closings for these institutions.[30] She dedicates her works to "those who have been there."

Traverse City, Michigan, seems to have avoided the need for a funeral for its state hospital. The asylum in Traverse City is located just one and a half miles from downtown, a fact that facilitated its revitalization. Local developer and history aficionado Ray Minervini headed plans to reuse the 1885 linear plan hospital, seven cottages, and several utility buildings on thirty-six acres of land abutting woods, farms, and parks. The Web site advertising the Village at Grand Traverse Commons boasts that the newly renovated structures offer "380,000 square feet of space in a tax-free Michigan Renaissance Zone."[31] These former state hospital buildings will be transformed into a "mixed-use walkable village environment." The historic Kirkbride building will be preserved for various uses, including restaurants, offices, and apartments. There is a two-story building from the 1960s where the center main once was: it now houses a coffee shop on the ground floor and professional offices on the second floor. The southview section, at the farthest southern end of the Kirkbride building, serves as home to an Italian restaurant and an art gallery. Minervini sees the development of the asylum site as a potential extension of the pedestrian area of downtown Traverse City and thus as an opportunity to create an environment where people can walk to work.[32] He also notes the exquisite workmanship behind the structure, saying, "It was built by the state at a time when buildings were meant to last."[33] The small town of Sykesville, Maryland, is in the process of saving its colonial-style state asylum; early plans include a police training facility and an arboretum.[34]

Two state universities have adopted asylum buildings for reuse. Camarillo State Hospital in California from the 1930s is among the few asylums that have already been successfully transformed; the cool white buildings are now incorporated into the California State University of the Channel Islands; the school's Web site proclaims without apology that it was built in the early part of the twentieth century "as the former Camarillo State Hospital, [and that the] sprawling 1930s Spanish revival buildings, cloistered hallways, Bell Tower, tiled fountains, open space, and many courtyards are being renovated to house our new state-of-the-art 21st century University."[35] (Jazz great Charlie Parker's "Relaxin' in Camarillo" refers to time spent in this facility.)[36] In Athens, Ohio, the 1874 asylum is now incorporated into Ohio University. Renamed Lin Hall, it includes offices for music and geology staff and faculty. The structure is also home to the Kennedy Museum of Art. Educational purposes are perhaps easier to accommodate than commercial ones in these buildings with difficult histories.

It need hardly be stated that there is a stigma attached to mental illness, and the stigma extends to those buildings that housed its sufferers. The marketing challenges for adaptive reuse are enormous. The popular image of a psych ward is the one from *One Flew over the Cuckoo's Nest*, and nobody wants to open a nail salon or a cookie shop in the shadow of Nurse Ratched. Even so, as Traverse City suggests, state mental hospitals, even those with terrible pasts, have emerged as fashionable among history buffs and preservation enthusiasts. In the middle of the twentieth century, though, the opposite was true. These Victorian buildings looked entirely unstylish, as they appeared hideously ornate, wasteful, irrational, and dark to eyes more accustomed to the simple forms and clean lines of modernism. In 1961, as a low-slung, flat-roofed modernist institution was constructed on the grounds of the Michigan State Hospital in Kalamazoo, a local newspaper described the creepy old building still standing: "warped wooden floors, narrow, steep stairwells, long windows and echo-bouncing high ceilings are the daily surroundings of almost 700 women who live in the victorian edifice" (Figure C.1). Costly, highly specific asylum architecture did not cause the demise of nineteenth-century psychiatry, but it did not help the profession's image, either. By the middle of the twentieth century, the buildings discussed in this book were rejected on both aesthetic and functional grounds. Nineteenth-century lunatic asylums took on the regrettable mantle of Bethlem: they were ugly; they did not work.

But what does it mean to say a building did not "work"? It's a common enough expression, used casually among nonspecialists, in historical debates, and at architecture school critiques. To say a building does not work connotes several meanings. For example, if a building, regardless of purpose, collapses because of a poorly designed structure, crushing its inhabitants, pundits agree that the building did not work. If a building is designed for a specific purpose, and that purpose can never be fulfilled because of errors in planning, discerning observers might reasonably agree that the building does not work. Given that in the past three decades almost every industrialized country has rejected the confinement of the mentally ill in large-scale buildings, one could argue that linear plan hospitals (reserving judgment for the cottage plan) did not work. Not one of the state mental hospitals discussed in this book

Figure C.1. *Kalamazoo Gazette*, September 21, 1961. Courtesy of Kalamazoo Public Library.

$700,000 UNIT FIRST STEP IN REPLACEMENT OF OLD FEMALE CENTER
Kalamazoo State Hospital Building Will House 120 in April

FIRST STEP IN MEETING NEEDS

Work Progresses on First Unit of State Hospital Female Center

When a building is still standing after 102 years, it probably is a historical site, elegant private home or, as in the case of the female center at Kalamazoo State Hospital, an obsolete, rickety, decaying structure.

Facility-bare as the old center is, its warped wooden floors, narrow, steep stairwells, long w i n d o w s and echo-bouncing high ceilings are the daily surroundings of almost 700 women who live in the victorian edifice.

THE S T A T I C condition is about to change soon. Since January, construction of the first of an anticipated three buildings has been moving along at a steady pace, and by April, 1962, about 120 patients from the old center will be transferred to the modern unit. It is 60 per cent completed now, and work will continue through the winter months on the interior.

Dr. Clarence M. Schrier, medi-

cal superintendent, has repeatedly told of the several wards in the original center which have been vacated and sealed off to patients and personnel as a safety necessity.

*　*　*

APPEALS FOR allotments for an additional two units to complete the first half of a long-range building program to replace the old female center have gone to the State Legislature in the past two years, without action. Cost of the new unit is set at approximately $70,000.

As Thomas Walker, business manager of the hospital mentioned, "This building composes only one-sixth of requirements needed to do away with the old center. We can start on the next unit only when we get the money. Until then all we can do is wait."

AGE: 102 YEARS; POPULATION: 700
Old Structure Now Partly Condemned

is currently in use for housing psychiatric patients, although many still have a few offices for the staff.[37] In this sense, one might also say the buildings did not work, because they had no lasting power to carry out the task for which they were designed.

But there is another, more generous interpretation of whether or not the buildings worked: that kinder interpretation is that we simply cannot know if the linear plan hospitals worked, because they were never used

in the way Kirkbride and his brethren envisioned. They were never given a chance to live up to the dreams of their builders. Buildings can be used or abused; they can be built for one type of occupation but used for another; they can be maintained well or left to deteriorate. Linear insane asylums are an extreme case of these changing fortunes over time: considered ideal at the time of their invention, they are now considered nearly useless.

I hope this examination of Victorian American asylum architecture has enriched the social history of mental illness and our knowledge of the plight of people who lived in these environments. Architects, historians, and psychiatrists still ask questions and search for answers about the built environment and its influence on human behavior, but most experts today soften their language and temper their claims. The environment might *influence* behavior but not *determine* behavior, and no one believes a changed environment will cure a mental disease. The architects and doctors in this book held particular beliefs about mental illness, preconceptions about cures and causes, and ideas about who deserved to be treated and how. All of them were encased within their own social world, and the nineteenth-century asylum was a microcosm of social realities outside its gates. Asylums were both punishing and welcoming; they took care and they held prisoners; they were curative and custodial. Even though today these institutions have

almost no credibility, social or medical, their buildings remain. They are witnesses to the history of medicine and testaments to a once-common faith in the power of architecture to shape behavior.

Coda: The Clubhouse Model

The struggles of the mentally ill to find a place in society are legion. To current and recovering patients, the hospitals represent confinement, separation from society, and loss of control. Patients clearly seek release from the hospital. But what constitutes a successful return to society? Staying healthy, reconnecting with family, making new friends, holding down a job, participating in a community—or merely staying off the street? Where does a recovered person (whether he or she has benefited from psychoactive drugs or from any other kind of therapy) go after a hospital stay?

Figure C.2. Fountain House, New York City, 2004. Photograph by the author.

In 1948, a group of men recently released from a state hospital began meeting casually to help each other adjust to their new lives. This group of friends, along with two philanthropists, began Fountain House in New York City as a response—both architectural and programmatic—to the problems of returning to society. Fountain House derives its name from a small fountain, a symbol of hope, that was located in the backyard of its original building, a nineteenth-century brick row house. In 1965, the organization moved across the street to a purpose-built neocolonial structure (Figure C.2). Fountain House originated the clubhouse model, the main concepts of which have been highly influential, spurring three hundred similar clubhouses worldwide. The basic policy premise of the clubhouse movement is that people with mental illness have a right to decent housing, meaningful employment, and social interaction, all of which were denied to hospitalized patients. The clubhouses provide members with a place to work and interact among supportive people. The Web site for Fountain House begins: "In 1948, a handful of men and women with major mental illnesses started a quiet revolution—in their own lives, as well as in the entire field of mental health care. Their idea was to join together, rather than to retreat in isolation, and to support one another in finding work and adjusting to life *beyond hospital walls*" (my emphasis).[38] Finding a place that was not a hospital, not walled, not confining: this was a desperate search. As described by the founders of Fountain House, "From the start, Fountain House was a very different kind of place. There were no bars on the windows or doors. No part of the building was restricted from members." Just as we saw in the nineteenth century, when observers like Frederick Law Olmsted noted that what improves life for the healthy also improves life for the sick, the first clubhouses were modeled on the gentlemen's clubs of New York. If healthy, wealthy people benefit from a civilized oasis in the city, a place to get away from both home and business, recovering mental patients could, too.

When patients were released because of deinstitutionalization policies, they needed further treatment interventions to allow them to adjust to life beyond the hospital walls. There were thousands of deinstitutionalized citizens who lacked practical access to housing and jobs. They had little sense of community and no

way of forming one. Psychiatric rehabilitation, in which individual counselors aid ex–mental patients in gaining vocational skills, securing housing, and attaining life skills, emerged in the 1980s as a way of retraining the severely mentally ill. In contrast to the clubhouses, psychiatric rehabilitation operates on a medical model, on one-on-one therapy, rather than focusing on building communities.[39] The clubhouses offer an architectural component by providing a casual environment for daily interaction. The mission statement of the International Center for Clubhouse Development notes: "As helpful as medications and therapies can be, such programs are not equipped to look beyond the 'patient' to the 'person,' nor to address the person's need for community, engagement, and investment in meaningful relationships and work." Members begin by simply watching the work of running the club; they join in work when they are able, often beginning in the dining hall, which may serve lunch to dozens of members each day (Figure C.3). Some members work as greeters at the front desk, and others help with clerical tasks necessary for the smooth maintenance of the club. The education unit focuses on enrollment in college classes and in honing computer skills. In a way, many of these activities are invented projects to keep members busy and improve their self-esteem. Called the "work-ordered day," this theory engages members and staff in the side-by-side running of the clubhouse.

It is easiest to describe the clubhouses by explaining what they are not: they are not mental hospitals, they are not lunatic asylums, and while they are institutions, they differ markedly from the institutions of the past. Importantly, the clubhouse is definitely not a residence. Although the staff assistants help members find housing, members cannot live there. The clubhouse is also not a treatment center: there are no doctors or nurses, and no drugs are administered. This policy was developed in order to separate the person from the disease. A person's relationship with his or her doctor is private and takes place away from the clubhouse. Even though 95 percent of Fountain House's members rely on some kind of psychoactive drug, their medical condition is not the responsibility of the clubhouse. Clubhouses cannot serve as offices for social workers, either. A member's diagnosis has nothing to do with his or her status at the clubhouse. The members have to obey certain rules

Figure C.3. Fountain House, interior of lunchroom, 2004. Courtesy of Fountain House, New York City, New York.

(no fighting, for example) and some codes of polite behavior (keeping oneself clean), and they have to be responsible members of the club community. The goal of these clubhouses, of which there are now examples in operation in forty-four U.S. states, is to allow the psychiatrically disabled person to achieve his or her potential, although, of course, that potential varies widely.

For this architectural study, the key concept is that clubhouses are spatially separated from the person's home. Kenneth Dudek, executive director of Fountain House, explains that he told the renovation architect to strive to create the appearance and feeling of a small hotel.[40] Fountain House does indeed capture that quality—it is a bit like the communal areas of a hotel (living rooms, snack bar, and dining hall) without the bedrooms; the common areas of many hotels, in turn, resemble gentlemen's clubs. A club, whether for the elite or the needy, ought to look and feel different from a home.

The recovering person lives in one neighborhood and must travel to the clubhouse, which, located elsewhere in the city, serves as a provisional office. It is, quite simply, a place to go during the day. The movement through the city, from home to club and back again, is one of the first steps for a person learning to live outside a mental hospital. The separation of work from home also dilutes the institutional quality of the place.[41] The nonresidential clubhouse represents a significant improvement over the nineteenth-century spatial arrangements of the insane hospital, where, whether in a linear building or a cottage, the patient spent most of his or her time in the same few rooms, either on one hallway or in one cottage. As one Victorian critic admonished, "he will breathe the same air, occupy the same space, and be surrounded by the same objects, night and day."[42] This remark illustrates one early example of a doctor conceptualizing the trouble with the institution—but the idea was not pursued, and almost all asylums continued to combine the day and night quarters.

The clubhouses share some of the main ideas of moral management—that work and recreation serve as therapy, that attendants and doctors should be kind to patients. (I am not suggesting, however, that the clubhouse represents a return to nineteenth-century treatment. Indeed, clubhouses would not be possible without modern psychotropic medication.)[43] The living room of Fountain House, with its old-fashioned upholstered furniture, patterned rugs, and small piano, resembles the parlors of many an insane asylum. Gardening was a common therapeutic practice in the nineteenth century, and so it is now at Fountain House, where participants in the horticulture department maintain five hundred houseplants, travel to the city's flower market to purchase cut flowers (donated by a philanthropist), and make floral arrangements for each table in the dining room.

Green Door, a renovated Victorian house in Washington, D.C., is based on the clubhouse model, and it serves the same clientele as Fountain House: people attempting to make the transition from a psychiatric hospital to society, or people who are too psychiatrically disabled to exist alone. The architect for the renovation of Green Door, Thomas Kerns, relished the nooks and crannies of the old Victorian house, because he was hoping to create casual and irregular spaces for small groups to congregate, and to facilitate different types of social interaction (Figures C.4 and C.5).[44] As

Figure C.4. Green Door Clubhouse, Washington, D.C. Thomas Kerns, renovation architect. The Richardsonian Romanesque house, formerly known as the Werlich Mansion, was designed by Fuller and Wheeler of Albany in 1886. Courtesy of Green Door, Washington, D.C.

at Fountain House, the dining room is an important site for gathering. A window seat is a particularly cherished corner for a chat among club members. Kerns maintained the details—fireplace, tilework, moldings—and the members take evident pride in the unusual house. Green Door is the daily destination for about 100 people, while Fountain House hosts 350 visitors and members per day. The sheer volume of people makes wear and tear on the furniture and carpets an issue, especially since the designers are aiming for a genteel appearance. Elsewhere in the city, the Green Door organization manages ten group homes and thirty-one apartments. The clubhouse model makes the occupation of a single spot impossible. Traversing the city, to get from home to the store and back, or from home to

the clubhouse and back, requires the recovering patient to encounter other people and new spaces. The clubhouses provide daily activities that prepare people with a mental illness to work and live independently.

Psychiatrists today reject the artificiality and orderliness of institutions and adapt their treatments to patients who may well live at home. Indeed, the large majority of schizophrenics and Alzheimer's patients are cared for at home by family members.[45] This home-based care causes enormous pressure for the caregivers, who serve all the roles of all the employees in a nineteenth-century asylum: the caregiver, usually a woman, must be nurse, cook, and superintendent in one. Schizophrenia usually hits at the time of late teens or early twenties; thus parents face decades of caring for a grown child.

Figure C.5. Green Door Clubhouse, dining room. Thomas Kerns, renovation architect. Kerns maintained the Victorian character of the structure while adapting it to its use as a clubhouse for mentally ill adults. The renovation design received a merit award from the Washington, D.C., chapter of the American Institute of Architects in 1990. Courtesy of Green Door, Washington, D.C.

If a schizophrenic patient responds well to pharma-ceuticals, there may be no need to move the patient outside of the family home.[46]

Dementia, on the other hand, strikes later in life, and in these cases a younger family member tends to the needs of an older one. (Dementia refers to a set of symp-toms related to a cluster of diseases, the most common being Alzheimer's disease.) People with Alzheimer's usually die within seven to ten years of the onset of dementia; thus their stays in residential facilities are long but not decades long. The decision to finally move an elderly loved one out of the home is very painful for caretakers, who tend to assume that no care is bet-ter than that offered at home.[47] Memory loss and con-fusion are common symptoms of dementia, and one of the major problems for Alzheimer's patients is that they cannot orient themselves in space.[48] They may get lost in their own home or on their own street. Researchers have found that people with dementia are particularly vulnerable to environmental influences.[49] Experts in de-signing for demented elderly patients stress the impor-tance of creating a homelike environment, eschewing institutional images and materials.[50] Because demented patients do not adapt easily to change, "the homelike qualities of a setting take on added importance. If the environment seems familiar, residents are more likely to be able to understand and cope with the change of relocating to a new place to continue their lives."[51] Hospitals and nursing homes are often immediately disorienting, and thus advocates for homelike special-care facilities argue that the entry hall should be warm, friendly, and decrease confusion. Similarly, large spaces can be overwhelming and intimidating, so big rooms are broken down into conversation areas that are more likely to be used by residents and visitors.[52] One of the most prevalent and negative images of any institution is the long corridor with its seemingly endless sequence of doors; a creative solution for making an Alzheimer's facility homelike is to eliminate corridors, both single-loaded and double-loaded. Patients' rooms may open directly onto a living room or eat-in kitchen.[53] Many facilities include a "wandering path," often a loop. Inte-rior designers insist the blank white walls and identical

rows of bedroom doors opening off a long corridor cause sensory deprivation; color, texture, and pattern are desired. Architects are encouraged to design small, human-scaled interconnected units rather than mono-lithic hospitals, recalling the logic of the cottage plan experts in the second half of the nineteenth century. Focus on the therapeutic influence of nature is another aspect of nineteenth-century design that carries for-ward into modern-day environments for dementia: access to the outdoors and views to the outside are cherished values for special-care facility designers.

With some trepidation, I present a viewpoint at the end of this book that undermines one of the central ideas that launched me on this project: that architec-ture is important to the care of the mentally ill. I have noticed in my historical research and in conversations with doctors and patients that the staff of a mental health facility is crucial to its success. A lovely building with an uncaring staff will surely fail. A poorly designed building with an excellent staff stands a good chance of succeeding. During the course of my research for this book, although I was mostly focused on the architec-ture, taking photographs, and studying the archives, I was incidentally struck by the friendliness of the staff in influencing my impression of each place. I think any sensible person would choose to reside in an awkward building with a great staff, rather than a beautiful building with mean-spirited personnel. I hope that my readers will not think this statement relegates the envi-ronments to meaninglessness or makes them unworthy of this extended study. Orderly, handsome buildings lent prestige to the entire field of asylum medicine. The parlors, billiard rooms, croquet courts, and picturesque gardens may not have cured anyone of anything, but I propose that those amenities did more good than harm. On the other hand, this is ultimately a book about buildings, and it was sometimes hard to find a balance between the importance of the architecture and other historical factors. I was gently put in my place by a member of Fountain House who, upon learning that I was an architectural historian, said, "This building is not so interesting. The architecture here is the rebuild-ing of lives, lives that are broken."[54]

Appendixes

Appendix A

NOTE ON TERMINOLOGY

I have followed the example set by Lynn Gamwell and Nancy Tomes in *Madness in America: Cultural and Medical Perceptions of Mental Illness before 1914,* in that I have chosen to use terms as they were used in their historical context. As Gamwell and Tomes point out, the reader must approach the subject of terminology gingerly, as the meanings of words changed, and most terms were used loosely anyway. Often new words were introduced in order to lessen the stigma associated with mental illness.[1] Some historical words (lunatic, for example) may be jarring to modern readers, but to use modern terms exclusively would have left too much unstated. I have nonetheless used some generic modern terms, such as "the mentally ill" and "psychiatric hospital," because their meaning is clear to today's readers.

The Buildings

Doctors preferred the term "hospital for the insane" to describe the buildings that housed the mentally ill, because the word "hospital" suggested that mental illness was a disease. The buildings were called "madhouses" in the eighteenth century and at the start of the nineteenth century, but this usage declined as the nineteenth century wore on. "Asylum" was widely used throughout the nineteenth century, and it suggested a refuge from the pressures of civilization. "Insane asylum" did not accrue negative associations until the end of the century.[2] The York Retreat in England and the Hartford Retreat in Connecticut used the term "retreat" just as we would understand it today—as a haven. The idea of health is indicated in the words "sanitarium" and "sanatorium," which did not come into usage until the second half of the nineteenth century; since the terms often refer to other types of establishments that offered medically supervised recuperation, such as those for tuberculosis, I chose not to use the terms here. By 1900, other phrases such as "center for nervous diseases" crept into the language. Today we use "psychiatric hospital" to denote institutions in which the seriously mentally ill are treated. A modern-day psychiatric ward is an area within a medical hospital that is designated for the care of the mentally ill. Psychiatric hospitals often operate as confining facilities. Not all the patients wished to be confined: "elopement" was the Victorian word for an escape from the asylum. Kirkbride disliked the word "asylum," as he wrote to Dorothea Dix, at a moment when the New Jersey legislature had refused further funding for the New Jersey State Lunatic Asylum: "I have regretted that their legislature failed to make the proper appropriations for extending the Asylum—I never write the word for the Trenton Institution that I do not regret that it cannot be called what it really is—a *hospital*."[3]

The Patients

The term "patient" was used in the same way then as now. The term "lunatic" actually had a legal definition in addition to its vernacular usage; it implied that the person was unable to conduct civil transactions. "Madmen" was also used to describe people, but it had an air of contempt about it, and doctors avoided it. Doctors used "the insane" to refer to the whole class of medical patients who were mentally alienated. Of course, colloquial language included countless insulting terms that do not bear repeating. Doctors did not use modern euphemisms such as "client," "customer," or "guest," although they often referred to "sufferers." "Inmate" appears in the annual reports and other documents without hint of negative association.

The Illness

There were many terms for what we now call mental illness—that is, any of a wide range of conditions characterized by loss of emotional or behavioral functioning. General terms included "madness," "lunacy," "insanity," "mental alienation," "mental derangement," "mental instability," and, later in the nineteenth century, "nervous disorder." The word "lunacy" derived from the ancient idea that occasional derangement was related to the phases of the moon, but doctors mocked this superstitious belief, even though they continued to use the term. The term lunacy frequently appeared in newspapers and literature, as did "madness." Gamwell and Tomes explain that madness was a vernacular term indicating "wildness, lack of restraint by reason, and loss of emotional control."[4] "Mania" and "frenzy" were used to describe furious, passionate rages. "Craziness" appears in colloquial language but not in medical journals. Mental illness was also described with adjectives set before "mind," such as "disturbed mind," "unsound mind," "troubled mind," and "unbalanced mind." Most of today's historians of

psychiatry shy away from attaching modern medical terms to the precise afflictions of nineteenth-century individuals; even so, historians conclude that patients in psychiatric hospitals suffered from serious mental illnesses, and the symptoms of diseases such as modern-day schizophrenia, bipolar disorder, psychotic depression, postpartum depression, and other severe forms of depression are evident in descriptions. Many asylum dwellers experienced delusions and hallucinations. "Refractory wards" were for those who were "frantic," "filthy," "obscene," or "profane."[5]

The Doctors

The people in charge of asylums were considered a type of physician or doctor; they were variously called "mad-doctors," "asylum doctors," "asylum superintendents," and "alienists." "Alienist" was derived from the term "mental alienation." Today alienist has a narrower definition: a psychiatrist who specializes in the legal aspects of mental disorders. For example, an alienist would be asked to determine a defendant's sanity or capacity to stand trial. Reformers referred to the body of knowledge they produced and legitimated as "asylum medicine," and they liked to be called "asylum doctors" or "asylum superintendents." The *place* where they worked dominated the name of their profession, reminding one of "factory worker" or "zoo keeper." The word "psychiatrist," referring to a physician who specializes in the diagnosis, treatment, and prevention of mental and emotional disorders, is derived from Psyche, the goddess of the soul; the term "psychiatrist" appeared first in Germany, and later in the United States and Great Britain, in the middle of the nineteenth century. Neurologists distinguished themselves from psychiatrists by seeking biological causes for nervous disorders. It was not until the twentieth century that the lexicon offered up words such as "analyst," "psychotherapist," and "headshrinker."

Appendix B

OCCUPATIONS OF PATIENTS IN 1850

Annual reports typically listed the occupations of patients. These lists offer an interesting, though flawed, glimpse at the social classes of patients. The merchants, clerks, teachers, and clergy represented here indicate the presence of middle-class patients. An occupation like "farmer" could cover many social levels. This list comes from the *Annual Report* at Trenton (1850), 22. The superintendent added a note to this chart commenting that the large number of farmers should not be misinterpreted: the agrarian life was still the best for mental health, and the high number of farmers merely reflected the high number of agricultural workers living in the vicinity of the hospital. For more on the social classes of asylum patients and the limits of using lists of occupations, see Nancy Tomes, *The Art of Asylum-Keeping,* 190.

Occupation	Men	Women	Total
Farmer	30		30
Farming	14		14
Laborer	6		6
Housekeeper		41	41
Housework		24	24
Shoemaker	4		4
Tailor	6		6
Merchant	3		3
Mason	2		2
Bookkeeper	1		1
Milliner		2	2
Weaver	1	1	2
Chair maker	1		1
Carpenter	3		3
Clerk	4		4
Painter	1		1
Teacher	2	1	3

Occupation	Men	Women	Total
Brick maker	1		1
Gold chain solderer		1	1
Piano forte manufacturer	1		1
Cabinet maker	2		2
Miller	1		1
Nurse		1	1
Student	1		1
Cooper	1		1
Artificial flower maker	1	1	2
Mantua maker (dressmaker)		2	2
Factory worker	1	1	2
Turner	1		1
Clergy	2		2
Blacksmith	2		2
Milkman	1		1
Writing master	1		1
Ship carpenter	1		1
Seamstress		1	1
Unknown	6	4	10
Total	101	80	181

Appendix C

COST OF LUNATIC ASYLUMS IN 1877

This list is based on a chart published in 1877 by Hervey B. Wilbur, an opponent of expensive insane hospitals. Wilbur summarized his findings by stating that on average these buildings cost $2,600 per bed, not including land or furniture, which was far more expensive than a luxury hotel. From *Buildings for the Insane, A Report* (Boston: Albert J. Wright, 1877), 13–14. This information was presented at the Saratoga Conference of Charities on September 6, 1877.

Location of Asylum	Number of Patients	Cost in Dollars
Worcester, Masschusetts	450	$1,250,000
Danvers, Massachusetts	450	1,600,000
Middletown, Connecticut	450	600,000
Poughkeepsie, New York	600	2,000,000
Buffalo, New York	500	1,800,000
Middletown, New York	300	900,000
Morristown, New Jersey	800	2,500,000
Danville, Pennsylvania	500	1,000,000
Maryland	300	803,000
Kentucky	375	162,000
Columbus, Ohio	900	1,800,000
Athens, Ohio	600	950,000
Kalamazoo, Michigan	580	653,000
Anna, Illinois	450	534,000
Oshkosh, Wisconsin	500	552,000
Iowa	300	600,000
St. Peter, Minnesota	500	480,000
Missouri	250	209,000
Nebraska	80	113,000
Napa, California	900	1,000,000
Total	9,785	$19,506,000

Appendix D
COMPARATIVE SIZES OF ASYLUMS, 1770–1872

These five lunatic asylums have been redrawn to one scale, thus showing the increase in overall size of such hospitals over the course of the late eighteenth and nineteenth centuries. The following asylums are shown here:

A. Public Hospital, Williamsburg, Virginia, 1770. 100 feet. From scale on drawing, Library of Virginia (Figure 1.15).

B. New Jersey State Lunatic Asylum, Trenton, 1847. 480 feet (before additions). From *Annual Report*, 1848.

C. St. Elizabeths Hospital, Washington, D.C., 1852. 750 feet. From Millikan, "Wards of the Nation," 10.

D. Greystone, Morristown, New Jersey, 1872. 1,243 feet. From *Commission to Select a Site and Build an Asylum*, 1872.

E. Buffalo State Hospital for the Insane, Buffalo, New York, begun 1871. 2,200 feet. From *Papers of Frederick Law Olmsted*, 6: 455.

A.

B.

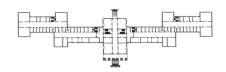

C.

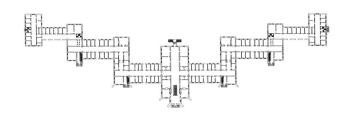

D.

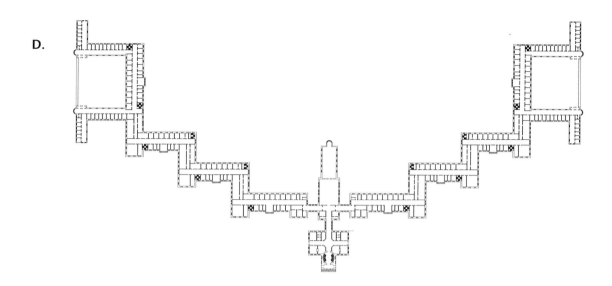

E.

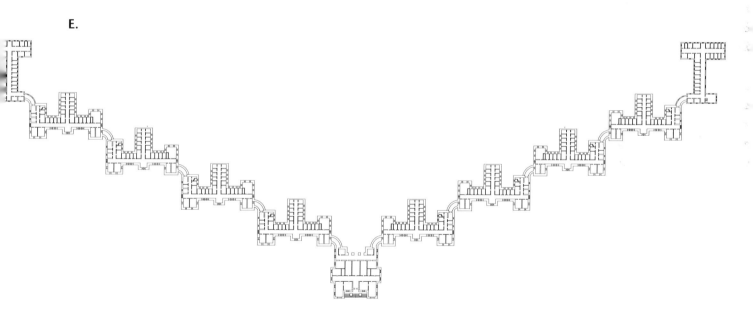

Notes

Introduction

1. *Annual Report* (Trenton), 1853, 13. The year listed for annual reports will be the year discussed in the report, not the year of publication, which is usually one year later than the report.

2. Porter, *Mind-Forg'd Manacles*, 16.

3. Porter, *Madness*, 4.

4. Similar lists may be found in the annual reports of many asylums, but this example is derived from *Annual Report* (Trenton), 1849, 23. Moran has analyzed indications of lunacy based on legal documents in "Historical Epidemiology of Insanity," 286.

5. Horwitz, *Creating Mental Illness*, 43.

6. Dwyer, *Homes for the Mad*, 69.

7. *Annual Report* (Morristown), 1876, 19.

8. Stearns, "The Relations of Insanity to Modern Civilization," 586. Stearns was the superintendent of the Hartford Retreat.

9. Ibid., 586.

10. Rothman, *The Discovery of the Asylum*, 112.

11. Tuke, "Does Civilization Favour the Generation of Mental Disease?" *Journal of Mental Science*, 4 (1857): 94, cited in Altschule, *Roots of Modern Psychiatry*, 122.

12. Hurd, *The Institutional Care of the Insane in the United States and Canada*, 1:373.

13. Stearns, "Relations of Insanity to Modern Civilization," 586.

14. Rosenberg, *Care of Strangers*, 4.

15. Grob, *The Mad among Us*, 24.

16. Ibid., 118.

17. Fox, *So Far Disordered in Mind*, 119.

18. Porter, *Mind-Forg'd Manacles*, 119–20.

19. Scull, *Social Order/Mental Disorder*, 242.

20. Scull, *The Most Solitary of Afflictions*, 352–55.

21. Galt, "The Farm of St. Anne," 354.

22. Seymour, "Observations on the Medical Treatment of Insanity," reprinted in Galt, *The Treatment of Insanity*, 203.

23. Scull, *Undertaker of the Mind*, 147.

24. Grob, *Mad among Us*, 80.

25. Grob, *Mental Illness*, 10.

26. Moran, "Asylum in the Community," 218.

27. Ibid., 219. See also the collected essays about British and Irish contexts in Bartlett and Wright, *Outside the Walls of the Asylum*.

28. Burdett, *Hospitals and Asylums of the World*, 1:536.

29. Wright, "Getting Out of the Asylum," 154.

30. Melling and Forsythe, *Insanity, Institutions, and Society*, 4.

31. Stevenson, *Medicine and Magnificence*, 210.

32. Porter, *Madness*, 116.

33. Battie, "Treatise on Madness," 68.

34. Rothman, *Discovery of the Asylum*, 133.

35. Woods, "Thomas Jefferson and the University of Virginia," 277.

36. O'Malley, "'Your Garden Must Be a Museum to You,'" 210.

37. John de Crèvecoeur, "Letters from an American Farmer," originally published in 1782, reprint, edited with an introduction by Albert Stone, 1981, 71, cited in O'Malley, "'Your Garden Must Be a Museum to You,'" 210.

38. Ibid.

39. Beveridge, "Frederick Law Olmsted's Theory of Landscape Design," 40.

40. Galt, "The Farm of St. Anne," 356.

41. Henry M. Hurd, an institutional psychiatrist himself, was the most important Whiggish historian who wrote about American mental hospitals. For an excellent summary of historiographical issues, see Moran, *Committed to the State Asylum*.

42. Scull, "A Failure to Communicate?" 157.

43. Ibid.

44. Horwitz, *Creating Mental Illness*, 1.

45. Wright, "Getting Out of the Asylum," 145.

46. Melling and Forsythe, *Insanity, Institutions, and Society*, 2.

47. Scull, *Social Order/Mental Disorder*, 12.

48. Two notable exceptions are historian Edward Shorter, who argues that psychiatric illness is a biological phenomenon, only

slightly affected by social definitions, and E. Fuller Torrey, M.D., a practicing psychiatrist, research scientist, and author, who believes that mental illness is entirely caused by biological factors. Both Shorter and Torrey claim that insanity increased over the past two hundred years; Torrey calls the increase an epidemic. The research institution that he manages is searching for a cure for schizophrenia and bipolar disorder by conducting basic neurological research. Shorter, *A History of Psychiatry*, and Torrey and Miller, *The Invisible Plague*.

49. Rothman, *Discovery of the Asylum*, xvii.

50. Ibid., 151.

51. Ibid., 133.

52. Ibid., 152.

53. Moran, "Asylum in Community," 224.

54. Ibid., 229.

55. Ibid., 235.

56. Hurd, *The Institutional Care of the Insane*. I reached these numbers by counting the entries in Hurd's table of contents.

57. Another line of inquiry, beyond the scope of this book, would be to study the oeuvres of architects who designed insane hospitals, to see if these practitioners made themselves into specialists or to identify personal variations on the type.

58. Van Slyck, *Free to All*, xxi.

59. Burdett, *Hospitals and Asylums of the World*, 2:59.

60. Conolly, *The Construction and Government of Lunatic Asylums and Hospitals for the Insane*, 34.

61. I also wrote little about buildings that are covered well by medical historians, such as the Worcester State Hospital. See Grob, *The State and the Mentally Ill*.

62. The Health Insurance Portability and Accountability Act, a patient confidentiality law passed in 2001, has made it difficult for anyone other than a family member to view unredacted patient records, thus restricting historians' access to these materials.

63. In *Homes for the Mad*, Dwyer made sure to give patients a voice, but her study of two hospitals, which focused on patient records and firsthand accounts, yields limited information about architecture.

64. Fairless, *Suggestions concerning the Construction of Asylums for the Insane*, 7.

1. Transforming the Treatment

1. Andrews et al., *The History of Bethlem*, 115.

2. Ibid., 204.

3. Ibid., 152.

4. Stevenson, "The Architecture of Bethlem at Moorfields," in ibid., 241.

5. Stevenson, *Medicine and Magnificence*, 34.

6. Andrews et al., *Bethlem*, 209.

7. Ibid., 215.

8. *Annual Report* (Poughkeepsie), 1871, 20.

9. *Annual Report* (Buffalo), 1885, 30.

10. Stevenson, *Medicine and Magnificence*, 206.

11. Ibid., 54.

12. Ibid., 61.

13. Andrews et al., *Bethlem*, 183.

14. Ibid., 193.

15. Ibid.

16. Stevenson, *Medicine and Magnificence*, 100.

17. Soane, *Memoirs of the Professional Life of an Architect between the Years 1768 and 1835* (London, 1835), cited in Brownell and Cohen, *The Architectural Drawings of Benjamin Henry Latrobe*, 2:9.

18. Stevenson, *Medicine and Magnificence*, 104.

19. Ibid., 206.

20. Reid, *Observations on the Structure of Hospitals for the Treatment of Lunatics*, 10–11.

21. Stevenson, *Medicine and Magnificence*, 210.

22. John Thompson and Grace Goldin refer to Stark's plan as "panoptical," but throughout their book they use the term "panoptical" to refer to cross-shaped plans. Stark's plan was actually a Greek cross, or four-armed radial plan, inscribed within a circle. Thompson and Goldin, *The Hospital*, 40.

23. Ibid., 54.

24. Brown, "Report of an Examination of Certain European Institutions for the Insane," 212.

25. Again, Thompson and Goldin claimed that Tuke would have "preferred a panoptical design," but by this they probably meant cross-shaped. Thompson and Goldin, *The Hospital*, 72. It is true that Samuel Tuke called Stark's Greek cross plan for the Glasgow Asylum "ingenious" (Tuke, *Description of the Retreat*, 106), but he did not specifically report that his grandfather would have preferred a cross-shaped plan. In this book, the term "panopticon" will be reserved for round buildings with towers at the center as specified by Jeremy Bentham.

26. Porter, *Mind-Forg'd Manacles*, 147.

27. Thompson and Goldin, *The Hospital*, 74.

28. Tuke, *Retreat*, 106

29. Ibid., 96.

30. Grob, *Mental Institutions in America*, 16.

31. Nineteenth-century American and British doctors debated restraining inmates; the British were more reluctant to use straitjackets and other devices, and they disparaged their American counterparts for relying heavily on mechanical restraints. See Nancy Tomes, "The Great Restraint Controversy," in Bynum, Porter, and Shepherd, eds., *Anatomy of Madness*, 191–225.

32. Sloane and Conant Sloane, *Medicine Moves to the Mall*, 36.

33. For a redrawn plan of the Pennsylvania Hospital, see ibid., 18.

34. Malin, *Some Account of the Pennsylvania Hospital*, 14, 17.

35. Ibid., 11.

36. Ibid., 12.

37. Ibid., 8.

38. Grob, *Mental Institutions in America: Social Policy to 1875*, 23.

39. Ibid., 25, quoting Francis Fauquier of 1766.

40. Thomas Jefferson, "Notes on the State of Virginia," in Roth, *America Builds*, 23.

41. Peterson, Greiff, and Thompson, *Robert Smith*, 134. See also McDonald, *Design for Madness*.

42. Kisacky, "An Architecture of Light and Air," 35.

43. Digby, *Madness, Morality, and Medicine*, 249.

44. The first building on the Friends Asylum site has been attributed to William Strickland in Tatman and Moss, *Biographical Dictionary of Philadelphia Architects*, 768. The structure has also been

attributed to Thomas Scattergood, a Quaker minister who was familiar with the York Retreat. Other scholars give credit to Isaac Bonsall, the asylum's first director.

45. Waln, *An Account of the Asylum for the Insane.*

46. McCandless, *Moonlight, Magnolias, and Madness,* 56.

47. Ibid., 57.

48. Bryan, *Robert Mills,* 179. Mills also built jails in Lancaster, S.C., Union, S.C., and Washington, D.C., plus a prison in Mount Holly, N.J.

49. Gallagher, *Robert Mills,* 54.

50. Bryan, *Robert Mills,* quoting Mills, *Statistics of South Carolina,* 704–5.

51. Liscombe, *Altogether American,* 122.

52. Bryan, *Mills,* quoting Mills, *Statistics of South Carolina,* 704–5.

53. Bryan, *Mills,* 182.

54. Tomes, *The Art of Asylum-Keeping,* 44.

55. Minutes of the Board of Managers, Pennsylvania Hospital Archives, volume 9, 1833–58, 190.

56. The term "pavilion" was used in numerous ways in the nineteenth century. Among asylum builders, the term referred to a two- or three-story building within a larger structure. In medical hospitals, the term pavilion was more precise, referring to a long thin structure, with windows on two sides, that was unencumbered on three sides. Such a pavilion was usually also part of a larger hospital.

57. *Annual Report* (Philadelphia), 1841, 8. The stone came from a quarry in Valley Forge, outside Philadelphia. Minutes of the Board of Managers, Pennsylvania Hospital Archives, volume 9, 1833–58, 190.

58. Ibid., 12.

59. Tomes, *The Art of Asylum-Keeping,* 117.

60. *Annual Report* (Philadelphia), 1841, 9–12.

61. Ibid.

62. Woods, "Thomas Jefferson and the University of Virginia," 277.

63. Brownell and Cohen, *The Architectural Drawings of Benjamin Henry Latrobe,* 2:538.

64. Grob, *State and the Mentally Ill,* 28.

65. Bagg, *The Pioneers of Utica,* 400, and Jones, *Annals and Recollections of Oneida County,* 594. There were two other commissioners, Francis E. Spinner and Elam Lynds. I thank Sandra Markham for guidance on this and many subjects.

66. Kirkbride, MS journal of "Visit to 9 Institutions for the Insane," 1845. Pennsylvania Hospital Archives.

67. Bagg, *Pioneers of Utica,* 400.

68. Hitchcock, *Architecture,* 86.

69. "Brief Description of the State Lunatic Asylum at Utica, N.Y."

70. Schuyler, *Apostle of Taste,* 78–79.

71. Ibid., 79. According to Schuyler, the reason why the managers chose the axial composition remains "unexplained in surviving documents." George B. Tatum noted that "until disease destroyed the stately elms, it proved every bit as majestic as Downing predicted." Tatum, "Nature's Gardener," in Tatum and MacDougall, *Prophet with Honor,* 70.

72. *Annual Report* (Utica), 1845, 13.

73. Bucknill, *Notes on Asylums for the Insane,* 38.

74. Brownell and Cohen, *The Architectural Drawings of Benjamin Henry Latrobe,* 2:98–112.

75. In a later postscript, Bentham relaxed his views on solitary confinement, allowing two persons to a cell. Bentham, *Panopticon,* 38.

76. Nicoletta, "The Architecture of Control," 375.

77. Johnston, *Forms of Constraint,* 75.

78. Ibid.

79. Ibid., 77.

80. Ibid., 71.

81. Ibid., 74. See also Nicoletta, "Architecture of Control," 375.

82. Johnston, *Forms of Constraint,* 71.

83. As Johnston explains, a proposal for a radial plan lunatic asylum for London is attributed to James Bevans, architect of the York Retreat. The proposal from 1814 was never built. Ibid., 56.

84. Bucknill, *Notes,* 19.

85. Earle, *A Visit to Thirteen Asylums,* 20.

86. Brown, "Report of an Examination of Certain European Institutions for the Insane," 203.

87. Ibid., 212.

2. Establishing the Type

1. Tomes, *Art of Asylum-Keeping,* 130.

2. Gollaher, *Voice for the Mad,* 195.

3. Buttolph, "Modern Asylums," 364.

4. Tomes, *Art of Asylum-Keeping,* 209.

5. Buttolph, "New Jersey State Lunatic Asylum," 3.

6. Kirkbride, *On the Construction,* 136.

7. "Report on the Construction of Hospitals for the Insane," 79–81. This report listed the propositions that had been voted into effect at the AMSAII's June 18, 1850, meeting.

8. Greiff, *John Notman,* 103. On the Trenton asylum, see also Coolidge, "The Architectural Importance of H. H. Richardson's Buffalo State Hospital," 88–90.

9. Greiff, *John Notman,* 103, quoting the *Pennsylvania Journal of Prison Discipline and Philanthropy* (1846): 60. In 1855–59, Notman oversaw a major renovation of Princeton's Nassau Hall; he did not build any other asylums after the one in Trenton.

10. *Annual Report* (Williamsburg), 1844, 25.

11. Moran, "Asylum in the Community," analyzes legal documents to reveal the intersection of community care, asylum life, and family decision making in pre–Civil War New Jersey.

12. Kirkbride, *On the Construction,* 1.

13. Grob, *Mental Illness,* 53.

14. *Annual Report* (Trenton), 1851, 31.

15. Scull, *Social Order/Mental Disorder,* 55.

16. Kisacky, "An Architecture of Light and Air," 106.

17. *Annual Report* (Trenton), 1853, 13.

18. Browne, *What Asylums Were, Are, and Ought to Be,* 182.

19. Ibid.

20. Buttolph, "New Jersey State Lunatic Asylum," 6.

21. Taylor, *The Architect and the Pavilion Hospital,* 59.

22. Buttolph, "New Jersey State Lunatic Asylum," 6.

23. Downing, *Cottage Residences,* as noted in Schuyler, *Apostle of Taste,* 63.

24. Downing, "A Chapter on School Houses," 395; quoted in Tatum, "Nature's Gardener," 78, and Schuyler, *Apostle of Taste,* 79.

25. Downing, *A Treatise on the Theory and Practice of Landscape Gardening*, 307–8.

26. Hawkins, *Made Whole*, 6.

27. Harold Cooledge notes that the "majority" of the building was "greatly altered," and, indeed, the center main was changed. But otherwise the building appears much as it did in early photographs. Cooledge, *Samuel Sloan*, 171.

28. Thompson and Goldin illustrated the sample asylum from Kirkbride's book, but labeled it the Alabama Insane Hospital. In 1891, Burdett described this asylum as an example of what in his terminology was the "corridor type." He did not much like this plan, because the double-loaded corridors and the offset wards did not offer sufficient ventilation, water closets were too close to the wards, and the ward hallways lacked bay windows. Burdett, *Hospitals and Asylums*, 2:94.

29. *Independent Monitor* (Tuscaloosa), June 25, 1857.

30. *Independent Monitor* (Tuscaloosa), June 25, 1857.

31. Ray, "American Hospitals for the Insane," 66.

32. There is some confusion about single rooms in American asylums: I believe the source of the confusion to be nineteenth-century alienist Isaac Ray, who promoted the ideal of single rooms for all patients. He is quoted in Elaine Showalter's *The Female Malady;* she then extrapolated the idea of single rooms to contrast American and British approaches to the treatment of the insane. Ray's ideal was not carried out in practice, so the comparison does not hold. British, American, and Canadian lunatic hospitals employed a mix of single and shared bedrooms. Conolly, *The Construction and Government of Lunatic Asylums,* 181–83, illustrates three asylums: the asylum at Derby housed approximately two-thirds of its inmates in singles and the rest in shared bedrooms. Conolly also illustrated the asylum in Kingston, Jamaica, which had singles as well as rooms for three, four, and ten beds. The same was true for the asylum in Halifax, Nova Scotia, which included a double-loaded hallway with singles on one side and shared bedrooms on the other.

33. Kirkbride, *On the Construction*, 2nd ed., 281.

34. Gamwell and Tomes, *Madness in America*, 56.

35. Sankey, "Do the Public Asylums of England, as at present Constructed, afford the Greatest Facilities for the Care and Treatment of the Insane?" 472.

36. Arlidge, *On the State of Lunacy and the Legal Provision for the Insane*, 202.

37. *Annual Report* (Tuscaloosa), 1872, 25.

38. Grob, *Mental Institutions in America*, 252. An exception was John M. Galt, of the Eastern Virginia State Hospital, who attempted to integrate wards in the 1850s.

39. Weaver, "Survival at the Alabama Insane Hospital," 27.

40. *Annual Report* (Tuscaloosa), 1878, cited in ibid., 18.

41. Brown, "Report," 213.

42. Cooledge, *Samuel Sloan*, 115.

43. Haskell, *The Trial of Ebenezer Haskell*, 25.

44. Ibid., 54.

45. Ibid., 45.

46. Ibid., 54.

47. Delilez, *The True Cause of Insanity Explained*, 146.

48. Scull, *Social Order/Mental Disorder*, 226.

49. Haskell, *The Trial of Ebenezer Haskell*, 43.

50. Ibid., 45.

51. Delilez, *The True Cause of Insanity Explained*, 136.

52. Packard, *The Prisoners' Hidden Life*, 59.

53. Ibid., 66.

54. Ibid., 68.

55. Packard was found "not insane" in a trial, and she spent the last years of her life living with one of her children and crusading for the rights of women.

56. Packard, *The Prisoners' Hidden Life*, 90.

57. Letter, Nichols to Dix, September 20, 1852. Dix Papers, Houghton Library, Harvard. Quoted in Millikan, "Wards of the Nation," 32.

58. Davis, "On the Bill to Organize an Institution for the Insane," 360–61.

59. Tiffany, *The Life of Dorothea Lynde Dix*, 154.

60. Senate. Ex. Doc II(32-2), serial 660; quoted in Millikan, "Wards of the Nation," 12.

61. Letter, Kirkbride to Dix, October 26, 1852, Kirkbride Papers, Pennsylvania Hospital Archives.

62. Nichols to Dix, August 15, 1853. Dix Papers, Houghton Library, Harvard, quoted in Millikan, "Wards of the Nation," 52.

63. Walter built several institutional buildings during his career, including Wills Hospital for the Blind and Lame, the Philadelphia City Prison in Moyamensing, Chester County Prison, the university buildings that later formed Bucknell, and the Pennsylvania Medical College.

64. Bucknill, *Notes*, 35.

65. Bird, "St Elizabeths Historic Resources Management Plan," section 3, 14.

66. "Proceedings," *American Journal of Insanity* 12 (July 1855): 89.

67. Ibid.

68. Bucknill, *Notes*, 35.

69. Gamwell and Tomes, *Madness in America*, 59.

70. Hurd, *The Institutional Care of the Insane*, 1:373. Hurd was quoting William Drewry, superintendent of the Central State Hospital for the Insane in Virginia, who made the comment in 1908.

71. Burdett, *Hospitals and Asylums of the World*, 2:ix. Annmarie Adams notes that around the turn of the twentieth century, and in the case of technologically advanced medical hospitals, architects like Edward Stevens were hired because of their expertise with planning, modern materials, and constructional techniques. Adams, "Modernism and Medicine." I agree with Jeremy Taylor's position that the pavilion plan hospital was necessarily constraining and "potentially stifling." Taylor, *The Architect and the Pavilion Hospital*, 30. Taylor's contribution is to explore the fascinating ways that architects worked *within* the constraints of the typology.

72. Tomes, *Art of Asylum-Keeping*, 129.

73. Kirkbride, "Description of the Pleasure Grounds," 348.

74. Gamwell and Tomes, *Madness in America*, 35.

75. Although it is commonly assumed there were more women than men in asylums, the numbers were about even. At the Pennsylvania Hospital for the Insane, between the years 1841 and 1883, 54 percent of the patients were male and 46 percent were female. Tomes, *Art of Asylum-Keeping*, 190.

76. *Annual Report* (Trenton), 1853, 16.

77. Delilez, *The True Cause of Insanity Explained*, 141.

78. *Annual Report* (Philadelphia), Pennsylvania Hospital for the Insane, 1844, 24.

79. *Annual Report* (Trenton), 1850, 29.

80. "Ball of Lunatics at the Asylum, Blackwell's Island," *Frank Leslie's Illustrated Newspaper*, December 9, 1865, 188.

81. Wilkins, *Insanity and Insane Asylums*, 108.

82. Charles Dickens, "American Notes," 99.

83. Cooledge, *Samuel Sloan*, 10.

84. Sloan, "Hospital for the Insane, St. Peter Hospital, Minnesota," 712.

85. Ibid., 715.

86. Hunter and Macalpine, *Psychiatry for the Poor*, 15.

87. Scull, *Mental Order/Social Disorder*, 234. In 1937, Colney Hatch's name was changed to Friern Hospital to dissociate the institution from its grim past.

88. Cooledge reported that Sloan received commissions for thirty-two lunatic asylums (Placzek, *Macmillan Encyclopedia of Architects*, vol. 4). To reach that number, Cooledge presumably counted some of Sloan's closely related institutional buildings, such as the Pennsylvania Training School for Feeble-Minded Children of 1857 or the west wing of the South Carolina Institute for the Deaf and Blind of 1884. The following list of buildings and projects, designated by town name and state, is restricted to institutions specifically for the insane that are confirmed Sloan designs: Pennsylvania Hospital for the Insane, with Holden, 1838; Tuscaloosa, Alabama, 1852; additions to Augusta, Maine, 1851–53; Pennsylvania Hospital for the Insane, Department for Males, 1856; additions to Trenton, New Jersey, 1855; Jacksonville, Illinois, west wing, 1857; Middletown, Connecticut, 1868; St. Peter, Minnesota, 1867; Indianapolis, 1866; second hospital in Indianapolis, for Women's Department, 1875; Morristown, New Jersey (Greystone), 1872–76; second hospital at Kalamazoo; addition to Raleigh, North Carolina (Dix Hill), 1874; Insane Department, addition to Blockley Almshouse, Philadelphia, 1870; Morganton, North Carolina, 1875; addition to campus of asylum for Columbia, South Carolina (Babcock Building), 1883; competition entry for Sheppard Asylum, Baltimore, Maryland, 1859.

3. Breaking Down

1. Scull, *Decarceration*, 112, 107.

2. Grob, *Mental Institutions in America*, 188.

3. Wright, "Getting Out of the Asylum," 154.

4. Grob, *Mental Institutions in America*, 188.

5. Wright, "Getting Out of the Asylum," 138, 143.

6. Dwyer, *Homes for the Mad*, 2.

7. *Annual Report* (Ovid), 1869, 13.

8. Ibid., 17.

9. Watrous, *The County between the Lakes*, 307. I thank Brian Clancy for his sharp eye with respect to this institution.

10. The brick main building projected a palatial quality, and the striking curved passages that connected its flanking structures to the main building recall precedents such as Palladio's Villa Badoer at Fratta Polesine (Book 2, 1556/7-63) and Robert Adam's Kedleston Hall of 1765.

11. *Annual Report* (Ovid), 1869, 17. Dwyer, *Homes for the Mad*, 3. She described Willard as "a central administrative unit and a large number of three-story detached cottages" (9).

12. The *Independent* (Ovid), June 30, 1875; quoted in Watrous, *The County between the Lakes*, 306.

13. Dewey, *Recollections of Richard Dewey*, 131.

14. Burdett, *Hospitals and Asylums of the World*, 2:59, 64–65. Burdett listed Willard among fifty-five "irregular or conglomerate" planned asylums in the United States.

15. For example, in 1872 at the ceremony for laying the cornerstone of the Buffalo State Asylum for the Insane, the governor of New York pronounced that "insanity is now conceded to be a curable disease in about seventy per cent of the cases properly treated in its first stages." *Proceedings in Connection with the Laying of the Cornerstone of the Buffalo State Asylum for the Insane* (Buffalo: 1872), 10.

16. Grob, *Mental Institutions*, 182.

17. *Annual Report* (Middletown, Conn.), 1877, 228.

18. Earle, "Provision for the Insane," 53.

19. Galt, "Farm of St. Anne," 354.

20. Grob, *State and Mentally Ill*, 211.

21. Like all tales of the saints, there are several versions of this story. William Parry-Jones gives the account I have repeated here in "The Model of the Geel Lunatic Colony," 201.

22. Ibid., 202.

23. Moore, "What Gheel Means to Me," 36.

24. Byrne, *Gheel*, 28.

25. Parry-Jones, "The Model of the Geel Lunatic Colony," 204.

26. Ibid.

27. Byrne, *Gheel*, 85.

28. Galt, "The Farm of St. Anne," 352.

29. McCandless, "Build! Build!" 561.

30. Earle, "A Visit to Gheel," 74.

31. Ibid., 75.

32. Parry-Jones, "The Model of the Geel Lunatic Colony," 206.

33. [Gray], "Hospital and Cottage Systems for the Care of the Insane," 83.

34. Ibid., 84–85. This essay, probably authored by John P. Gray, appears as an introduction to the article by John B. Tuke on cottages in Scotland, "The Cottage System of Management of Lunatics as Practiced in Scotland."

35. Ibid., 94.

36. Burdett, *Hospitals and Asylums of the World*, 1:128.

37. Grob, *Mad among Us*, 167.

38. Brown, "Report," 213.

39. Grob, *Mental Institutions in America*, 328. Illinois Board of State Commissioners of Public Charities, *Biennial Report* (1869/70), 82–85. Whittingham asylum was yet another model.

40. Grob, *State and the Mentally Ill*, 210. Bemis was the doctor to whom Richardson referred in his sketchbook, as discussed in chapter 4.

41. Scull, *Decarceration*, 113.

42. Galt, "Farm of St. Anne," 356; Lee, "Provision for the Insane Poor," 14.

43. Grob, *Mad among Us*, 111.

44. Grob, *State and the Mentally Ill*, 220.

45. Ibid., 223.

46. The phrase "a village for the insane" appeared in a celebratory pamphlet produced in conjunction with the World's Columbian Exposition, possibly handed out to fairgoers at the Illinois State

Pavilion. Board of World's Fair Commissioners, *Committee on State Charitable Institutions*, 6.

47. Grob, *Mental Institutions in America*, 324.

48. Illinois Board of State Commissioners of Public Charities, *Biennial Report*, I (1869–70), 95.

49. Grob, *Mad among Us*, 113.

50. "James Rowland Willett. F.A.I.A.," *Quarterly Bulletin of Obituaries* 8 (1907): 105–6. Willett's partner's name appears on the bird's-eye drawing, but he is not recognized in the annual reports.

51. "Obituary, James R. Willett," *Inland Architect and News Record* (May 1907): 1.

52. Willett, "Architect's Report," in *Annual Report* (Kankakee), 1878, 11.

53. Burdett, *Hospitals and Asylums of the World*, 1:127.

54. Board of World's Fair Commissioners, *Committee on State Charitable Institutions*, 8.

55. Turner, *Campus*, 21, 23. By 1655, Harvard had four buildings.

56. Ibid., 37.

57. Horowitz, *Alma Mater*, 30.

58. Kowsky, *Country, Park and City*, 30. After Downing's death, Vaux designed a second house for Vassar. Kowsky maintains that Vaux also built a log cabin on the grounds of Vassar's estate (74).

59. Milo P. Jewett, "Origin of Vassar College," March 1879, typed copy, 5, Vassar College Library, Poughkeepsie, N.Y.; quoted in Horowitz, *Alma Mater*, 32.

60. Horowitz argues that for Renwick, the "most significant precedents for Vassar [were] hospitals and asylums"; *Alma Mater*, 31.

61. Longstreth, "From Farm to Campus," 155.

62. Horowitz, *Alma Mater*, 357.

63. Baker, *Cottage Hospitals*, 5. Cottages appeared on college campuses as well as on insane hospital grounds; among English doctors, "cottage hospitals" was a term used for small village medical hospitals run by country doctors, such as the one built in Cranleigh in 1859. These were dedicated but tiny facilities with eight or ten beds for the treatment of acute illnesses, and they were touted for their fresh air and sunlight. Many were retrofitted into existing dwellings, and others were adapted for children. The rural hospitals acted as a sort of neighborhood medical clinic, allowing country practitioners to avoid traveling great distances from one house call to the next. Since the patients in cottages hospitals were often children, were not ambulatory, and did not stay for very long, the country cottage hospital, in spite of its similar name, is not directly related to the architecture of the cottage system for insane asylums.

64. Fisher and Little, *Compendium and History*, 100–101. In 1854, before the asylum had opened, the trustees in Michigan hired John P. Gray, then an assistant physician in Utica, to oversee the construction. Gray's stay in Michigan was brief, because he was enticed back to Utica for the chief's job in 1856. See chapters 1 (Utica) and 4 (Buffalo) for more on Dr. Gray.

65. *Annual Report* (Kalamazoo), 1895–96, 53.

66. Ibid., 54.

67. Ibid.

68. Ibid., 55. The Chicago architects Holabird and Roche designed at least one cottage for the Kalamazoo State Hospital in Michigan. Bruegmann, *Holabird and Roche, Holabird and Root*, vol. 1, entry 252, 166. A surviving drawing from 1896 represents a two-story brick building with a raised basement and a cruciform plan. The lower floor included communal rooms, and the second floor was reserved for sleeping. According to Bruegmann, the interior framing was metal.

69. Report of the Board of Trustees of the Michigan Asylum for the Insane (Kalamazoo), 1895–96, 54. In a twist that must have chagrined Kirkbride, since the most volatile patients could never live in cottages, when they added cottages to existing campuses, the linear hospital became a de facto refractory ward, a purpose for which it had not been designed.

70. Ibid., 55.

71. Galt, "Farm of St. Anne," 354.

72. Galt, *Essays on Asylums*, 15.

73. *Annual Report* (Poughkeepsie), 1872, 12.

74. Arlidge, *On the State of Lunacy*, 201–2.

75. *Biennial Report* (Mount Pleasant, Iowa), 1961, 20.

76. Schuyler, *Apostle of Taste*, 95.

77. Rockefeller Library, Colonial Williamsburg, MS 78.3, miscellaneous papers 1862–1941, folder 3 of 6, "Architecture Notes and Drawings." The drawing is too lightly sketched to allow for reproduction.

78. Kowsky, "Downing's Architectural Legacy," 262.

79. *Illinois Board of State Commissioners of Public Charity*, I (1869–79), 100.

80. Galt, "Farm of St. Anne," 352–57.

81. Ibid., 354.

82. Grob, *State and the Mentally Ill*, 217.

83. Ibid., 227.

4. Building Up

1. Tomes, *Art of Asylum-Keeping*, 286.

2. Ibid., 287.

3. Dewey, *Recollections of Richard Dewey*, 130.

4. Scull, *Social Order/Mental Disorder*, 240–42; MacKenzie, *Psychiatry for the Rich*, 6.

5. Tomes, *Art of Asylum-Keeping*, 124.

6. Ibid., 125.

7. Ibid., 124.

8. Scull, *Social Order/Mental Disorder*, 240–42.

9. Wright, "Getting Out of the Asylum," 154.

10. Scull, *Social Order/Mental Disorder*, 8.

11. Porter, *Mind-Forg'd Manacles*, 117–19.

12. Grob, *Mental Institutions*, 71.

13. McCandless, *Moonlight, Magnolias, and Madness*, 162.

14. Grob, *Mental Institutions*, 76.

15. [Butler] *Annual Report* (Hartford), 1867, 33; quoted in Grob, *Mental Institutions*, 79.

16. Grob, *Mental Institutions*, 71.

17. Packard, *Modern Persecution*, 2:346–47. Packard was here recounting the testimony of a woman who wished to keep her identity a secret.

18. Goodheart, *Mad Yankees*, 158. Quotations are from the *Annual Report* (Hartford), 1864 and 1861.

19. Beam, *Gracefully Insane*, 23–25.

20. Hawkins, "The Therapeutic Landscape," 264.

21. Butler to Olmsted, December 3, 1872, quoted in ibid., 267.

22. Weidenmann, *Beautifying Country Homes*.

23. Weidenmann, quoting Butler, n.p., precedes plate XVIII.

24. Quoted in Hawkins, "Therapeutic Landscape," 267–68. Hawkins also notes that Olmsted served as consultant to D. Tilden Brown of Bloomingdale Asylum, New York City, in late 1860 or 1861. In particular, Olmsted gave the doctor "valuable counsel" regarding the "line of enclosure," possibly some sort of plantings that would serve as a visual screen and fence. See chapter 3 for more on Butler's role as a consultant to the Sheppard Asylum.

25. Goodheart, *Mad Yankees*, 163.

26. Kowsky, *Country, Park, and City*, 153.

27. Ibid.

28. "Announcement of the Sheppard Asylum," 30.

29. Kowsky, *Country, Park, and City*, 153–54. Kowsky (34) notes that Vaux used similarly dramatically curved towers, which Vaux considered "Rhenish," in a house for Joel Headley that appeared as the frontispiece of the 1852 edition of *Cottages, Residences*.

30. "Announcement of the Sheppard Asylum," 6. Brown to Olmsted, October 12, 1868, quoted in Hawkins, "Therapeutic Landscape," 283.

31. Kirkbride, "Remarks on Cottages," 378.

32. Platt, *The Eagle's History of Poughkeepsie*, 208.

33. Ibid.

34. I thank Robert H. Wozniak for conversations about this important topic, and many other subjects in the history of psychiatry and postcard collecting.

35. *Annual Report* (Poughkeepsie), 1867, 7.

36. Olmsted to Mary Perkins Olmsted, September 21, 1862. Olmsted, *Papers*, 4:423.

37. Kowsky, *Country, Park, and City*, 200. Brown committed suicide in 1889 after an exposé of the doctor's ongoing depression appeared in the *New York World*.

38. Roper, *FLO*, 474.

39. *Annual Report* (Poughkeepsie), 1867, 10. Vaux's role in the Hudson River State Hospital is unclear, but we know from *Annual Report* (Poughkeepsie), 1872, 17, that Withers designed the elevation. Vaux could certainly have participated in the planning. Kowsky also gives credit to Withers alone; see "Architecture, Nature and Humanitarian Reform," 47.

40. *Annual Report* (Poughkeepsie), 1867, 7. The firm of Vaux and Withers may have been selected because Withers knew a commissioner, Joseph Howland; Howland lived in a Withers-designed house, Tioranda, on the Hudson River at the junction of the Fishkill Creek, and he was married to architect Richard Morris Hunt's sister. Baker, *Richard Morris Hunt*, 196.

41. Alex, *Calvert Vaux*, illustrates a line drawing that does not correspond to earliest known photographs, probably because it shows a tower over the chapel that was never built. Hawkins described the plan this way: it "met AMSAII guidelines for a central administration block with flanking patient wings, but separated them into a series of discrete pavilions connected by covered passages." Hawkins, "Therapeutic Landscape," 283. "Covered passages" correctly identifies the links between the center main and the first two pavilions, but the other return wings, which included usable hospital spaces, are more complex than the term "passage" suggests. Vaux and Withers also worked on the renovation of the Hartford Retreat in 1870. *Annual Report* (Hartford), 1870, 15. This was ten years after Olmsted's proposal for the landscape.

42. *Annual Report* (Poughkeepsie), 1867, 9, and "Hudson River State Hospital," 110.

43. "Hudson River State Hospital," 110.

44. Ibid.

45. Ibid.

46. *Annual Report* (Poughkeepsie), 1872, 12.

47. Ibid.

48. *Life in the Asylum*, 15.

49. *Annual Report* (Morristown, N.J.), 1876, 7.

50. Bucknill, *Notes*, 16.

51. *Report of the Commissioners*, 6; Sloan, "New Jersey Asylum for the Insane." Sloan had earlier worked out a plan and elevation, presumably for the competition for this building in March 1869. He illustrated a plan of one story and a bird's-eye view with the caption "Proposed Asylum for the State of New Jersey" in his self-published journal.

52. *Report of the Commissioners*, 6.

53. Sloan, "New Jersey Asylum for the Insane," 552.

54. *Annual Report* (Morristown, N.J.), 1876, 26.

55. For more on these magic lantern shows, see Gamwell and Tomes, *Madness in America*, 95, and Gage and Harper, *The Magic Lantern of Dr. Thomas Story Kirkbride*.

56. *Annual Report* (Morristown, N.J.), 1876, 26.

57. *Annual Report* (Worcester), 1840, reprinted in Grob, *The Origins of the State Mental Hospital in America*, 43.

58. *Annual Report* (Washington, D.C.), 1866–67.

59. Tomes, *Art of Asylum-Keeping*, 222.

60. Bucknill, *Notes*, 16.

61. Ibid.

62. Ibid.

63. Wilbur, *Buildings for the Insane*, 14.

64. Ibid., 9. Wilbur had his own charity cases to protect. Most noted as the promoter of rights for developmentally disabled children, he founded the New York State Asylum for Idiots in Syracuse, which resembled an Italianate villa. He perceived a wide range of dependents in need of state support, and it seemed to him that lunatics received far more funding than people with developmental disabilities. He believed that such people, who had been systematically excluded from insane hospitals because they were incurable, could nonetheless be educated in morality and taught to perform simple occupations.

65. *Annual Report* (Poughkeepsie), 1870, 10.

66. *Annual Report* (Poughkeepsie), 1872, 13.

67. Taylor, *The Architect and the Pavilion Hospital*, 6.

68. Burdett, *Hospitals and Asylums of the World*, 4:40. Three models of pavilion plan hospitals were Lariboisière in Paris, the colossal St. Thomas Hospital in London, and Nightingale's preferred Herbert Hospital in Woolwich.

69. Before the Civil War, many patients were ambulatory, because hospitals had a greater mix of uncategorized impoverished, sick, and deranged people (Rosenberg, *Care of Strangers*, 36). In the period after the Civil War, patients were confined to bed until the final stages of their hospital stay (ibid.).

70. Kisacky, "An Architecture of Light and Air," 121. Kisacky explains that Nightingale's "solution to hospital disease was two-fold: ventilation and nursing."

71. Natural (as opposed to artificial) ventilation employed openings such as windows, fireplaces, and flues as well as changes in temperature to encourage the movement of air. Although mechanical ventilation existed in the nineteenth century, fans and other equipment were costly. For greater details on air circulation, ventilation, and the spread of disease, see Kisacky, "An Architecture of Light and Air," chapters 1 and 2.

72. Ibid., 182.

73. Ibid., 142. Nightingale suggested there be two hospital types: smaller urban hospitals scattered throughout the city for acute care, and larger general hospitals.

74. Ibid., 110.

75. Concern about contagion was central to both building types, the medical and mental hospital, although contagion was far more serious in a regular hospital. In a mental hospital the patients were not initially infectious, but if they did catch a communicable disease it was important to contain the spread of that disease by moving the inmate to an infirmary within the asylum.

76. Billings and Hurd, *Hospitals, Dispensaries, and Nursing,* 439.

77. Billings, *Description of the Johns Hopkins Hospital,* 19.

78. Two private rooms were also located on northern end of the common ward block.

79. Burdett, *Hospitals and Asylums of the World,* 4:153–55.

80. Insanity caused by syphilis could be considered contagious.

81. Burdett, *Hospitals and Asylums of the World,* 4:155.

82. Forty, "The Modern Hospital in England and France," 75.

83. Bucknill, *Notes,* 17.

84. Lee, *Provision for the Insane Poor,* 16. Lee was quoting Samuel Gridley Howe of Massachusetts.

85. Olmsted, *Papers,* 6:454.

86. Ochsner, *H. H. Richardson,* 78; Olmsted, *Papers,* 6:455.

87. Ochsner, *H. H. Richardson,* 78.

88. Coolidge, "The Architectural Importance of Richardson's Buffalo State Hospital," 92, and Olmsted, *Papers,* 6:455.

89. Beveridge and Rocheleau, *Frederick Law Olmsted,* 94.

90. Ochsner, *H. H. Richardson,* 71.

91. I agree with Francis Kowsky in giving much credit to the doctor. Kowsky writes: "The rambling plan, which had been dictated to Richardson by Dr. Gray, consisted of five independent pavilions on either side of the central administration building." Kowsky, *Buffalo Projects,* 9.

92. "Insane Asylum," *Daily Courier* (Buffalo), November 7, 1880.

93. O'Gorman, *H. H. Richardson and His Office,* 212, and Ochsner, *H. H. Richardson,* 78. His wife wrote, "He expects to go to Buffalo— Did you know he met Dr. Grey [*sic*] of Utica about the Insane Asylum?"

94. *Annual Report* (Buffalo), 1875, 10.

95. Gray submitted a plan, presumed lost, that was approved by the board of managers of the Buffalo State Asylum in 1870. On July 7, 1871, the board of managers rejected Gray's plan and adopted Richardson's. Olmsted, *Papers,* 6:454.

96. Hurd, *The Institutional Care,* 4:415.

97. O'Gorman, *H. H. Richardson and His Office,* 212. O'Gorman wrote that the "doctor whose name begins with a B remains unidentified," but I believe the note says "Dr. Bemis." Richardson's use of the word "ward" almost certainly meant a long hallway with rooms on either side of it, not an open ward as one would find in a medical hospital. O'Gorman referred to the sketch as the "first study of the Buffalo State Hospital," and this is certainly the logical conclusion, given the note. But the relationship between the sketch and the note remains mysterious to me, given that the sketch illustrates *neither* a typical Gray plan nor a typical cottage or farm asylum. One possibility is that although it appears next to a note about Buffalo State, it is actually a sketch for the general medical hospital at Worcester.

98. Richardson might have made Bemis's acquaintance when he worked in Worcester on a different building, the Worcester General Hospital in 1869.

99. Hitchcock, *The Architecture of Henry Hobson Richardson.* Hitchcock's dubiously teleological approach to architectural history is beyond the scope of this chapter; his primary interest in Buffalo State Hospital was that in a series of three stages of elevation design, he could demonstrate the young architect coming to his protomodernist senses. The rose window drawing, he said, "shows the worst peculiarities of the vernacular Victorian Gothic, in a form as corrupt as on the Worcester High School" (120), and the second drawing, as Hitchcock noted, looks like an administrative block rather than a chapel, which he admired, yet he found the details "rather fussy and too small in scale for the rest of the composition" (123).

100. Curved corridors appear in the following country houses, all illustrated in Campbell, *Vitruvius Britannicus:* Cliefden, vol. 1, plate 71; Hopton, vol. 1, plate 75; Stokepark, vol. 2, plate 9; Houghton, vol. 2, plate 29; Goodwood, vol. 2, plate 53; Nostell, vol. 4, plate 70; Fonthill, vol. 4, plate 82; Latham, vol. 4, plate 94; Oakland, vol. 5, plate 16.

101. Hitchcock, *Architecture of H. H. Richardson,* 123. Two of Hitchcock's assertions hold little merit. In 1936, he wrote that the precedents for the Buffalo State Hospital were French and that the state hospital in Connecticut was an immediate source, and he repeated both these claims in the 1966 edition of his book on Richardson: "According to tradition, it was based on the scheme of similar French institutions. It also follows very closely that of the older buildings of the Connecticut State Hospital in Middletown" (118). In fact, there were no shallow-V plans in France. Richardson had dozens more obvious choices in the United States than the one in Middletown to draw on for inspiration, but Hitchcock taught at Wesleyan University, within sight of the state asylum in Middletown, Connecticut.

102. The year 1871 was a busy one for the asylum board and its designers: Olmsted and Vaux undertook a preliminary survey of the grounds in January 1871; at an asylum board meeting in March 1871, the board made Richardson architect and Warner supervising architect; in May, Olmsted visited the site with both Richardson and Warner; and in July 1871, Olmsted submitted a site plan and full report. The groundbreaking was in June 1871, but the laying of the center main's cornerstone did not take place until September 1872. Olmsted, *Papers,* 6:454–58.

103. Ibid., 6:454.

104. Hawkins, "Therapeutic Landscape," 287. In the commentary that accompanies Olmsted, *Papers,* 6:454, Hawkins points out that the committee rejected Gray's plan and accepted Richardson's instead.

105. Hawkins, "Therapeutic Landscape," 287.

106. Ibid., 288.

107. Ibid. This planting plan is illustration 7.8 in Hawkins's dissertation. The drawing is held by the National Park Service, Olmsted National Historic Site, Brookline, Mass. Olmsted and Vaux had dissolved their partnership by the time Olmsted began consultations at Buffalo.

108. *Morning Express* (Buffalo), September 19, 1872.

109. O'Gorman, *H. H. Richardson*, 42.

110. *Daily Courier* (Buffalo), September 19, 1872.

111. *Daily Courier* (Buffalo), November 7, 1880.

112. Ibid.

113. *Annual Report* (Buffalo), 1871, 17.

114. Bucknill, *Notes*, 17.

115. Ibid. It is not clear why Bucknill described the passages as glass-covered. He may have meant simply that they were glazed, or that they had a lot of windows, compared to the rest of the structure. There is no evidence that the passages were intended to have skylights or were constructed of iron and glass, like an exhibition building. It is possible Bucknill saw the 1870 drawing in which the passages appear to be iron and glass, but by 1875 when he visited, that plan had been superseded.

116. Burdett, *Hospitals and Asylums of the World*, 1:110.

117. *Annual Report* (Buffalo), 1871, 17.

118. The supervising architect was A. J. Warner of Rochester; drawings for the brick pavilions were made in 1876–77; the western range for women was opened in 1895; the outer pavilions of brick were completed not by Richardson but by several building superintendents, including Peter Elmslie, "a leading Buffalo engineer." Kowsky, *Buffalo Projects*, 9.

119. This cross shape was unusual for any asylum in the United States and had no obvious precedent other than Stark's Glasgow asylum of ninety years earlier.

120. *Second Biennial Report of the Trustees and Treasurer of the Illinois Asylum for Incurable Insane at Peoria*, 1898, 11–12. I thank Fabio Barry for his insights about this structure based on close scrutiny of vintage photographs.

121. Ibid., 11.

122. Ibid.

123. Zeller, "World Gasped When Shackles Were Removed." Bartonville is a small town outside of Peoria.

124. Ibid.

125. Tomes, *Art of Asylum-Keeping*, 288.

126. Board of World's Fair Commissioners, *Committee on State Charitable Institutions*, 6.

127. Dewey, *Recollections of Richard Dewey*, 135.

128. Sankey, "Do the Public Asylums," 472.

129. Delilez, *The True Cause of Insanity Explained*, 141.

130. Bly, *Ten Days in a Mad-House*, 54.

131. Ibid.

132. Hammond, *Insane Asylum Reform I*, 1–2; quoted in Scull, *Decarceration*, 111.

133. Grob, *Mental Illness and American Society*, 52.

134. Mitchell, "The Treatment by Rest," 2037; quoted in Caplan, *Mind Games*, 3.

135. Caplan, *Mind Games*, 58.

136. Mitchell, "Address," 414; quoted in Grob, *Mental Illness and American Society*, 61.

Conclusion

1. Melling and Forsythe, *Insanity, Institutions and Society*, 18.

2. Javitt and Coyle, "Decoding Schizophrenia."

3. Ibid.

4. Ibid.

5. Ibid.

6. Rosenberg, *Care of Strangers*, 10.

7. Grob, *Mental Illness and American Society*, 53.

8. Fairless, *Suggestions concerning the Construction of Asylums for the Insane*, 7.

9. Grob, *Mad among Us*, 167.

10. George Kline, "Presidential Address," 4; quoted in Shorter, *A History of Psychiatry*, 161.

11. Grob, *Mental Illness and American Society*, 120–21.

12. Horwitz, *Creating Mental Illness*, 1.

13. Grob, *Mental Illness and American Society*, 121.

14. Horwitz, *Creating Mental Illness*, 2.

15. Lerman, *Deinstitutionalization and the Welfare State*, 98.

16. Ibid., 93.

17. Scull, *Decarceration*, 140, 150.

18. Horwitz, *Creating Mental Illness*, 187.

19. Scull, *Decarceration*, 139.

20. Porter, *Madness*, 211.

21. Kusner, *Down and Out on the Road*, 243. Some advocates for the homeless point out that there are many overlapping conditions that plague America's extreme poor: unemployment, addiction, physical disability, and family conflict. Also, advocates for the homeless suggest that living on the street causes psychiatric despair, so it is not correct to assume, as many people do, that a mentally ill homeless person has been discharged from a state hospital.

22. Edmondson, "St. Elizabeths Hospital," 18.

23. preserve.bfn.org/bam/archs/rich/statekowsky. Francis Kowsky contributed to this Web site.

24. Ceraulo, "N.Y. Designates Funds."

25. Ragonese, "Finding a Future for Greystone," 14.

26. James and Noakes, *Hospital Architecture*, 2.

27. Boursaw, "Seeking Asylum," 23, and www.calthorpe.com, the Web site for Calthorpe Associates.

28. Lewis, "Historic Asylums at Rest."

29. Anna Schuleit, artist statement, www.1856.org.

30. Schuleit, interview with author, January 18, 2005.

31. www.thevillagetc.com/site. The 380,000 square feet figure refers only to the Kirkbride building, known as Building 50. Residents will still have to pay federal taxes, but they will be exempt from state personal income taxes and local real estate taxes. Business owners who choose to relocate are similarly exempt from certain state and local taxes. I thank Chris Miller for assistance.

32. Boursaw, "Seeking Asylum," 25.

33. Lewis, "Historic Asylums at Rest."

34. Ibid.

35. www.csuci.edu.

36. Lewis, "Historic Asylums at Rest."

37. The unusually well-funded Sheppard Pratt Hospital does accommodate patients in its Victorian buildings. Warren Psychiatric Hospital is a Kirkbride plan hospital with all the oldest parts of the hospital in full use. Schuleit, interview with author, January 18, 2005.

38. www.fountainhouse.org/history. The Web site is written and maintained by members.

39. Jackson, *The Clubhouse Model*, 27. As an architectural historian, I am not qualified to compare clubhouses to psychiatric rehabilitation in terms of effectiveness; but since the clubhouse model was founded on certain spatial and architectural assumptions, I have focused on it rather than psychiatric rehabilitation.

40. Kenneth Dudek, executive director of Fountain House, interview with author, January 29, 2004.

41. Clubhouse rhetoric downplays the importance of diagnoses. Nonetheless, it might be helpful for readers outside the field of psychiatry to know the conditions affecting the majority of clubhouse members. These are schizophrenia, bipolar disorder (also known as manic-depressive illness), and major depression. Schizoaffective disorder refers to people who have symptoms of both schizophrenia and bipolar disorder. Jackson, *Clubhouse Model*, 25.

42. Arlidge, "On the State of Lunacy," 201–2.

43. As Jackson explains in *Clubhouse Model*, "Many major medical disorders can be treated through the use of psychiatric medications. With careful and controlled use, medications are generally effective in dampening and diminishing symptoms of major thought and mood disorders. Most professionals consider medication essential for permitting individuals to manage their mental illness and more fully access their own skills and abilities" (26).

44. Thomas Kerns, architect in charge of the renovation of Green Door, interview with author, March 7, 2003.

45. Harvard Medical School, Consumer Health Information, www.intelihealth.com. Seventy percent of dementia sufferers are cared for at home. Yale–New Haven Psychiatric Hospital, www.ynhh.org, reports that one in four American households care for an elderly or a disabled relative.

46. Stephen Verderber and David J. Fine explain that from 1946 to the 1980s, "the healthcare industry has done everything in its power to supplant the home as the center of the care universe." Verderber and Fine, *Healthcare Architecture*, 331. In the following decade of the 1990s, however, hospitals and HMOs pushed medical patients out of the hospital and back into the home. This historical shift in medical care (from home to hospital to home again) does not correspond precisely to the historical care of the mentally ill. It is not clear that there are any more insane patients cared for at home now than in the nineteenth century. The doctors' rhetoric, however, has most certainly changed. No psychiatrist working today would claim hospitalization is the single path to a cure; instead, doctors try to keep the ill person in the home while treating them with medication. Hospitalization is typically reserved for people who pose a threat to themselves or others.

47. Brawley, *Designing for Alzheimer's Disease*, 38.

48. Cohen and Day, *Contemporary Environments for People with Dementia*, 12.

49. Ibid., 8.

50. Ibid., 11.

51. Brawley, *Designing for Alzheimer's Disease*, 159.

52. Ibid., 161.

53. Cohen and Day, *Contemporary Environments*, 187.

54. Jonathan F., clubhouse member, Fountain House interview with the author, April 17, 2004.

Appendix A. Note on Terminology

1. Gamwell and Tomes, *Madness in America*, 9.

2. Ibid.

3. Letter, Kirkbride to Dix, April 9, 1857, Pennsylvania Hospital Archives.

4. Gamwell and Tomes, *Madness in America*, 9.

5. Goodheart, *Mad Yankees*, 65.

Bibliography

Published Sources from the Eighteenth and Nineteenth Centuries

"Announcement of the Sheppard Asylum: A Hospital for Mental Diseases." Baltimore: n.p., 1891.

Arlidge, John T. *On the State of Lunacy and the Legal Provision for the Insane, with Observations on the Construction and Organization of Asylums.* London: John Churchill, 1859.

Bagg, M. M. *The Pioneers of Utica: Being Sketches of Its Inhabitants and Its Institutions, with the Civil History of the Place, from the Earliest Settlement to the Year 1825—the Era of the Opening of the Erie Canal.* Utica: Curtiss and Childs, 1877.

Baker, Lucius W. *Cottage Hospitals, Read before the Massachusetts Medical Society.* West Gardner, Mass.: Record Office, 1882.

Battie, William. "Treatise on Madness." 1758. Reprinted in Richard Hunter and Ida Macalpine, *A Treatise on Madness by William Battie, M.D., and Remarks on Dr Battie's Treatise on Madness by John Monro M.D.: A Psychiatric Conversation in the Eighteenth Century.* London: Dawsons of Pall Mall, 1962.

Bentham, Jeremy. *Panopticon; or, The Inspection House.* 3 vols. London: T. Payne, 1791.

Billings, John Shaw. *Description of the Johns Hopkins Hospital.* Baltimore: Johns Hopkins Hospital, 1890.

———, and Henry M. Hurd, eds. *Hospitals, Dispensaries, and Nursing: Papers and Discussions in the International Congress of Charities, Corrections, and Philanthropy, Section III.* Baltimore: The Johns Hopkins University Press, 1894.

Bly, Nellie. *Ten Days in a Mad-house; or, Nellie Bly's Experience on Blackwell's Island.* New York: Munro, [1887].

Board of World's Fair Commissioners, Committee on State Charitable Institutions. *Brief History of the Charitable Institutions of the State of Illinois,* "Brief History of Illinois Eastern Hospital for the Insane Located in Kankakee" (n.p.: 1893), 6.

"Brief Description of the State Lunatic Asylum at Utica, N.Y." *American Journal of Insanity* 4 (April 1847): 96.

Brown, D. Tilden. "Report of an Examination of Certain European Institutions for the Insane." *American Journal of Insanity* 20 (1863–64): 200–216.

Browne, William Alexander Francis. *What Asylums Were, Are and Ought to Be, Being the Substance of Five Lectures Delivered before the Managers of the Montrose Royal Lunatic Asylum.* 1837. Reprint, New York: Arno Press, 1976.

Bucknill, John Charles. *Notes on Asylums for the Insane in America.* London: J. & A. Churchill, 1876.

———, and Daniel H. Tuke. *A Manual of Psychological Medicine.* Philadelphia: Blanchard & Lee, 1858.

Burdett, Henry C. *Hospitals and Asylums of the World: Their Origin, History, Construction, Administration, Management and Legislation.* 4 vols. London: J. A. Churchill, 1891–93.

Buttolph, Horace. "Historical and Descriptive Account of the New Jersey State Lunatic Asylum." *American Journal of Insanity* 6 (1849–50): 1–22.

———. "Modern Asylums." *American Journal of Insanity* 4 (1847–48): 364–78.

Byrne, Julia C. *Gheel, City of the Simple.* London: Chapman Hall, 1869.

Campbell, Colin. *Vitruvius Britannicus.* London: 1715–71.

Chadbourne, Paul, ed. *Public Service of the State of New York,* vol. 1. Boston: James R. Osgood, 1882.

Conolly, John. *The Construction and Government of Lunatic Asylums and Hospitals for the Insane.* 1847. Reprint, London: Dawsons Press, 1968.

Davis, John G. "On the Bill to Organize an Institution for the Insane of the Army and Navy of the United States, and of the District of Columbia." *American Journal of Insanity* 11 (1854–55): 358–65.

Delilez, Francis. *The True Cause of Insanity Explained; or, The Terrible Experiences of an Insane, Related by Himself, The Life of a Patient in an Insane Asylum, by a Patient of the Northern Wisconsin Hospital at Winnebago, Wisconsin.* Minneapolis, Minn.: L. Kimball & Co., Printers, 1888.

Dickens, Charles. "American Notes," 1842. In *American Notes and Pictures from Italy.* London: Oxford University Press, 1957.

Dix, Dorothea Lynde. *Memorial of D. L. Dix Praying for a Grant of Land for the Relief and Support of the Indigent, Curable, and Incurable Insane in the United States.* [Washington: Tippin & Streeper, printers], 1848.

———. *Memorial Soliciting a State Hospital for the Insane.* Montgomery, Ala.: n.p., 1849.

———. *On Behalf of the Insane Poor: Selected Reports.* New York: Arno Press, 1971.

Downing, Andrew Jackson. *The Architecture of Country Houses Including Designs for Cottages, Farm-Houses, and Villas.* New York: D. Appleton, 1850.

———. *Cottage Residences: A Series of Designs for Rural Cottages and Cottage Villas.* New York: Wiley and Putnam, 1842.

———. *A Treatise on the Theory and Practice of Landscape Gardening, Adapted to North America.* New York: Wiley and Putnam, 1841.

Earle, Pliny. "The Curability of Insanity." *American Journal of Insanity* 33 (1876–77): 1483–533.

———. "Provision for the Insane." *American Journal of Insanity* 25 (1868–69): 51–65.

———. "A Visit to Gheel." *American Journal of Insanity* 8 (1851–52): 67–77.

———. *A Visit to Thirteen Asylums for the Insane in Europe.* Philadelphia: J. Dobson, 1841.

Fairless, William Dean. *Suggestions Concerning the Construction of Asylums for the Insane.* Edinburgh: Sutherland and Knox, 1861.

Galt, John M. *Essays on Asylums for Persons of Unsound Mind.* Richmond, Va.: H. K. Ellison's Power Press, 1850.

———. "The Farm of St. Anne." *American Journal of Insanity* 11 (1854–55): 352–57.

———. *The Treatment of Insanity.* 1846. Reprint, New York: Arno Press, 1973.

[Gray, John P.] "Brief Description of the State Lunatic Asylum at Utica, N.Y." *American Journal of Insanity* 4 (1847–48): 96.

———. "Hospital and Cottage Systems for the Care of the Insane." *American Journal of Insanity* 27 (1870–71): 80–92.

Hammond, George F. *A Treatise on Hospital and Asylum Construction with Special Reference to Pavilion Wards.* Cleveland, Ohio: n.p., 1891.

Hammond, William A. *Insane Asylum Reform I: The Non-Asylum Treatment of the Insane.* New York: G. P. Putnam & Sons, 1879.

Haskell, Ebenezer. *The Trial of Ebenezer Haskell, in Lunacy, and His Acquittal Before Judge Brewster, in November, 1868.* Philadelphia: E. Haskell, 1869.

Hawkins, H. *Made Whole: A Parting Address to Convalescents on Leaving an Asylum.* London: Society for Promoting Christian Knowledge, [1871].

"Hudson River State Hospital, Poughkeepsie, N.Y." *American Architect and Building News,* March 30, 1878, 110.

"Insane Asylum." *Daily Courier* (Buffalo), November 7, 1880.

Jarvis, Edward. "Comparative Liability of Males and Females to Insanity." *American Journal of Insanity* 7 (1850–51): 142–71.

Jefferson, Thomas. "Notes on the State of Virginia, 1782–1785." In *America Builds: Source Documents in American Architecture and Planning,* edited by Leland Roth, 22–25. New York: Harper & Row, 1983.

Jones, Pomroy. *Annals and Recollections of Oneida County.* Rome, N.Y.: n.p., 1851.

Kirkbride, Thomas S. "Description of the Pleasure Grounds and Farm of the Pennsylvania Hospital for the Insane." *American Journal of Insanity* 4 (1847–48): 347–54.

———. *On the Construction, Organization, and General Arrangements of Hospitals for the Insane.* Philadelphia: Lindsay & Blakiston, 1854 (1st ed.) and J. B. Lippincott & Co., 1880 (2nd ed.). Reprint, New York: Arno Press, 1973.

———. "Remarks on Cottages." *American Journal of Insanity* 7 (1850–51): 374–79.

Lee, Charles A. *Provision for the Insane Poor of the State of New York, and the adaptation of the Asylum and Cottage Plan to Their Wants, as Illustrated by the History of the Colony of FitzJames, at Clermont, France.* Albany: Van Benthuysen's Steam Printing House, 1866.

Life in the Asylum: An Autobiographical Sketch. London: Houlston & Wright, 1867.

Malin, W. G. *Some Account of the Pennsylvania Hospital, Its Origin, Objects, and Present State.* Philadelphia: Thomas Kite, 1832.

Mayhew, Henry, and John Binny. *The Criminal Prisons of London and Scenes of Prison Life.* New York: A. M. Kelley, 1868.

Mills, Robert. *Statistics of South Carolina, Including a View of Its Natural, Civil, and Military History.* Charleston, S.C.: Hurlbut and Lloyd, 1826.

Mitchell, S. Weir. "Address before the Fiftieth Annual Meeting of the American Medico-Psychological Association." *Journal of Nervous and Mental Diseases* 21 (July 1894): 413–37.

Olmsted, Frederick Law. *The Papers of Frederick Law Olmsted,* vols. 1–5, Charles Capen McLaughlin and Charles Beveridge, eds.; vol. 6, David Schuyler and Jane Turner Censer, eds. Baltimore: The Johns Hopkins University Press, 1977–1992.

Packard, Elizabeth Parsons Ware. *Modern Persecution; or, Insane Asylums Unveiled.* 2 vols. Hartford, Conn.: Case Lockwood & Brainard, 1873.

———. *The Prisoners' Hidden Life; or, Insane Asylums Unveiled as Demonstrated by the Report of the Investigating Committee of the Legislature of Illinois, Together with Mrs. Packard's Coadjutors' Testimony.* Chicago: A. B. Case, printer, 1868.

Palladio, Andrea. *The Four Books on Architecture* [ca. 1570], translated by Robert Tavernor and Richard Schofield. Cambridge, Mass.: MIT Press, 1997.

"Proceedings of the Tenth Annual Meeting of the Association of Medical Superintendents of American Institutions for the Insane." *American Journal of Insanity* 12 (1855–56): 39–101.

Pugin, Augustus, and Thomas Rowlandson. *Microcosm of London.* London: Ackerman, 1808–11.

Ray, Isaac. "American Hospitals for the Insane." *North American Review* 19 (July 1854): 67–91.

Reid, Robert. *Observations on the Structure of Hospitals for the Treatment of Lunatics and on the General Principles on Which the Cure of Insanity May Be Most Successfully Conducted.* Edinburgh: James Ballantyne, 1809.

Report of the Commissioners Appointed to Select a Site and Build an Asylum for the Insane of This State. Trenton, N.J.: True American Office, 1873.

"Report on the Construction of Hospitals for the Insane, made by the Standing Committee of the Association of Medical Superintendents of American Institutions for the Insane." *American Journal of Insanity* 8 (1851–52): 79–81.

Sankey, W. H. O. "Do the Public Asylums of England, as at present Constructed, Afford the Greatest Facilities for the Care and Treatment of the Insane?" *Journal of Mental Science* (1856): 466–79.

Seymour, Edward J. "Observations on the Medical Treatment of Insanity." 1832. Reprinted in John M. Galt, *The Treatment of Insanity*. 1846. Reprint, New York: Arno Press, 1973, 260–66.

Sloan, Samuel. *City and Suburban Architecture: Containing Numerous Designs and Details for Public Edifices*. 1859. Reprint, New York: Da Capo Press, 1976.

———. "Hospital for the Insane, St. Peter, Minnesota." *Architectural Review and American Builders' Journal* 1 (1869): 551–54.

———. "New Jersey Asylum for the Insane." *Architectural Review and American Builders' Journal* 2 (1870): 712–17.

Soane, John. *Memoirs of the Professional Life of an Architect between the Years 1768 and 1835*. London, 1835.

Stark, William. *Remarks on Public Hospitals for the Cure of Mental Derangement*. Edinburgh: James Ballantyne, 1807.

Stearns, Henry P. "The Relations of Insanity to Modern Civilization." *Scribner's Monthly* 17 (February 1879): 582–86.

Tiffany, Francis. *The Life of Dorothea Lynde Dix*. Boston: Houghton, Mifflin, 1890.

Tuke, Daniel H. "Does Civilization Favour the Generation of Mental Disease?" *Journal of Mental Science* 4 (1857): 94–110.

———. *The Insane in the United States and Canada*. 1885. Reprint, New York: Arno Press, 1973.

Tuke, John B. "The Cottage System of Management of Lunatics as Practiced in Scotland." *American Journal of Insanity* 27 (1870–71): 92–103.

Tuke, Samuel. *Description of the Retreat, An Institution near York, for Insane Persons of the Society of Friends*. 1813. Reprint, with introduction by Richard Hunter and Ida Macalpine, London: Dawsons of Pall Mall, 1964.

———. *Letter on Pauper Lunatic Asylums*. New York: Samuel Wood and Sons, 1815.

Waln, Robert. *An Account of the Asylum for the Insane, Established by the Society of Friends Near Frankford in the Vicinity of Philadelphia*. Philadelphia: Benjamin and Thomas Kite, 1825.

Weidenmann, Jacob. *Beautifying Country Homes: A Handbook of Landscape Gardening*. New York: O. Judd, 1870.

Wilbur, Hervey Backus. *Buildings for the Insane: A Report Read at the Saratoga Conference on Charities*. Boston: A. J. Wright, 1877.

Wilkins, E. T. *Insanity and Insane Asylums: Report of E. T. W., Commissioner in Lunacy for the State of California*. Sacramento: T. A. Springer State Printer, 1872.

Secondary Sources

Adams, Annmarie. *Architecture in the Family Way: Doctors, Houses and Women, 1870–1900*. Montreal: McGill Queens University Press, 1996.

———. "Modernism and Medicine: The Hospitals of Stevens and Lee." *Journal of the Society of Architectural Historians* 58 (March 1999): 42–61.

Alex, William. *Calvert Vaux: Architect and Planner*. New York: Ink, 1994.

Altschule, Mark D. *Roots of Modern Psychiatry*. New York: Grune and Stratton, 1965.

Andrews, Jonathan, Asa Briggs, Roy Porter, Penny Tucker, and Keir Waddington. *The History of Bethlem*. London: Routledge, 1997.

———, and Andrew Scull. *Undertaker of the Mind: John Monro and Mad-Doctoring in Eighteenth-Century England*. Berkeley and Los Angeles: University of California Press, 2001.

Baker, Paul R. *Richard Morris Hunt*. Cambridge, Mass.: MIT Press, 1980.

Bartlett, Peter, and David Wright. *Outside the Walls of the Asylum: The History of Care in the Community, 1750–2000*. London: Athlone Press, 1999.

Baxter, William E., and David W. Hatchcox. *America's Care of the Mentally Ill: A Photographic History*. Washington, D.C.: American Psychiatric Press, 1994.

Beam, Alex. *Gracefully Insane: The Rise and Fall of America's Premier Mental Hospital*. New York: Public Affairs, 2001.

Beveridge, Charles E. "Frederick Law Olmsted's Theory of Landscape Design." *Nineteenth Century* 3 (Summer 1977): 38–43.

———, and Paul Rocheleau. *Frederick Law Olmsted: Designing the American Landscape*. New York: Rizzoli, 1995.

Bird, Betty. "St. Elizabeths Historic Resources Management Plan." *District of Columbia Office of Business and Economic Development* (n.p., 1983).

Boursaw, Jane Louise. "Seeking Asylum." *Planning* 68 (November 2002): 22–23.

Brawley, Elizabeth C. *Designing for Alzheimer's Disease: Strategies for Creating Better Care Environments*. New York: Wiley & Sons, 1997.

Brown, Thomas E. "Dance of the Dialectic? Some Reflections (Polemic and Otherwise) on the Present State of Nineteenth-Century Asylum Studies." *Canadian Bulletin of Medical History* 11 (1994): 267–95.

Brownell, Charles E., and Jeffrey A. Cohen, eds. *The Architectural Drawings of Benjamin Henry Latrobe*. 2 vols. New Haven: Yale University Press, 1994.

Bruegmann, Robert. *Holabird and Roche, Holabird and Root: An Illustrated Catalogue of Works, 1880–1940*. 3 vols. New York: Garland Press, 1991.

Bryan, John M. *Robert Mills: America's First Architect*. New York: Princeton Architectural Press, 2001.

Caplan, Eric. *Mind Games: American Culture and the Birth of Psychotherapy*. Berkeley and Los Angeles: University of California Press, 1998.

Ceraulo, Maria. "N.Y. Designates Funds to Restore Buffalo Psychiatric Center, Wright House." www.preservationonline.org (February 21, 2006).

Cohen, Uriah, and Kristen Day. *Contemporary Environments for People with Dementia*. Baltimore: The Johns Hopkins University Press, 1993.

Cooledge, Harold N., Jr. *Samuel Sloan: Architect of Philadelphia 1815–1884*. Philadelphia: University of Pennsylvania Press, 1986.

Coolidge, John. "The Architectural Importance of H. H. Richardson's Buffalo State Hospital." In *Changing Places: Remaking Institutional Buildings*, edited by Lynda Schneekloth, Marcia Feuerstein, and Barbara Campagna, 85–105. Fredonia, N.Y.: White Pine Press, 1992.

Dewey, Richard. *Recollections of Richard Dewey, Pioneer in American Psychiatry: An Unfinished Autobiography with an Introduction by Clarence B. Farrar, M.D.* Chicago: University of Chicago Press, 1936.

Digby, Anne. *Madness, Morality and Medicine: A Study of the York Retreat, 1796–1914.* Cambridge: Cambridge University Press, 1985.

Dwyer, Ellen. *Homes for the Mad: Life inside Two Nineteenth-Century Asylums.* New Brunswick, N.J.: Rutgers University Press, 1987.

Edmondson, Brad. "St. Elizabeths Hospital." *Preservation,* December 2004.

Evans, Robin. *The Fabrication of Virtue: English Prison Architecture, 1750–1840.* Cambridge: Cambridge University Press, 1982.

Fisher, David, and Frank Little, eds. *Compendium and History and Biography of Kalamazoo County Michigan.* Chicago: A. W. Bowen, 1906.

Floyd, Margaret Henderson, and Paul Rocheleau. *H. H. Richardson: A Genius for Architecture.* New York: Monacelli Press, 1997.

Forbush, Bliss, and Byron Forbush. *Gatehouse: The Evolution of the Sheppard and Enoch Pratt Hospital, 1853–1986.* Baltimore: The Sheppard and Enoch Pratt Hospital, 1986.

Forty, Adrian. "The Modern Hospital in England and France: The Social and Medical Uses of Architecture." In *Buildings and Society: Essays on the Social Development of the Built Environment,* edited by Anthony King, 61–93. London: Routledge & Kegan Paul, 1980.

Foucault, Michel. *Madness and Civilization: A History of Insanity in the Age of Reason.* Abridged and translated by Richard Howard. New York: Pantheon, 1965. Originally published as *Folie et déraison; histoire de la folie* (1961).

Fox, Richard. *So Far Disordered in Mind: Insanity in California, 1870–1930.* Berkeley and Los Angeles: University of California Press, 1978.

Gage, Frances, and Carolyn Harper. *The Magic Lantern of Dr. Thomas Story Kirkbride.* Philadelphia: Atwater Kent Museum, 1993.

Gallagher, H. M. Pierce. *Robert Mills: Architect of the Washington Monument, 1781–1855.* New York: Columbia University Press, 1935.

Gamwell, Lynn, and Nancy Tomes. *Madness in America: Cultural and Medical Perceptions of Mental Illness before 1914.* Ithaca, N.Y.: Cornell University Press and Binghamton University Art Museum, 1995.

Gerlach-Spriggs, Nancy, Richard Enoch Kaufman, and Sam Bass Warner, Jr. *Restorative Gardens: The Healing Landscape.* New Haven, Conn.: Yale University Press, 1998.

Gollaher, David. *Voice for the Mad: The Life of Dorothea Dix.* New York: Free Press, 1995.

Goodheart, Lawrence B. *Mad Yankees: The Hartford Retreat for the Insane and Nineteenth-Century Psychiatry.* Amherst: University of Massachusetts Press, 2003.

Greiff, Constance M. *John Notman, Architect, 1810–1865.* Philadelphia: The Athenaeum of Philadelphia, 1979.

Grob, Gerald. *From Asylum to Community: Mental Health Policy in Modern America.* Princeton, N.J.: Princeton University Press, 1991.

———. *The Mad among Us: A History of the Care of America's Mentally Ill.* New York: Free Press, 1994.

———. *Mental Illness and American Society, 1875–1940.* Princeton, N.J.: Princeton University Press, 1983.

———. *Mental Institutions in America: Social Policy to 1875.* New York: Free Press, 1973.

———, ed. *The Origins of the State Mental Hospital in America.* New York: Arno Press, 1973.

———. *The State and the Mentally Ill: A History of Worcester State Hospital in Massachusetts, 1830–1920.* Chapel Hill: University of North Carolina Press, 1966.

Hawkins, Kenneth. "The Therapeutic Landscape: Nature, Architecture, and Mind in Nineteenth-Century America." Ph.D. diss., University of Rochester, 1991.

Hitchcock, Henry-Russell. *Architecture: Nineteenth and Twentieth Centuries.* Baltimore: Penguin Books, 1958.

———. *The Architecture of H. H. Richardson and His Times.* Cambridge, Mass.: MIT Press, 1966. [Revision of 1935 edition.]

———. *The Architecture of Henry Hobson Richardson and His Times.* Harmondsworth: Penguin Books, 1935.

———. *Richardson as a Victorian Architect.* Baltimore: Smith College at the Barton-Gillet Co., 1966.

Horowitz, Helen. *Alma Mater: Design and Experience in the Women's Colleges from Their Nineteenth-Century Beginnings to the 1930s.* New York: Alfred A. Knopf, 1984.

Horwitz, Allan V. *Creating Mental Illness.* Chicago: University of Chicago Press, 2002.

Hunter, Richard, and Ida Macalpine. *Psychiatry for the Poor, 1851. Colney Hatch Asylum, Friern Hospital 1973: A Medical and Social History.* London: Dawsons of Pall Mall, 1974.

Hurd, Henry Miles. *The Institutional Care of the Insane in the United States and Canada.* 4 vols. 1916–17. Reprint, New York: Arno Press, 1973.

Jackson, Robert L. *The Clubhouse Model: Empowering Applications of Generalist Practice.* Belmont, Calif.: Brooks Cole, 2001.

James, Paul, and Tony Noakes. *Hospital Architecture.* London: Longman House, 1994.

"James Rowland Willett. F.A.I.A." *Quarterly Bulletin of Obituaries* 8 (1907): 105–6.

Javitt, Daniel C., and Joseph T. Coyle. "Decoding Schizophrenia: A Fuller Understanding of Signaling in the Brain of People with This Disorder Offers New Hope for Improved Therapy." *Scientific American* (January 2004), www.sciam.com/article.cfm?articleID=000EE239-6805-1FD5-A23683414B7F0000.

Johnston, Norman Bruce. *Forms of Constraint: A History of Prison Architecture.* Urbana: University of Illinois Press, 2000.

———. *The Human Cage: A Brief History of Prison Architecture.* New York: Institute of Corrections, 1973.

King, Anthony, ed. *Buildings and Society: Essays on the Social Development of the Built Environment.* London: Routledge & Kegan Paul, 1980.

Kisacky, Jeanne. "An Architecture of Light and Air: Theories of Hygiene and the Building of the New York Hospital, 1771–1932." Ph.D. diss., Cornell University, 2000.

Kline, George. "Presidential Address." *American Journal of Psychiatry* 7 (1927): 1–22.

Kowsky, Francis R. "The Architectural Legacy of Andrew Jackson Downing." In *Prophet with Honor: The Career of Andrew Jackson Downing,* edited by George B. Tatum and Elisabeth McDougall, 259–90. Washington, D.C.: Dumbarton Oaks, 1989.

———. "Architecture, Nature, and Humanitarian Reform: The Buffalo State Hospital for the Insane." In *Changing Places: Remaking Institutional Buildings*, edited by Lynda Schneekloth, Marcia Feuerstein, and Barbara Campagna, 43–63. Fredonia, N.Y.: White Pine Press, 1992.

———. *The Architecture of Frederick Clarke Withers and the Progress of the Gothic Revival in America after 1850.* Middletown, Conn.: Wesleyan University Press, 1980.

———. *Buffalo Projects: H. H. Richardson.* Buffalo, N.Y.: Burchfield Center, 1980.

———. *Country, Park, and City: The Architecture and Life of Calvert Vaux, 1824–1895.* New York: Oxford University Press, 1998.

Kromm, Jane. *The Art of Frenzy: Public Madness in the Visual Culture of Europe, 1500–1850.* London: Continuum, 2002.

Kusner, Kenneth L. *Down and Out on the Road: The Homeless in American History.* New York: Oxford University Press, 2002.

Lerman, Paul. *Deinstitutionalization and the Welfare State.* New Brunswick, N.J.: Rutgers University Press, 1982.

Lewis, Laura. "Historic Asylums at Rest." www.nationaltrust.org/magazine/archives/arch_story/091201.htm.

Liscombe, Rhodri Windsor. *Altogether American: Robert Mills, Architect and Engineer, 1781–1855.* New York: Oxford University Press, 1994.

Longstreth, Richard. "From Farm to Campus: Planning, Politics, and the Agricultural College Idea in Kansas." *Winterthur Portfolio* 20 (Summer 1985): 149–79.

MacKenzie, Charlotte. *Psychiatry for the Rich: A History of Ticehurst Private Asylum.* London: Routledge, 1992.

Markus, Thomas. *Buildings and Power: Freedom and Control in the Origin of Modern Building Types.* London: Routledge, 1993.

McCandless, Peter. "Build! Build! The Controversy over the Care of the Chronically Insane in England 1855–1870." *Bulletin of the History of Medicine* 53 (1979): 553–74.

———. *Moonlight, Magnolias, and Madness: Insanity in South Carolina from the Colonial Period to the Progressive Era.* Chapel Hill: University of North Carolina Press, 1996.

McDonald, Travis C., Jr. *Design for Madness: An Architectural History of the Public Hospital in Williamsburg Virginia.* Williamsburg, Va.: Colonial Williamsburg Foundation, 1986.

Melling, Joseph, and Bill Forsythe. *Insanity, Institutions and Society, 1800–1914: A Social History of Madness in Comparative Perspective.* London: Routledge, 1999.

Millikan, Frank Rives. "Wards of the Nation: The Making of St. Elizabeths Hospital, 1852–1920." Ph.D. diss., George Washington University, 1990.

Mitchell, S. Weir. "The Treatment by Rest, Seclusion, etc., in Relation to Psychotherapy." *Journal of the American Medical Association* 50 (June 20, 1908): 2033–37.

Moore, John D. J. "What Gheel Means to Me." *Look* 25 (May 23, 1961): 36.

Moran, James E. "Asylum in the Community: Managing the Insane in Antebellum America." *History of Psychiatry* 9 (June 1998): 217–40.

———. *Committed to the State Asylum: Insanity and Society in Nineteenth-Century Quebec and Ontario.* Montreal: McGill-Queen's University Press, 2000.

———. "Historical Epidemiology of Insanity." *History of Psychiatry* 14 (September 2003): 281–301.

Nicoletta, Julie. "The Architecture of Control: Shaker Dwelling Houses and the Reform Movement in Early-Nineteenth-Century America." *Journal of the Society of Architectural Historians* 62 (September 2003): 352–87.

"Obituary, James R. Willett." *Inland Architect and News Record* (May 1907): 1.

Ochsner, Jeffrey. *H. H. Richardson: Complete Architectural Works.* Cambridge, Mass.: MIT Press, 1982.

O'Gorman, James F. *H. H. Richardson: Architectural Forms for an American Society.* Chicago: University of Chicago Press, 1987.

———. *H. H. Richardson and His Office: A Centennial of His Move to Boston, 1874: Selected Drawings.* Cambridge, Mass.: Harvard University, Fogg Art Museum, 1974.

O'Malley, Therese. "'Your Garden Must Be a Museum to You': Early American Botanic Gardens." *Huntington Library Quarterly* 59 (1997/98): 207–31.

Parry-Jones, William Ll. "The Model of the Geel Lunatic Colony and Its influence on the Nineteenth-Century Asylum System in Britain." In *Madhouses, Mad-doctors, Madmen: The Social History of Psychiatry in the Victorian Era*, edited by Andrew Scull, 201–17. Philadelphia: University of Pennsylvania Press; London: Athlone, 1981.

Peterson, Charles E., Constance Greiff, and Maria M. Thompson. *Robert Smith: Architect, Builder, Patriot, 1722–1777.* Philadelphia: Athenaeum of Philadelphia, 2000.

Pevsner, Nikolaus. *A History of Building Types.* Princeton, N.J.: Princeton University Press, 1976.

Placzek, Adolf K., ed. *Macmillan Encyclopedia of Architects.* 4 vols. New York: Free Press; London: Collier Macmillan, 1982.

Platt, Edmund. *The Eagle's History of Poughkeepsie.* Poughkeepsie, N.Y.: Dutchess County Historical Society, 1987.

Porter, Roy. *Madness: A Brief History.* Oxford: Oxford University Press, 2002.

———. *Mind-Forg'd Manacles: A History of Madness in England from the Restoration to the Regency.* London: Athlone, 1987.

Ragonese, Lawrence. "Finding a Future for Greystone." *Star-Ledger* (October 15, 2002): 14.

Reaume, Geoffrey. *Remembrance of Patients Past: Patient Life at the Toronto Hospital for the Insane, 1870–1940.* New York: Oxford University Press, 2000.

Roosens, Eugeen. *Mental Patients in Town Life: Geel, Europe's First Therapeutic Community.* Beverly Hills, Calif.: Sage, 1979.

Roper, Laura Wood. *FLO: A Biography of Frederick Law Olmsted.* Baltimore: The Johns Hopkins University Press, 1973.

Rosenberg, Charles E. *The Care of Strangers: The Rise of America's Hospital System.* New York: Basic Books, 1987.

Roth, Leland M., ed. *America Builds: Source Documents in American Architecture and Planning.* New York: Harper & Row, 1983.

Rothman, David. *The Discovery of the Asylum: Social Order and Disorder in the New Republic.* Boston: Little, Brown, 1971.

Russell, William Logie. *The New York Hospital: A History of the Psychiatric Service, 1771–1936.* New York: Columbia University Press, 1945.

Schneekloth, Lynda, Marcia Feuerstein, and Barbara Campagna, eds. *Changing Places: Remaking Institutional Buildings.* Fredonia, N.Y.: White Pine Press, 1992.

Schuyler, David. *Apostle of Taste: Andrew Jackson Downing, 1815–1852.* Baltimore: The Johns Hopkins University Press, 1996.

Scull, Andrew. *Decarceration: Community Treatment and the Deviant—a Radical View.* Englewood Cliffs, N.J.: Prentice Hall, 1977.

———. "A Failure to Communicate? On the Reception of Foucault's *Histoire de la folie* by Anglo-American Historians." In *Rewriting the History of Madness: Studies in Foucault's "Histoire de la folie,"* edited by Arthur Still and Irving Velody, 150–63. London: Routledge, 1992.

———, ed. *Madhouses, Mad-doctors, Madmen: The Social History of Psychiatry in the Victorian Era.* Philadelphia: University of Pennsylvania Press; London: Athlone, 1981.

———. *The Most Solitary of Afflictions: Madness and Society in Britain, 1700–1900.* New Haven, Conn.: Yale University Press, 1993.

———. *Museums of Madness: The Social Organization of Insanity in Nineteenth-Century England.* London: Allen Lane, 1979.

———. *Social Order/Mental Disorder: Anglo-American Psychiatry in Historical Perspective.* Berkeley and Los Angeles: University of California Press, 1989.

———. *Undertaker of the Mind: John Monro and Mad-Doctoring in Eighteenth-Century England.* Berkeley and Los Angeles: University of California Press, 2001.

———, Charlotte MacKenzie, and Nicholas Hervey. *Masters of Bedlam: The Transformations of the Mad-doctoring Trade.* Princeton, N.J.: Princeton University Press, 1996.

Shorter, Edward. *A History of Psychiatry from the Era of the Asylum to the Age of Prozac.* New York: John Wiley and Sons, 1997.

Showalter, Elaine. *The Female Malady: Women, Madness, and English Culture, 1830–1980.* New York: Pantheon, 1985.

Sloane, David, and Beverlie Conant Sloane. *Medicine Moves to the Mall.* Baltimore: The Johns Hopkins University Press, 2003.

Stein, Susan, ed. *The Architecture of Richard Morris Hunt.* Chicago: University of Chicago Press, 1986.

Stevenson, Christine. *Medicine and Magnificence: British Hospital and Asylum Architecture, 1660–1815.* New Haven, Conn.: Yale University Press, 2000.

———. "Robert Hooke's Bedlam." *Journal of the Society of Architectural Historians* 55 (September 1996): 254–75.

Still, Arthur, and Irving Velody, eds. *Rewriting the History of Madness: Studies in Foucault's "Histoire de la folie."* London: Routledge, 1992.

Stone, Albert E., ed. *Letters from an American Farmer; and, Sketches of Eighteenth-Century America, by J. Hector St. John de Crèvecoeur.* New York: Penguin, 1981.

Tatman, Sandra L., and Roger W. Moss. *Biographical Dictionary of Philadelphia Architects, 1700–1930.* Philadelphia: The Athenaeum, 1985.

Tatum, George B. "Nature's Gardener." In *Prophet with Honor: The Career of Andrew Jackson Downing,* edited by George B. Tatum and Elisabeth MacDougall, 43–80. Philadelphia: The Athenaeum; Washington, D.C.: Dumbarton Oaks Research Library, 1989.

———, and Elisabeth MacDougall, eds. *Prophet with Honor: The Career of Andrew Jackson Downing.* Philadelphia: Athenaeum of Philadelphia; Washington, D.C.: Dumbarton Oaks Research Library, 1989.

Taylor, Jeremy. *The Architect and the Pavilion Hospital: Dialogue and Design Creativity in England, 1850–1914.* London: Leicester University Press, 1997.

———. *Hospital and Asylum Architecture in England, 1840–1914.* London: Mansell, 1991.

Thompson, John D., and Grace Goldin. *The Hospital: A Social and Architectural History.* New Haven, Conn.: Yale University Press, 1975.

Tomes, Nancy. *The Art of Asylum-Keeping: Thomas Story Kirkbride and the Origins of American Psychiatry.* Philadelphia: University of Pennsylvania Press, 1994. Originally published as *A Generous Confidence: Thomas Story Kirkbride and the Art of Asylum-Keeping.* Cambridge: Cambridge University Press, 1983.

———. "The Great Restraint Controversy: A Comparative Perspective on Anglo-American Psychiatry in the Nineteenth Century." In *The Anatomy of Madness,* edited by W. F. Bynum, Roy Porter, and Michael Shepherd, 3:191–225. London: Routledge, 1986.

Topp, Leslie. "An Architecture for Modern Nerves: Josef Hoffman's Purkersdorf Sanatorium." *Journal of the Society of Architectural Historians* 56 (December 1997): 414–37.

———. "Otto Wagner and the Steinhof Psychiatric Hospital: Architecture as Misunderstanding." *Art Bulletin* 87 (March 2005): 130–56.

Torrey, E. Fuller. *The Invisible Plague: The Rise of Mental Illness from 1750 to the Present.* New Brunswick, N.J.: Rutgers University Press, 2001.

Turner, Paul Venable. *Campus: An American Planning Tradition.* Cambridge, Mass.: MIT Press, 1984.

Verderber, Stephen, and David J. Fine. *Healthcare Architecture in an Era of Radical Transformation.* New Haven, Conn.: Yale University Press, 2000.

Watrous, Hilda R. *The County between the Lakes: A History of Seneca County, New York, 1876–1982.* Waterloo, N.Y.: Seneca Board of Supervisors, 1982.

Weaver, Bill L. "Survival at the Alabama Insane Hospital, 1861–1892." *Journal of the History of Medicine and Allied Sciences* 51 (January 1996): 5–28.

Woods, Mary. "Thomas Jefferson and the University of Virginia: Planning the Academic Village." *Journal of the Society of Architectural Historians* 44 (October 1985): 266–83.

Wright, David. "Getting Out of the Asylum: Understanding the Confinement of the Insane in the Nineteenth Century." *Social History of Medicine* 10 (1997): 137–55.

Yanni, Carla. "The Linear Plan for Asylums in the United States before 1866." *Journal of the Society of Architectural Historians* 62 (March 2003): 24–49.

Zeller, George A. "World Gasped When Shackles Were Removed: Bartonville Institution Grew from False Start to Be Model." *The Peoria Transcript: Special Seventieth Anniversary Edition.* Peoria, Ill.: n.p., 1925.

Zukowsky, John. "New York State Inebriate Asylum." *Apochrypha* 3 (1978): 43–44.

Archives and Collections of Rare Books, Manuscripts, and Drawings

Alabama (University of), Special Collections, Tuscaloosa

Alpha Park Public Library, Bartonville, Illinois

Athenaeum, Philadelphia, Pennsylvania

Bentham Papers, University College London, UCL Library, Special Collections, London

The Office of Betty Bird, Architectural Historian, Washington, D.C.

British Library, London

Buffalo and Erie County Public Library, Buffalo, New York

Buffalo Psychiatric Center, Buffalo, New York

Chicago Historical Society, Chicago, Illinois

Oskar Diethelm Library, Institute for the History of Psychiatry, Weill Medical College, Cornell University, New York, New York

Free Library of Philadelphia, Philadelphia, Pennsylvania

Green Door, Washington, D.C.

Greystone Psychiatric Center, Morristown, New Jersey

Houghton Library, Harvard College, Harvard University, Cambridge, Massachusetts

Hudson River Psychiatric Center, Poughkeepsie, New York

Kalamazoo Public Library, Kalamazoo, Michigan

Library of Congress, Washington, D.C.

Library of Virginia, Richmond

National Archives, Washington, D.C., and College Park, Maryland

National Library of Medicine, Bethesda, Maryland

New York Academy of Medicine Library, New York

New York Public Library, New York, New York

Pennsylvania Hospital Archives, Philadelphia

Peoria Public Library, Peoria, Illinois

Princeton University Library Rare Books, Princeton, New Jersey

Rockefeller Library, Colonial Williamsburg, Virginia

Shapiro Developmental Center, Kankakee, Illinois

Sheppard and Enoch Pratt Hospital, Baltimore

South Carolina Department of Archives, Columbia

Trenton Psychiatric Center, Trenton, New Jersey

Vassar College Library, Poughkeepsie, New York

Wellcome Library, London

The Robert H. Wozniak Postcard Collection, Bryn Mawr, Pennsylvania

Index

Carla Yanni is associate professor of art history at Rutgers University. She is the author of *Nature's Museums: Victorian Science and the Architecture of Display*.